Pot Roast, Politics, and Ants in the Pantry

Pot Roast, Politics, and Ants in the Pantry

Missouri's Cookbook Heritage

Carol Fisher and John Fisher

University of Missouri Press   Columbia and London

Copyright © 2008 by
The Curators of the University of Missouri
University of Missouri Press, Columbia, Missouri 65201
Printed and bound in the United States of America
All rights reserved
5 4 3 2 1   12 11 10 09 08

Library of Congress Cataloging-in-Publication Data

Fisher, Carol, 1949–
   Pot roast, politics, and ants in the pantry : Missouri's cookbook heritage / Carol Fisher and John Fisher.
       p. cm.
   Includes bibliographical references and index.
   Summary: "A revealing look at the history of Missouri cookbooks from the 1800s to today. From Julia Clark's simple frontier recipes to Irma Rombauer's encyclopedic Joy of Cooking to Missouri producers' online recipe collections, the Fishers show how cookbooks provide history lessons, document changing foodways, and demonstrate the cultural diversity of the state"— Provided by publisher.
   ISBN 978-0-8262-1791-2 (alk. paper)
   1. Cookery—History. 2. Cookery—Missouri—History. 3. Cookery—Missouri—Bibliography. I. Fisher, John C., 1949– II. Title.
   TX648.F57 2008
   641.509—dc22   2007052492

Designer: Kristie Lee
Typesetter: BookComp, Inc.
Printer and binder: Thomson-Shore, Inc.
Typefaces: Adobe Caslon, Big Caslon, and Onyx

The University of Missouri Press gratefully acknowledges Paul Newman for his generous contribution in support of the publication of this book.

*This book is dedicated to Becky and Adolf Schroeder, avid
Missouri historians, who have inspired us to learn more about
Missouri, our home state, and to Jean Chambers Gibbs,
who enjoyed cooking pot roast for the family.*

Contents

Introduction 1

Chapter 1 Cookbooks Come to Missouri 3

Chapter 2 A Taste of Nineteenth-Century Publications 11

Chapter 3 Community Cookbooks 28

Chapter 4 A Serving of Ethnic Cookbooks 52

Chapter 5 Missouri Cookbooks Record History 65

Chapter 6 Individually Authored and Edited Cookbooks 88

Chapter 7 Producer and Festival Cookbooks 105

Chapter 8 Company/Product Cookbooks 119

Chapter 9 Cookbooks from Restaurants Past and Present 140

Chapter 10 World Events and Politics in Missouri Cookbooks 153

Chapter 11 Kitchen Medicine, Housekeeping Tips,
and Cookbook Literature 165

Chapter 12 A Final Perspective 180

Appendix: Selected Recipes 183

Notes 197

Bibliography 209

Index 225

Acknowledgments

We are thankful for our mothers, Wilma Chambers and Eunice Fisher, who provided good Missouri food for our families, served with valuable food stories that connected us to our past.

Numerous organizations and individuals have contributed to the project by donating cookbooks, answering questions, and sharing helpful information. As well, let us not forget Missouri's cookbook authors, editors, compilers, and cooks, who have preserved and who continue to preserve not only their kitchen ways but also their lives through their contributions to the state's buffet of cookbooks.

Special thanks to the Blue Owl Restaurant and Mary Hostetter, the Campbell Chamber of Commerce, Eagle Family Foods, Inc., Farmland Foods, the First United Methodist Church Women Unionville and Jean Pratt, Hammons Products Company, Harter House in Springfield, the Missouri Bison Association and Fred Neumann, the Missouri Pork Association, Missouri SOS Archives and Laura Jolley, the Missouri State Teachers Association, the Missouri State Bee Keepers Association and Neil Bergman, the Pennytown Freewill Baptist Church Cookbook Committee and Virginia Huston, the Principia and Peter Shay, the Richmond Chamber of Commerce, St. James Winery, the Soy Bean Merchandising Council, Stone Hill Winery, Unity and Sharon M. Sartin, Wicker's Food Products, and the Independence Junior League and Alison Hill.

Thanks to Sylvia Forbes, John and Mary German, Nancy H. Grant, Sue Hall, Jean Hamacher, Angie Thompson Holtzhouser, Jean Mowrer, Anne Moyer, Dean and Lois Preuett, Jean Rissover, Tina Waibel, Barbara Willenberg, Twila Melton, Patricia Shell, and Carol Habgood.

Appreciation also goes to valuable archivists and librarians and to libraries and historical societies, in particular the Augusta Historical Society and Ellen Knoernschild, the Dunklin County Library staff, Michigan State University

Libraries and Ruth Ann Jones, the Missouri Historical Society staff, Park University Archives and Carolyn Elwess, the St. Louis Mercantile Library and Charles Brown, the State Historical Society of Missouri staff, and Unity archivist and reference librarian Eric E. Page.

Pot Roast, Politics, and Ants in the Pantry

Introduction

Within the pages of Missouri cookbooks, readers find more than recipes for culinary creations; they find solutions to common household problems: Dad has dyspepsia; there are ants in the pantry; the hens have quit laying; the brass fixtures are dull; the children have a cough—and there's still supper to cook. What's a busy housewife to do? Throughout the pages of their cookbooks, Missouri's early authors and compilers invited readers into their kitchens to share details of demanding household duties, daily farm activities, and ongoing medical problems as well as to deliver their cooking instructions. Additionally, Missouri cookbooks have documented the effect that world events, societal changes, and technological advancements have had on those who gather around the kitchen table. Cookbooks have also been an important part of fairs and festivals and have even appeared in the political arena.

The community/charity cookbooks, organized and published by groups throughout the state, often include local historical community vignettes blended with recipes for such old-time favorites as jam cake, vinegar pie, corn pone, pot roast, and dandelion wine, thus preserving important community historical details along with instructions for delectable fare. Fortunately, Missourians have also seen fit to record ethnic food preferences in recipe contributions to community recipe collections, thus allowing Missourians to visit the kitchens of the past in order to enjoy or retrieve Aunt Martha's directions for fruitcake, Mom's special technique for making flaky piecrust, or Great Grandma's recipe for liver dumplings.

Missouri's cookbook history presents a table set with platters, bowls, and dishes of simple, hearty foods prepared with fruits and vegetables grown on Missouri farms, meats from animals raised on farms or game hunted in Missouri's woods and fields, and fish caught in its lakes, streams, and rivers. In modern times, cookbooks have added recipes using items purchased at a plethora of stores, public markets, farmers' markets, and roadside stands. Even though the state's cooks use similar food products, ethnic cookbook authors and compilers in the state assure readers that indeed there was and continues to be variety on the Missouri table with cooks detailing ethnic and regional cooking styles and techniques, adding ingredients, spices, and flavorings to suit their specific cultural tastes. Missouri's cookbook authors and compilers have also brought the state into the twenty-first century with stylish works, brimming with sophisticated recipes using updated food products, some reflecting current health issues of the day, others preserving regional fare and encouraging ethnic options. Aware of the wealth of the past, individuals and groups in the state continue to dish up servings of cookbooks packed with historical information.

Pot Roast, Politics, and Ants in the Pantry examines a representative sampling of this generous array of culinary works, noting and sharing historical information about people, places, events, foods, and cooking practices included in the cookbooks. The project benefits from supplemental historical and informational notes concerning subjects mentioned in the cookbooks. Primarily, the cookbooks selected for discussion are written or assembled by Missouri authors and compilers, although certain publications may simply use a Missouri theme or fall into a category of early cookbooks published in the state.

Chapter 1

Cookbooks Come to Missouri

Mrs. Hancock says the best way to make those roles, is to work up the Dough very well at night, when made and handle it as lightly as possible in the morning then make it in roles She thinks working it over in the morning kills the dough.—Julia Clark Memoranda Book, 1820

Culinary records indicate that it was not until the latter half of the nineteenth century that printed cookbooks by Missouri authors, Missouri community groups, and Missouri businesses became a part of America's cookbook history. Very early colonial cooks simply arrived in America with a working knowledge of cooking practices acquired through experience in their kitchens in the Old World. Some carried with them a collection of handwritten family "receipts." As the pool of literate women expanded in the colonies, the audience grew for cookbooks marketed by European cookbook publishers. Books by English authors such as Eliza Smith (*The Compleat Housewife*), Hannah Glasse (*The Art of Cookery Made Plain and Easy*), Elizabeth Raffald (*The Experienced English Housekeeper*), and Susannah Carter (*The Frugal Housewife*) gained popularity in eighteenth-century America. As publishing became cost-effective in the New World, cookbooks were not only marketed to the colonies from outside but were also printed within the colonies. Smith's, although English, was the first to be printed here in 1742. It was followed by Carter's. There were no others between 1742 and 1796.

It was not until 1796 that a cookbook written by an American author for American cooks became available with the publication of Amelia Simmons's *American Cookery*. Simmons, who refers to herself as an orphan, could not write, but she was willing to share the secrets of her culinary talent, and she enlisted other individuals to pen the cookbook for her. This was the first cookbook to include recipes for dishes using unique American foodstuffs readily found in the colonies in addition to the expected recipes typical of English cookbooks of the day. Breaking new ground in the world of cookbooks, this small American volume records adaptations that had taken place over the previous years in the kitchens of colonial cooks as they learned to modify their recipes or to develop new recipes as they prepared breads and dishes for their families using the native produce, particularly corn, beans, and squash, as well as game found in the New World.

The nineteenth century produced American cookbook authors who continued to offer works with an American flavor. A sampling of these publications begins with *The Virginia House-Wife* (1824), by Mrs. Mary Randolph, who treats cooks to a collection of recipes, including those typical of southern kitchens. Significant works of influential culinary writers from the Northeast follow. Eliza Leslie offers a baking cookbook, *Seventy-Five Receipts for Pastry Cakes and Sweetmeats,* published in 1828. Lydia Maria Child's *The American Frugal Housewife* (1829) focuses on being conservative, and Sara Josepha Hale advocates healthy eating in *The Good Housekeeper* (1839). Catharine Beecher, the sister of author Harriet Beecher Stowe, promotes the principles of domestic science in one of her cooking and housekeeping guides as midcentury approaches in *The Domestic Receipt Book* (1846). Marion Harland, also a native of Virginia, wrote *Common Sense in the Household* in 1871. The last three decades of the century produced successful cookbooks written by notable cooking teachers also from the Northeast: Juliet Carson from the New York Cooking School; Miss Parloa, Mrs. D. A. Lincoln, and Fannie Farmer from the famous Boston Cooking School; and Sarah Tyson Rorer from the Philadelphia Cooking School.

America's cookbook offerings became more diversified as enthusiastic authors and civic-minded individuals added their projects to the pool of culinary works. The community cookbook, so popular with Missouri cooks today, arrived on the cookbook scene with *A Poetical Cook Book,* Maria J. Moss's contribution to the Great Sanitary Fair held in Philadelphia in 1864, a benefit for the Civil War soldiers from the North. By the end of the nineteenth century, American cooks could purchase a variety of cookbooks, some large works complete with recipes, medical information, and housekeeping directions.

At the time of the 1796 publication of Simmons's cookbook, Missouri, then the western frontier, was under the control of the Spanish but had maintained a French culture with French settlers dominating the population. About this time, Anglo-American settlers started moving into Missouri with the major influx beginning in 1804 following the Louisiana Purchase. During the first half of the century, Kentucky provided the greatest number of settlers coming into Missouri with many others moving in from Tennessee, Virginia, and the Carolinas. During the 1830s, '40s, and '50s, large numbers of German immigrants further diversified Missouri's growing population.

Early Missouri cooks who had learned to read and write preserved their families' recipes in manuscript cookbooks. Two written in the 1820s serve as representative examples of manuscript cookbooks recording the foodways of notable families in the state. The *Julia Clark Household Memoranda Book,* a part of the Clark family papers archived at the Missouri Historical Society in St. Louis, was assumed until recent years to have been written by Julia, the wife of William Clark of the Lewis and Clark Expedition. However, researchers Robert Stone and David Hinkley, after examining the structure of the work and comparing the handwriting in it to William Clark's handwriting in his Expedition journals, propose in *Clark's Other Journal* that this early collection of Julia's recipes may have been recorded by Clark himself. Stone and Hinkley discuss details relating to the lives of the Clarks at the time the cookbook was compiled, which led them to their conclusion.[1] They reproduce the Clark recipes and personal inventories in their project. Whether the recipes were recorded by Clark or by his wife, the collection allows Missourians to learn about the foodways of this famous Missouri family. The other cookbook carries the name of Harriet O'Fallon, the wife of Clark's nephew, John O'Fallon.

Capt. William Clark, after returning from the now-famous Lewis and Clark Expedition, rekindled a friendship with Julia Hancock, a young woman from Fincastle, Virginia, whom he had met prior to the Expedition. The two were married in 1808, when she was in her mid-teens, and they went on to have five children. Clark worked in Indian Affairs and served as the final governor of the Missouri Territory while he and his wife lived in St. Louis, then the largest city in the state.

In addition to recipes credited to family and friends, the *Julia Clark Household Memoranda Book* offers detailed lists of the family's items of clothing. It appears that the lists were written at a time when Julia was either preparing to return or had returned to Virginia in 1820. The notes on her personal wardrobe allow modern readers to get a sense of fashions worn by women of means in St. Louis at that time. The work also lists which clothes her husband took on the trip to Virginia as well as what clothing he left behind in St. Louis. There is a similar list of wardrobe items for Meriwether Lewis, the Clarks' first son, named after William Clark's friend and partner in the Expedition. Readers learn which clothes were taken for "ML" for the Virginia trip and which were left behind in St. Louis. The section also lists infant clothing taken to Virginia. Unfortunately, Julia died in Virginia that same year.

The "receipt" section includes a variety of dishes prepared for the St. Louis family's table. An assortment of pudding recipes appear in the collection, including Indian meal pudding, carrot pudding, transparent pudding, and one for boiled pudding. In the food preservation section, the collection provides instructions for making "orrange" preserves, green sweetmeats, and pickle peaches. Two recipes explain how to make catsup, not with tomatoes, but with Missouri walnuts. A recipe labeled "Mrs. Hancock's receipt for Light Roles" demonstrates the "recipe voice" of the day.

Mrs. Hancock's receipt for Light Roles

To one quart of flour, take a pint of new milk, a large bit of butter, warm your milk and butter together then, put to your flour four spoons full of yeast and three eggs, beat this in your flower [*sic*] with your milk and butter warm make it in a batter and set to rise in the morning work it well, make out your roles lay them on a tin plate to rise, when enough risen, bake them quick they are very light and [fare or fine?]

A note follows the recipe:

Mrs. Hancock says the best way to make those roles, is to work up the dough very well at night, when made and handle it as lightly as possible in the morning and then make it in roles She thinks working it over in the morning kills the dough.[2]

In her study of "Missouri Women in the 1820s," historian Jerena East Giffen reacts to recipes in the Clark manuscript cookbook as she compares them to manuscript recipes by women who were living in areas of Missouri away from larger communities like St. Louis. "Spices, available in Missouri only by import, were found in the recipes of Mrs. Clark indicative of her early years spent in more developed areas of Virginia." She points out the use of a variety of spices included in the instructions for "Mrs. N. Prestons receipt for Catchup." "Menus of mid-Missourians in the early 1820s were not as varied as the foods served by French and American cooks in St. Louis. Foodstuff available to the log cabin cook was much more limited, except in those areas of southeast Missouri bordering the Mississippi river where steamboats would stop. Steamboat traffic on the Missouri River was just starting when the state was admitted to the Union." Giffen believes Julia Clark's recipe for Indian meal pudding reflects a more "refined" way of cooking than one might have found in the kitchens of Missouri's log cabins.[3] A look at her recipe reveals a generous use of sugar, the addition of "orrange" peel, and the addition of a glass of wine.

"Take four ounces Indian meal searched [?] fine, ten eggs, ten ounces of sugar, ten ounces of butter a little orange peel beat fine and sifted, a glass of white wine—this in an excellent pudding." Giffen reminds readers, "Refined sugar was a great luxury and Missouri's early wives used honey and some-times maple sugar to sweeten their foods." The Clark collection includes a recipe for "orrange" preserves. "Pare the rine down in as many quarters as you found thick, leave the orrange whole in the middle get of all the white skin, preserve it in a rich surrip be carefull not to brake of the rine, it looks beau-tifull when done nice, when you preserve the rine alone, boil it but a moment in the surrip as it hardens it, soak in warm water."[4]

Harriet Stokes O'Fallon, wife of Col. John R. O'Fallon, a native of Ken-tucky, penned the second Missouri manuscript cookbook mentioned. "The History of O'Fallon" offers personal background information and highlights of her husband's successful business career. O'Fallon's mother was William Clark's sister. O'Fallon himself came to St. Louis after his engagement in the War of 1812 to work with Clark in Indian Affairs, and in 1818 he resigned his commission in the army in favor of a business career. He became the first president of the Missouri Pacific, the Baltimore and Ohio, and the Wabash Railroads. The city of O'Fallon is named after him, and his contributions to St. Louis included one million dollars in charitable donations. As well, he donated the land for St. Louis University and financed the construction of Pope Medical College, which later became Washington University Medical School.[5] O'Fallon married Harriet Stokes in 1820, and the following year she recorded her recipes in a manuscript cookbook.

Mrs. O'Fallon's diverse collection includes instructions for preparing such dishes as stuffing for veal, calves' feet, and pigs' feet and ears. Readers also find recipes for "beef boullie," "mutton collops," and "an omeltte." The "omeltte" instructions call for eight eggs seasoned with pepper, salt, a shallot, and some shredded parsley. Not skimping on the butter, she suggests putting "into a frying pan a quarter of a pound of butter" and "when it boils throw in the eggs and stir it over a clear fire." She adds, "When browned on the under side double it and put it on a dish pour gravy over it." Perhaps familiar with the popular English cookbook written by Glasse, O'Fallon includes a recipe found in that cookbook which tells how to preserve English peas. "To keep green pease [*sic*] till Christmas shell and throw them into boiling water and salt let them boil five or six minutes drain them then lay a cloth four or five times double and . . . dry them well put them in dry bottles cork and melt wax over them then tie them down with a bladder."[6]

Like the Clark manuscript, O'Fallon's collection of recipes offers helpful noncooking information sandwiched between regular recipes. At one point, she records a recipe for a mixture designed to promote the growth of apple trees and one to be used in cleaning a harness. Briefly shifting to kitchen medicine, the author follows with recipes for dealing with dysentery and bilious "stomack" and then immediately returns to recipes for pickled beef and how to make green preserves. She comments on the value of pulverized charcoal for medicinal purposes and follows with newspaper clippings that explain how to save cucumbers from bugs and how to keep flowers from fading. After supplying a recipe for blackberry cordial, O'Fallon offers an "Excellent Embrocation for the Whooping Cough," which she believes to be a cure. Next comes a recipe for "Tomatoe [*sic*] or Love apple Catsup." She wraps up her culinary collection with detailed instructions for how to preserve fruits without sugar, helping cooks to reduce their need for expensive sugar.

Historic cookbook bibliographies show evidence of cookbook publishing in Missouri during the final decades of the nineteenth century, specifically in St. Louis and Kansas City. In 1764 St. Louis was established by Pierre Laclede as a trading post. His young clerk, Auguste Chouteau, supervised the construction of its first buildings. When the British took control of Illinois country, many French settlers chose to move across the river to St. Louis rather than live under British rule.[7]

St. Louis's location at the junction of the Mississippi and Missouri Rivers made it an ideal site for a major commercial center. Initially, trade in furs and

> four pound of loaf sugar and four
> pints juice fills twelve tumblers
>
> Tomatoe or Love apple Catsup
>
> Slice the apples thin and over every layer sprinkle
> a little salt cover them and let them lie 24
> hours then beat them well and simmer them
> 1/2 an hour in a bell metal kettle add
> mace and allspice strain through a sieve and
> simmer again when cold add 2 cloves of shallots
> cut small and half a gill of brandy to every
> Bottle which must be corked tight and kept in
> a cool place
>
> Apple Jelly
>
> Peel and quarter a 1/2 bushel of white pippin
> apples and throw them into cold water to prevent
> their becoming dark coloured when all are done put
> them into boiling water and let them remain in it

This 1821 recipe for "Tomatoe or Love apple Catsup" is from a book by Harriet O'Fallon, a St. Louis cook. (John O'Fallon Collection, reproduced courtesy Missouri Historical Society, St. Louis)

hides with the Indians brought wealth. St. Louis also became the primary shipping center for products such as hemp, tobacco, corn, and pork produced on farms along the Missouri River, and the young city served as the major supplier of goods needed by farms and settlements in the same area. Following the Civil War, St. Louis's importance as a trade and manufacturing center grew rapidly, sparked in part by railroad building and by the construction of the Eads Bridge, which provided improved access to eastern markets. The increased number of manufacturers and the wages they paid brought a high level of prosperity to St. Louis in the 1880s and 1890s.

Kansas City had its beginnings in the 1820s with the establishment of a trading post by the Chouteaus from St. Louis.[8] In the late 1830s the Town of Kansas Company laid out lots for the Town of Kansas near the Kansas River. By 1850 the company was no longer in existence. The town, however, had already started to grow; it was officially organized that year and chartered a few years after that as the City of Kansas. It later became Kansas City.[9] The city benefited from western trade and from outfitting wagon trains carrying settlers westward. Kansas City's growth following the Civil War was phenomenal. Its population rose from 5,000 in 1865[10] to 32,000 in 1870.[11] The cattle trade fueled much of this growth. Cattle were driven from ranches in the West to Kansas City, where they were loaded on trains for shipment to the East. In addition, during the 1870s and 1880s the city became a major meatpacking center with beef and pork being either canned for distribution or shipped to eastern markets in refrigerated rail cars. Milling became a second important factor stimulating Kansas City's rapid growth. The city's mills received Kansas wheat and processed it into flour. During this time, every major milling company had a facility in Kansas City.

It isn't surprising that printers and publishers in St. Louis and Kansas City turned out some of the first printed cookbooks in Missouri. *The Kitchen Directory and American Housewife* (1841), originally printed in 1839 in New York as the *American Housewife*, traveled through numerous printings in various cities, including St. Louis in 1858 and 1859.[12] The 1896 *Granite Iron Ware Cook Book* printed in St. Louis includes testimonials tracking back to 1878, which suggests it may have been copyrighted as early as that date.[13] A community cookbook was published in St. Louis as early as 1875 with similar projects surfacing in various areas of the state in the '80s and '90s and on into the twentieth century. Individually authored cookbooks also showed up as early as the '70s and '80s.

Chapter 2

A Taste of Nineteenth-Century Publications

This book will render divorce Courts an expensive luxury, instead of a
social necessity. It is the housekeeper's Magna Charta. Her Emancipation
Proclamation. . . . The recipes gathered into this priceless volume have
been sent from all parts of the known world; several even from New
Jersey.—*My Mother's Cook Book*, Ladies of St. Louis, 1880

In 1875 and again in 1880 a group called the Ladies of St. Louis sold *My
Mother's Cook Book,* compiled for the benefit of the Women's Christian
Home located in their community. Modern-day Missourians turning the
pages of this early Missouri cookbook will find instructions for dishes similar to those served in their own kitchens as well as some not-so-familiar
recipes. In the soup section, the St. Louis ladies offer recipes for familiar
gumbo soups; bean, pea, and potato soups; and corn soup and corn chowder.
On the other hand, of special interest is a detailed recipe for the preparation
of mock turtle soup, a multiple-step culinary process requiring two days to
complete.

Day one begins with the purchase of one large calf's head, with skin on. The
recipe notes that the butcher has removed the eyes and nose and has opened
the head. A thorough washing follows in addition to the removal of the brains,
which are tied in a thin cloth and put in a pot of boiling water with the head.
While the head is cooking, one old hen is placed in a second pot with a knuckle
of veal. Both pots of meat simmer for seven hours and are then allowed to
stand overnight. On the morning of day two, the fat is removed from each pot
and the contents combined with butter, vegetables, and a variety of spices. The

My Mother's Cook Book, first published in 1875, is one of Missouri's very early community cookbooks, compiled by the Ladies of St. Louis for the benefit of the Women's Christian Home.

mixture simmers for two additional hours. Toward the end of the process, the cook is instructed to make meatballs the size of pigeon's eggs out of the brains and then add them to the soup prior to serving. The soup also benefits from a cup of Madeira wine and the juice of a lemon.[1]

Mrs. E. F. Richards, one of the project organizers, seemingly adept at food presentation, offers her suggestions for a "handsome" way to serve raw oysters. "Take a nice clear square piece of ice, about ten pounds, and with hot flat irons melt out a deep dish in the middle of the ice, leaving an edge about one inch wide all around to keep in the oysters, it is not at all necessary to keep the inside edge straight or square, for the more jagged it is the prettier it will look; while doing it I keep two or three irons heating on the stove."[2] At serving, the ice bowl filled with oysters was placed on a towel-draped tray. Richards indicates that the base of the ice bowl may be decorated with parsley or carrot tops.

It is apparent from the collection of recipes that nineteenth-century cooks in St. Louis prepared a wide range of meat, poultry, and seafood dishes, from tenderloin and fried kidneys to roast beef and jellied chicken to simple fried fish and fancy turbot à la creme. The cookbook provides recipes for cooking an old chicken and instructions for preparing snipes, woodcocks, stuffed quail, and potted pigeons. Not to be overlooked is a recipe for fried pigs' feet and one for a simple ham sandwich.

The canning and preserving section offers tips for success relating to this important aspect of supplying year-round food for the family. Modern-day readers accustomed to the convenience of purchasing a jar of jelly or preserves at a local supermarket learn about concerns associated with home canning and preserving at this time in Missouri kitchens. Dealing with the problem of spoilage, the St. Louis ladies present their solution to "mould on the surface" of preserves. "You need not throw them away until you have first tried to recover them by adding a little more sugar and boiling them over again: but if they have an unpleasant smell and insects about them, then they must be thrown away."[3]

Early in the cookbook, the editors promise in grandiose prose that the book will solve the problem of new cooks having to compete with the standards set by their more experienced mothers and mothers-in-law who have had the benefit of practice and experience in the kitchen. To help a cook deal with "the way mother used to do it" in the kitchen, these early Missouri ladies offered their collection of recipes in a "priceless volume." The cookbook recipes "have been sent from all parts of the known world; some even from New Jersey." They say, "Here is a wilderness of pies, puddings, pickles, jellies and jams; here are more cookies and cream pies than could be found at a charitable Sunday school picnic." The ladies promise the book to be "A genuine cook book. Not a series of experimental conjectures evolved from the consciousness of a brilliant theorist in cooking, but a batch of practical recipes that have been embodied in luscious dishes, and bear the credential of gratified appetites."[4]

Indeed, *My Mother's Cook Book* also promised the housekeeper "every species of pie." Without a doubt, this cookbook must have been a worthy kitchen companion for the late-nineteenth-century Missouri cook, especially (also noted in introductory remarks) if the wife, after practicing the skills served up in the cookbook, heard from her husband, "Wife, your cooking of this (or that) dish has outdone our mothers—a thing we considered impossible."[5]

During the second half of the nineteenth century, the publishing industry produced in addition to smaller cookbooks also larger compendium-type cookbooks, which included extensive medicinal sections and housekeeping sections as well as large collections of recipes, some running into thousands of entries. The very well educated Mrs. Mary Foote Henderson, while living in St. Louis in 1876, wrote *Practical Cooking and Dinner Giving.* She comments on the disadvantages of these larger types of publications compared to the smaller cookbook that she proposes. "There are generally only two or three good modes of cooking a material, and one becomes bewildered and discouraged in trying to select and practice from books which contain often from a thousand to three thousand receipts." Having identified what she considers to be an element missing from cookbooks of the time, instructions relating to serving food and entertaining, she intends to address this omission. "The aim of this book is to indicate how to serve dishes, and to entertain company at breakfast, lunch and dinner, as well as to give cooking receipts." She says that she hopes she has selected recipes which "stood the test of time" and that her cookbook will "show how it is possible with moderate means to keep a hospitable table." She believes her credentials, "having pursued courses of study with cooking teachers in America and in Europe" will serve her well in the project.[6]

Her cooking-school training surfaces as she discusses exact ways of serving and entertaining, indicating the current style of entertaining to be somewhat of a compromise between the English and Russian styles. "The English mode is to set the whole of each course, often containing many dishes, at once upon the table."[7] Henderson omits no detail in instructing Missourians regarding serving styles and entertaining skills, devoting the first twenty-plus pages of her work to these tasks.

Before explaining how to serve a dinner one course at a time under the "new plan" more in the Russian style, she discusses table settings and table arrangements. According to Henderson, the ideal table "best calculated to show off a dinner" is a round table five feet in diameter. Among her "setting" instructions, she advises that the napkins not be starched and that a baize be placed under the tablecloth to prevent noise. "The finest and handsomest table-linen looks comparatively thin and sleazy on a bare table."[8]

Under the pen of the author, the table comes to life as Henderson offers dining experience details. "The table-linen is of spotless purity, and the dishes and silver are perfectly bright." She discusses options for the placement of eating utensils—whether to place all on the original table design or to have the server add necessary utensils as each course is served—and says she personally favors hiring a French waiter to do the carving at the side table.[9]

Mrs. Mary Henderson combined recipes with tips on proper presentation and helpful explanations of tools for the cook in *Practical Cooking and Dinner Giving*.

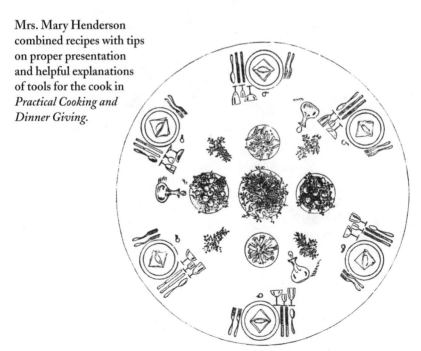

Table set for Serving from the Side.

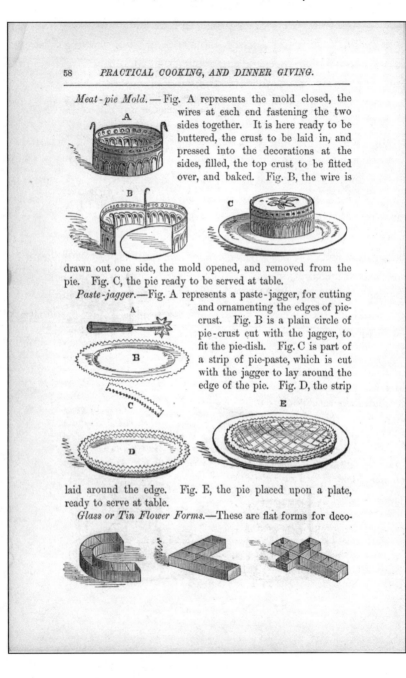

Meat - pie Mold. — Fig. A represents the mold closed, the wires at each end fastening the two sides together. It is here ready to be buttered, the crust to be laid in, and pressed into the decorations at the sides, filled, the top crust to be fitted over, and baked. Fig. B, the wire is drawn out one side, the mold opened, and removed from the pie. Fig. C, the pie ready to be served at table.

Paste - jagger. — Fig. A represents a paste - jagger, for cutting and ornamenting the edges of pie-crust. Fig. B is a plain circle of pie - crust cut with the jagger, to fit the pie-dish. Fig. C is part of a strip of pie-paste, which is cut with the jagger to lay around the edge of the pie. Fig. D, the strip laid around the edge. Fig. E, the pie placed upon a plate, ready to serve at table.

Glass or Tin Flower Forms. — These are flat forms for deco-

106   *PRACTICAL COOKING, AND DINNER GIVING.*

repeat the receipts for each particular one. I will only suggest the best manner for cooking certain kinds, and will add certain receipts not under the general rule:

SALMON

is undoubtedly best boiled. The only exception to the rule of boiling fish is in the case of salmon, which must be put in hot instead of cold water, to preserve its color. A favorite way of boiling a whole salmon is in the form of a letter S, as in plate.

It is done as follows: Thread a trussing-needle with some twine; tie the end of the string around the head, fastening it tight; then pass the needle through the centre part of the body, draw the string tight, and fasten it around the tail. The fish will assume the desired form.

For parties or evening companies, salmon boiled in this form (middle cuts are also used), served cold, with a *Mayonnaise* sauce poured over, is a favorite dish. It is then generally mounted in style, on an oval or square block pedestal, three or four inches high, made of bread (two or three days old), called a *croustade*, carved in any form with a sharp knife. It is then fried a light-brown in boiling lard. Oftener these *croustades* are made of wood, which are covered with white paper, and brushed over with a little half-set aspic jelly. The salmon is then decorated with squares of aspic jelly. A decoration of quartered hard-boiled eggs or of cold cauliflower-blossoms is very pretty, and is palatable also with the *Mayonnaise* sauce. The best sauces for a boiled salmon served hot are the *sauce Hollandaise*, lobster, shrimp, or oyster sauces — the *sauce Hollandaise* being the favorite.

If lobster sauce is used, the coral of the lobster is dried, and

The overall serving plan enlists the aid of a butler, a maid, and a cook. When the meal is ready, she indicates, "It should be announced by the butler or dining-room maid. Never ring a bell for a meal. Bells do very well for country inns and steamboats, but in a private house, the ménage should be conducted with as little noise a possible."[10] She sees successful dining and entertaining based on routine, a routine that the help, the hostess, and the host should all know. According to Henderson, a bill of fare is posted in the kitchen, and the cook systematically plans ahead and prepares one course at a time. It is delivered to the table, served, and enjoyed, and plates are then removed, and the next course is brought in. If this routine is followed, she believes the dining experience will be enjoyed by guests and hosts down to the dessert course when the butler removes the last plates and exits the room. This style she believes to be superior to the English way and should be followed in each meal of the day.

In 1868, Henderson came from New York to Louisiana, Missouri, as the bride of John B. Henderson, who was then serving as United States senator from Missouri. Mrs. Henderson more than once was featured in the news in St. Louis. On one occasion, the Sunday magazine of the *St. Louis Post-Dispatch* featured Mrs. Henderson and her husband, contributing information about the couple. The article explains that when they were not in Washington during his term of office, the two lived in boardinghouses and in a hotel in Louisiana, Missouri, the senator's hometown. The author of the article details Senator Henderson's political career, pointing out that he "had the distinction of drafting the constitutional amendment which, supplementing Abraham Lincoln's proclamation of emancipation, liberated the remaining slaves and killed deader than any doornail the institution of slavery in the United States" and also believes that Henderson's "vote to keep Andrew Johnson in the presidency retired him to private life."[11]

After Henderson left office, the couple moved to St. Louis and then back to Washington, where before his death, he became one of Washington's richest men. Mrs. Henderson became very active in her community when she lived in St. Louis and in later years in Washington. In 1886 in St. Louis, she was elected president of the Missouri State Suffrage Association, and that same year she organized the St. Louis School of Design. Three years later, she founded the Woman's Exchange of St. Louis. While in Washington, she successfully managed the couples' acquired wealth after her husband's death, investing aggressively and shrewdly in real estate especially in building and selling large estates. Known for "doing things out of the ordinary," at one time she proposed donating one of her mansions to be used as the home of the vice president,[12] an offer that, it was later reported, had been turned down because it was supposed that his salary would have to be raised in order to maintain the large home.[13] On another occasion, after moving toward the side of the prohibitionists, when asked about the use of wines and brandies as ingredients in her St. Louis cookbook, she "repudiated those recipes years later" and as well "poured the contents of her husband's wine cellar into the gutters of fashionable Washington."[14]

A second nineteenth-century individually authored cookbook, *Health in the Household: or Hygienic Cookery* (1883), written by Susanna W. Dodds, is one of Missouri's early health-related cookbooks. Dr. Dodds became professionally associated with her sister-in-law, Mary Dodds, also a doctor. The 1914 edition of *Notable Women of St. Louis* details the careers of the two women, indicating that they were successful once they overcame the initial resistance to women in the medical profession, explaining that St. Louisians weren't quite accustomed to women doctors at the time they set up their practices. Readers learn that there had been only two female doctors in St. Louis before the Drs. Dodds set up their practice in the city: Dr. Grennan, a homeopath, and Dr. Lavelle, an allopath.[15]

Dodds's cookbook carries a hygienic cookery theme. Her interest in the hygienic way of eating developed when she became acquainted with and later married Andrew Dodds. Her husband, a vegetarian, espoused the hygienic method of treating diseases, one that emphasized meatless meal plans among additional strict dietary restrictions for disease prevention and healthy living. Dodds and her husband trained at the Hygeo-Therapeutic College of New York after attending classes at Antioch College in Ohio. Susanna completed her course of study in 1866. They then moved to St. Louis with their families, where her husband and brother-in-law established A. and G. Dodds Granite and Stone Company.[16]

After Andrew's death, Susanna joined with Mary, who had also attended hygienic classes in New York, to organize a health sanitarium, Dodds' Hygeian Home, in St. Louis in 1878. According to the editors of *Notable Women of St. Louis*, the two doctors focused on "natural methods of treatment: diet, exercise, massage, electricity and hydrotherapy in all of its manifold applications, and had phenomenal success in the curing of both acute and chronic patients."[17] Women doctors at the time, many of them hygienic practitioners, generally were not accepted into the mainstream medical community dominated by men. Therefore, they established their own medical institutions in order to deliver their services.

As Susanna Dodds's career moved forward, she turned to writing as a means of promoting her teachings with *Hygienic Cookery* beginning her twenty-year writing career. She also became dean of the St. Louis Hygienic College of Physicians and Surgeons, which was incorporated by the State of Missouri in 1887. After Susanna's death in 1911, Mary continued their work until she sold the business in 1912.[18] In his discussion of the entrance of women into the practice of medicine in the nineteenth century, Dr. Herbert M. Shelton, also a popular hygienist, proposes that Susanna Dodds was "Perhaps the most outstanding woman graduate of the Hygeo-Therapeutic College" and that her "writing and lecture upon the subject of Hygiene constitute a valuable addition to Hygienic literature." He also indicates that in addition to her role in medicine of the time, she, taking a stand for dress reform for women, "continued to shock the prudish of her era by wearing pants instead of dresses.[19]

Dodds divides her cookbook into three sections: part one explains the principles and methods of a strict hygienic diet, one that does not allow the use of white flour, soda, baking powder, milk, sweeteners, spices, condiments, and flesh foods; part two offers recipes primarily following these concepts, although some modifications not strictly hygienic are allowed in some recipes in this section; part three includes a wide selection of more "worldly recipes." It appears that she developed part three, "The Compromise," somewhat reluctantly. Its recipes utilize more common ingredients, which were restricted in part one. Dodds lets readers know that even though she utilizes these ingredients in recipes in the cookbook, she doesn't approve of them and strongly suggests that the dishes should be prepared sparingly.

A little more than decade after Henderson offered her entertaining guide and directions for preparation of dishes in St. Louis, a group called the Ladies of Kansas City published their cookbook, *Housekeeping and Dinner Giving in Kansas City* (1887), for the advancement of Presbyterianism and for the support of benevolent institutions in the city. More than a cookbook, this project provides exact instructions for the inexperienced housekeeper as well as specific comments relating to entertaining. Mrs. T. F. Willis seems to be the primary voice in narrative sections of the project, although Mrs. W. S. Bird is also credited as an editor. Both provide introductions to sections in the cookbook and contribute numerous recipes to the collection. The Kansas City ladies share the goals of the cookbook: "to indicate how to serve dishes as well as to give the receipts for preparing them; how to systematize in housekeeping and entertaining, so that you may be enable to conquer your work, instead of allowing it to conquer you."[20] This delightful cookbook allows modern readers to experience housekeeping and entertaining in Kansas City through personal narratives and generous recipe comments by a group of civic-minded ladies under the leadership of Mrs. Willis as their community moves toward the last decade of the century.

If a young housewife in Missouri, be she in the city or the country, knew very little about taking care of her house, her ignorance would be remedied by reading Mrs. Willis's twelve-page opening narrative. Mrs. Willis guides the reader from room to room and duty to duty in her lessons and recipe comments. Over one hundred years after the book's publication, twentieth-first-century readers have the opportunity to experience a virtual tour of what appears to be a Kansas City home staffed with at least one servant. Willis begins by discussing the changing servant situation at the time. "The days of trained servants seem to have passed away, and it is necessary for every housekeeper to know something more than the theory of work. She must know how to put her knowledge to practical use, that she may be enabled to teach and control her servants." Willis continues. "Servants are quick to see the incapacity of the mistress and few are slow to take advantage of her ignorance." Finally, "If a girl knows anything about cooking, she can readily learn the way you prefer to have yours done, if you know how yourself, so as to give her some instructions."[21] It certainly seems that Mrs. Willis, in her attention to detail in her instructions, knew what she was talking about. That knowledge was presumably developed through personal housekeeping experience.

She takes the young housekeeper through the house, offering advice on the proper way to keep a house in order. Steps for effectively cleaning in the bedroom involve thorough cleaning techniques and processes. Bedclothes and pillows must be hung before an open window, and once each month mattresses should be taken into the open air. She suggests laying them on the banisters of a porch where they can be beaten with an old broom handle and then swept and dusted with a clean broom. Of concern is the problem of bedbugs. She offers steps for ridding the bed of the invaders, warning against poisons "as they only serve to compel the bugs to leave the bed and seek other quarters in the room." Instead, she advocates washing the bed, slats, and sides and ends of the mattress with a wet cloth soaked in brine; if this plan is executed two or three times a week, she says the eggs will be destroyed. She believes that proper dusting in this manner should both rid the bed of bugs and prevent their returning in the future.[22]

She next scrutinizes the bathroom. Cleaning agents and equipment of choice include oxalic acid and pumice stone for the bathtub, pounded sapolio mixed into a paste for cleaning marble basins and tops of washstands, and lumps of copperas to be placed in the water closet every night. She explains, "A liberal allowance of water is poured into the closet every morning after the contents of the slop jars have been emptied into it" and insists that the windows be raised "to let fresh air in and foul air out" and only water closets with an outside opening in the room should be allowed in homes.[23]

Considering the kitchen to be the most important room in the house, Mrs. Willis lines out her ideas for its care and maintenance. Key points of discussion include a well-lit area, hardwood floors because they are easiest to clean, and a room wainscoted to a height of four feet. Her list continues: a closet with shelves for cooking utensils, a clean sink, and a clean floor. Continued discussion of the kitchen area nets descriptions of equipment used in a Kansas City kitchen at the time. She points out the importance of a tin safe in the kitchen to keep food cold and suggests storing salt, bread crumbs, spices, and cornstarch in jars. Her answer for keeping ants out of the tin safe is to place the legs of it in tin cups filled with water. Even though some houses of which she is aware are overrun with roaches, she indicates she has been keeping house for over eighteen years and never has had a problem with them and recommends the use of powdered borax to "keep them away." Mrs. Willis is not into the "new fangled flour and meal boxes," preferring the use of a barrel with a tight-fitting cover for her flour and a wooden sugar bucket for meal.[24]

Dishing out numerous housekeeping details, she believes that washtubs should be stored with water in them to keep them from drying and shrinking (and then leaking), and irons should be stored in dry places to prevent rusting. Both may be kept in the cellar. Regarding the disposal of kitchen refuse, she favors burning parings and hulls after the meal is over and doesn't "see a need for a swill bucket if you don't have hogs." She offers a warning if one is used: "Be sure that it is washed and scalded every day, or you may have a case of typhoid fever." Addressing freezing temperatures in Kansas City in the winter, she indicates that one should "saturate a cloth with lard, lay it in a pie pan and light it and hold it under the pipes" to thaw frozen pipes or avoid the inconvenience by simply turning the water off at night when it appears that there will be freezing weather.[25]

In the housekeeping narration, two additional important areas warrant the instruction of Mrs. Willis—how to manage a spring cleaning and how to prepare and serve breakfast. Given the climate in Kansas City, May seems to be the target date for beginning the spring-cleaning process. Duties include cleaning the garret and closets. Winter clothes not being stored in cedar closets benefit from camphor and tobacco placed among them during storage. The removal of rugs to yard areas where they may be cleaned by beating and sweeping appears to be a major part of the spring-cleaning effort. After hanging rugs on a line and beating them with a contraption described as a "leather strap, two inches wide and four or five feet long on a wooden handle" they are spot cleaned with a suds of soap tree bark or beef gall. Dry rugs are then repositioned on the floors with a carpet stretcher and tacked back down until the next spring cleaning.[26]

The role of the hired cook becomes evident in a discussion of how to prepare and serve breakfast. Obviously considering breakfast to be an important meal, Mrs. Willis modifies an old adage and includes it in her introductory comments in the cookbook. "Time and tide ('and my breakfast table') wait for no man," she explains. A Kansas City breakfast in her opinion sports a hearty bill of fare: broiled beefsteak, Saratoga potatoes, scrambled eggs, yeast powder biscuits, tea, and coffee. She explains that a first course of fruit or oatmeal is acceptable and that sliced tomatoes in season add to the breakfast choices. Willis offers tips for teaching the cook how to prepare the bill of fare in stages so that items are the temperature desired when serving. Of interest is a gadget in the home that she uses to communicate with the cook. "I have a regular hour for breakfast, but sometimes we might not be ready when it was announced, so I have a speaking tube to the kitchen, and I call to the cook to serve breakfast; that means to put the steak on to broil, and all the household know they have twenty minutes to get ready for breakfast."[27]

What were Kansas City cooks preparing for meals other than breakfast? Recipes for such familiar dishes as breaded pork chops, baked ham, salmon croquettes, baked potatoes, cauliflower with cheese, green peas, macaroni and tomatoes, boiled cabbage, stewed okra, cherry pie, and lemon pie make appearances in the cookbook. Recipes modern Missouri cooks may not have experienced include salt rising bread, beaten biscuits, cornmeal mush, sheep's tongue, hog brains, baked pigeons, prairie chickens, hickory nut candy, transparent pie, and vinegar pie.

It seems that raising chickens wasn't limited to Missouri's rural areas during the time the Kansas City ladies compiled their cookbook. Mrs. Willis takes time to offer words in the section devoted to meat recipes about "spring chickens." She explains, "The excellence of spring chickens depends as much upon feeding as cooking them." She suggests placing them in the yard in a coop about four or five feet square. They should be fed corn or wheat and table scraps for about a week prior to the chicken dinner so that "They will be plump and white, and the flavor quite different from the skinny, bony chickens from the market." She also proposes an interesting alternative plan for fattening up chickens: "If you have several rooms in the cellar, use one for the chickens, sprinkle the floor with a little gravel and keep it clean." Her final tip—"If it is to be cooked in the morning, dress the night before."[28] Mrs. Bird follows with a recipe for the ever-popular fried chicken, proposing that it be served with a bowl of cream gravy.

Like Mrs. Henderson's cookbook, the Kansas City cookbook includes recipes written in single paragraph style with ingredients and limited instructions embedded within the sentences. Mrs. Henderson's cookbook, however, does include more dishes with a foreign flair possibly as a result of her European cooking-school training. Additionally Mrs. Henderson's cookbook includes several pages of illustrations of nineteenth-century cooking utensils and directions for their use, including, among others, one of a bain marie for keeping cooked dishes warm, a Saratoga potato-cutter, a meat-squeezer for pressing out the juice of beef for invalids, a butter roller for forming individual serving balls, and a finally a potato, carrot, or turnip cutter for making vegetable curls.

Mrs. Willis's cookbook offers readers an opportunity to become familiar with late-nineteenth-century Kansas City businesses through the advertisement section of the project. Landis Transfer and Livery Company, 811 Wyandotte Street, details transportation services they have available within the city. "To and from Depot for 50 cents each. Baggage free to any point within limits. Limits. North of Twenty Third Street and west of Woodland Avenue. To points beyond this limit and within city limits, $1.00 will be charged for each passenger. All drivers in livery. Elegant calling carriages. Reasonable charges and prompt attention." Mrs. R. Sach's ad for her Fashionable Millinery and Hair Goods business states, "Orders for all parts of the country are promptly attended to." H. H. Shepard's Bookstore promotes books, fine stationery, artistic novelties, fine fancy goods, leather goods, and opera glasses. Robert Keith Furniture and Carpet Company boasts that their warerooms are the largest in the United States, occupying ten floors with a total of eighty thousand feet of floor room. M. B. Wright advertises as the oldest jewelry house in Kansas City. Huggins Cracker and Candy Company promotes graham and oatmeal crackers, handmade cakes, sea foams, and Jersey butters. Readers can see the specifications and an illustration of the latest Leonard Hardwood Refrigerator in the Hall and Willis Hardware Company ad.

American cookbook authorities Eleanor and Bob Brown explain the significance of a late-nineteenth-century Missouri company cookbook also published in St. Louis. They believe that this promotional cookbook set the style for kitchen utensils across the country.[29] A small sixty-four-page cookbook packed with information and printed in 1896 (and possibly first printed as early as 1878), *The Granite Iron Ware Cook Book* includes numerous illustrations of the company's Granite Iron cooking goods within the pages of recipes. Through these illustrations, Missouri cooks, as well as cooks in other states, were able to learn about the St. Louis company's cookware. Testimonials in the cookbook proclaimed the safety and suitability of the merchandise for cooking. One professor assures cooks that the cookware is "free from lead, arsenic, and other metals injurious to health."[30]

Comments in the cookbook appeal to society-conscious women who entertain and who do so properly. Information in an early section of the publication offers a glimpse of the social "do's and don'ts" of Missourians who traveled in elevated social circles at the time. Regarding planning and hosting dinners, the cookbook explains, "Persons invited to a dinner party should be of the same standing in society. They need not be acquaintances, yet they should be such as move in the same class. Good talkers and good listeners are equally invaluable at a dinner. Among your guests always have one or more musicians. This will add greatly to the entertainment before and after dinner."[31]

Detailed instructions pertaining to invitations and judgments relating to the success of a dinner party follow. Readers learn that gentlemen cannot be invited without their wives, unless it is to a dinner given only for gentlemen, and ladies should not be invited without their husbands when other ladies

The Granite Iron Ware Cook Book, published in 1896, includes images of popular kitchen items and other household utensils marketed throughout the country by this St. Louis company.

are invited with their husbands. Concerning the proper time for a dinner party, the cookbook suggests that after business hours or from five to eight o'clock is best for city entertaining. However, an hour or two earlier is acceptable in the country. An additional note proposes, "The success of a dinner party is readily judged by the manner in which conversation has been sustained. If a stream of talk has been kept up, it shows that the guests have been entertained."[32]

Because of limited space, this cookbook offers only a sampling of recipes in each division, covering the range of main dishes, soups, salads, breads, entrees, and desserts. Recipes written in single-paragraph style with limited process instructions necessitate that Missouri cooks of the time fill in the details for mixing and baking from their own experience, as the following recipe for fruitcake demonstrates:

Fruit Cake
Twelve eggs, one pound of flour, one pound sugar, one pound butter, two pounds raisins, two pounds currants, one pound citron, two tablespoons cinnamon, four nutmegs, on cup sweet milk, one cup molasses, one teaspoon cream tarter, one teaspoon soda, one gill brandy. Bake two hours or more.[33]

The back cover of the cookbook features a page of the latest Granite Iron toilet articles, including slop jars, water carriers, foot tubs, and chamber pots—certainly essential items; however, they are not the sort of items one would find being advertised on the cover of a modern Missouri cookbook.

This taste of nineteenth-century Missouri cookbooks whets the appetite for more to come. Of special interest is the involvement of church groups, civic organizations, educational institutions, and medical auxiliaries as they join the state's community cookbook foray.

Chapter 3

Community Cookbooks

Grandmothers tell us that if we make good, brisk fires we are sure
of a smart partner for life.—*Park College Cook Book,* George S. Park and
Ella Park Lawrence, 1883

It is obvious that good news travels fast when it comes to the popularity of the community cookbook. One might imagine that women attending the Great Sanitary Fair in 1864 who browsed the books and stationery booth were impressed when they picked up a copy of *A Poetical Cookbook,* now recognized as America's first community cookbook, and found that it was written by one of their own, a Philadelphia woman, Maria J. Moss. They might have been aware that Moss was involved in the organization of the fair, serving on several women's committees, and might have felt that she was to be commended for donating a previously written cookbook to be sold for the benefit of the needs of the Northern soldiers. It also might have crossed their minds that they and their organizations could raise money in the same way, especially if other members of their group could be enlisted to contribute some of their favorite recipes, making the project easier and less time-consuming.

Apparently, more than a few civic-minded women felt that compiling cookbooks and selling them to raise money had potential. When, at the end of the Civil War, they transferred their charitable efforts to a variety of causes in their towns and cities, they added community cookbook projects to their fund-raising agendas. In *America's Charitable Cooks,* Margaret Cook demonstrates the growth and popularity of the community cookbook from its inception toward the end of the Civil War through 1915, as she chronologically details cookbook projects in communities by state. A survey of her representative listings shows that by the mid-1870s and 1880s, organizations across the country, including some in Missouri, were developing and promoting cookbooks through their church and civic organizations.

Taking advantage of the popularity of these projects in the late nineteenth century, Missouri communities joined Kansas City and St. Louis, two of the first communities to produce fund-raising cookbook projects. A sampling of known nineteenth-century Missouri community cookbooks during these two decades shows cookbook publications in Parkville, Fayette, Lexington, Mount Vernon, Carthage, Kahoka, Sedalia, Knob Noster, and Butler.

Moving into the first decade of the twentieth century, enthusiasm for the community cookbook continued. In addition to new publications in St. Louis and Kansas City, historical records indicate that church cookbooks also surfaced in such communities as Canton, Hannibal, Liberty, Springfield, Columbia, Sheridan, and Cape Girardeau. Alexandria, Monroe City, Neosho, Meadville, Jefferson City, and Webb City joined the parade with their own publications. During the second decade, Monett, Webster Groves, Memphis, Kirksville, Liberty, Paris, and Joplin also produced cookbooks.

Several factors likely contribute to this widespread enthusiasm for community cookbooks. Since they were developed by the cooks themselves, recipe collections reflected foods that were actually being prepared in the contributors' own kitchens. Generally speaking, community cookbooks listed easily obtainable, locally grown ingredients.

Additionally, because her name commonly appeared with the recipe, each cook was certain to donate her favorite tried-and-true recipes. In St. Louis in 1910, the ladies of the church in the *Union Avenue Christian Church Cook Book* address their patrons in opening comments: "The best recipes are those that have been tried and tested before they are recommended as such [and we believe our cookbook] is made up of the best recipes known to our ladies, hence we can recommend them to you with all confidence that they will prove to be first aid to the digestion."[1] Members of the Helen Richardson Mission Band of the St. Louis Lafayette Park M. E. Church, South, in selecting *The Kitchen Oracle* (1889) as the name of their project seem to be alluding to the worthwhile culinary information contained in their cookbook.

Opening remarks in two Kansas City cookbooks and in one from Pocohontas discuss the merits of their recipes. The ladies of the Fifth Presbyterian Church in Kansas City titled their cookbook *Choice and Tested Recipes*

(1905) and share their selection philosophy: "A favorite recipe is a part of the home atmosphere. We associate certain 'dishes' with one who bore a loving thought for us when she made it, and as long as we live will remember with keen pleasure the dishes mother made which were just a little better than any others."[2] The project includes recipes contributed by mothers, recipes that merit, in their opinion, being handed down to future generations. In *Our Own Cookbook* (Kansas City, 1920) members of Woman's City Club refer to "grandmother's cook book, the little blank book in which she copied the recipes collected from other friends" and indicate that their recipes, like grandmother's, are "tried and dependable recipes."[3] Taking the same approach, in Pocahontas the *St. John's Evangelical Lutheran Church Cookbook* (1977) committee offers this message: "The recipes in this book may not have been laboratory tested, but their merit has been established by church and civic groups and the most critical group of all Husbands and Family!"[4]

Church projects represent a significant portion of Missouri's community cookbooks. Because many of the recipes contributed to collections had been carried to church potlucks, it is quite possible that members of the congregation and residents of the community had already had an opportunity to sample dishes detailed in the cookbooks, and an awareness of the food-preparation skills of the women of the church certainly may have boosted cookbook sales.

In Missouri, especially during the first half of the nineteenth century, church activities were a significant part of the social lives of individuals who lived in small towns and on surrounding farms. Rural Missourians gathered at their churches not only for Sunday services but also for social events and other church activities. Frequently, the events featured foods prepared by members either for a dinner or a supper or to be served as light refreshments at women's circles, ladies' aid activities, and youth gatherings.

Communal meals, whether in city or rural churches, provided a time for members to relax and visit with friends and neighbors on topics related to church, cooking, sewing, child rearing, tractors, jobs, schools, and taxes. Members enjoyed the social interaction as well as the variety of food shared at church potlucks, carry-in dinners, and dinner-on-the-grounds events. Not to be overlooked, summertime ice cream socials provided welcome relief on hot and humid Sunday afternoons or evenings in Missouri.

To help their communities and to contribute to their larger mission programs, congregations organized food events to raise money for various needs: upkeep of the church cemetery, the building fund, the minister's salary, youth activities, the church's overseas mission program, or repairs on some aspect of the church sometimes called for additional funding over and above the Sunday offering. In Missouri, some staples of such events included chicken and dumplings, kettle beef, bratwurst, fried chicken, ham and beans, pancakes and sausage, spaghetti, fish, barbecue, chili, or soup. Main dishes were typically flanked by generous side dishes, homemade breads, and desserts prepared and baked by church members. More recently, church food events have featured ethnic dinners and baked potato bars. Even today, several churches around the state raise money by orchestrating apple-butter-making events in the fall. For over thirty years, members of the Arcadia Valley Methodist Church in Ironton, under the direction of Dot Owens and according to a recipe passed down by her grandmother, have been stirring up batches of apple butter for a yearly money-making project.

Fund-raising church cookbooks became a natural for women who attended churches where events and activities were celebrated and companioned with food. Since cooking and recipes were so much a part of their lives, organizing a church cookbook project would have been a relatively simple feat for members of a women's circle or of a Sunday school class. At a regular meeting members would kick off the project with a request for cooks to select and contribute several recipes to the collection. Willing cooks delivered their recipe choices to the cookbook committee or to those who had agreed to serve as editors of the project. Church cookbooks often included recipes from members' friends in the area as well as those from distant states who were not members themselves. The 1926 *Chaffee Cook Book,* organized by the ladies of the Circle of the Methodist Church, included recipes sent in from Keytesville and Lee's Summit in Missouri; East St. Louis, Illinois; Longmont, Colorado; Akron, Ohio; and Santa Ana, California. Likewise, the group moved outside their city limits to sell advertising space in the cookbook, in this case to Benton and Cape Girardeau.

As the recipe-collecting process wound down, decisions had to be made regarding the addition of extra information and determinations made concerning duplication and printing processes. It was not uncommon for project organizers to include information about their church. At a minimum cookbook organizers might add a bit of information about themselves, include a picture of their church, and add the times of their services and the name of their minister. Members of the Martha Mary Circle at the Belleview

Methodist Church, dressed in their Sunday-morning best, took time to have their picture snapped for inclusion in their cookbook, *A Book of Favorite Recipes* (1986), and also added the times of worship services. In 1996 St. Paul's Lutheran Ladies' Aid Society in New Melle opened *St. Paul's Country Recipes* with a photo of their church gracefully nestled in a snow-covered lawn flanked by an ice-covered tree reflecting a bright crisp winter day. They note that their church was established in 1844 and also offer sample table prayers before moving to the recipe collection. Compiled by the United Methodist Youth, the *Senath United Methodist Church Cookbook* (1981) includes a message from the pastor at the end of the collection of recipes. Reverend Roberson points out, "How good God is to us . . . and how good the green earth which he has designed to satisfy us with good things with just a little skill and effort. Such is the culinary art."[5]

Groups with more enthusiastic writers, photographers, and illustrators detail church histories and place images of their buildings in cookbooks or on covers. The *Arcadia Valley Cook Book* (1920), compiled by the Ladies' Aid Society, features numerous photographs, among them a photo of the First Baptist Church in Ironton. Other photos spotlight several sites in the area, including Lake Killarney, a shut-in near Arcadia, Bungalow Block in Arcadia, and the elegant W. H. Thomson "Valley Home" country residence in Arcadia. Cooks have an opportunity to visualize church-camp life offered at Arcadia Heights, the Baptist assembly grounds. Of special interest is a large in-ground swimming pool, no doubt quite an attraction at the time.

A. J. Sheahan Granite Company ads include a photo of a working granite quarry as well as one of the famous Elephant Rocks. About this now-popular state attraction, the Missouri Department of Natural Resources notes on its Web site that "Architects and developers discovered the elephants . . . in the 1800s"; the description indicates that the Elephant Rocks area, dating back geologically over a billion years, moved from private ownership to Missouri state park status when Dr. John S. Brown, a retired St. Joseph Lead Company geologist, purchased the property and then in 1966 deeded the 135-acre site to the state for use as a recreation area and park.[6]

Arcadia Valley, nestled among the rugged peaks of the St. Francois Mountains, is considered by tourists to be one of the most picturesque areas of Missouri, especially in the fall. This area, like Belleview Valley to the north, was one of the first areas inland from the Mississippi River to be settled. Looking for farmland, settlers moved into these areas in the late 1700s and early 1800s.[7] While French settlers dominated nearby areas such as Mine La Motte, Fredericktown, Old Mines, and Potosi, settlers moving into the Belleview and Arcadia Valley areas were primarily of Scotch-Irish descent. Many of the early settlers had obtained Spanish land grants. Arcadia Valley and the towns that developed there—Iron Mountain, Arcadia, Ironton, Graniteville, and Pilot Knob—became important to the development of the state because of the presence of mineral deposits. As early as 1815, iron was mined near Ironton, and more serious commercial iron mining began in the early 1840s.[8]

Because of the mineral resources in this area, the St. Louis and Iron Mountain Railroad was chartered to build a line to Pilot Knob to haul ore and iron to St. Louis in 1851.[9] This made Arcadia Valley of strategic importance during the Civil War, resulting in a significant battle at Fort Davidson in Pilot Knob. Granite, another mineral resource of importance to the region, was quarried as early as the 1860s at several small quarries. Between 1900 and 1930 the area provided large quantities of granite for use as paving stones for St. Louis streets and in the construction of the Eads Bridge. Granite is still quarried at Graniteville.[10]

The look of community cookbooks has undergone significant change as printing and publishing options have evolved. Early Missouri community cookbooks seem rather plain when compared to more colorful modern editions. Cookbook covers in the early years simply featured the name of the cookbook and in some cases a graphic design that complemented the title.

Publishing and printing credits in early Missouri community cookbooks indicate that they were commonly printed at local print shops and at newspaper-printing facilities, although some groups found printing options outside their communities. The Faithful Workers of the Presbyterian Church in Caruthersville hired Cashion and Cashion, Printers in Perryville, to print their project, *The Twentieth Century Cook Book* (1902), and the Ladies' Aid Society of the First Baptist Church in Ironton enlisted the Western Baptist Publishing Company in Kansas City to print the 1920 edition of the *Arcadia Valley Cook Book*. Some organizers cut expenses by designing and duplicating their own cookbooks and covers, as in the cases of the *Centennial Cookbook* (1956), under the direction of editor Dorothy Reese, and *Favorite Recipes,* prepared by the Miriam Circle of the Ascension Lutheran Church in Kansas City. The first includes a simple stapled fold-over mimeographed cover made of paper that was slightly heavier than that used for the pages. The second cover seems to have been constructed by sewing wallpaper onto pieces of cardboard through which two metal rings were then run to hold this creative homemade cookbook together.

In the early decades of the century, cookbook compilers chose both hard and soft covers to encase their collections. Hardcover editions were not limited to city printings as *The Kitchen Oracle* and the *Arcadia Valley Cook Book* demonstrate. *The Campbell Cook Book* (1910), a seventy-four-page hardcover publication compiled by the Ladies of the Baptist Church, seems to have been printed by a local printing establishment, the Campbell Citizen Shop. A final message from the printer touts the local printing available in this southeast Missouri town. "No one can send a job of printing away and get it done for the same money that the home man charges for a better job. We have compared printing from every state in the Union with that produced by Dunklin county shops, and find that home printing is superior in nearly every instance. And a mighty big per cent of Dunklin's good printing is the product of the Campbell Citizen Shop."[11]

Early cookbook organizers seeking to finance publication expenses obviously realized the benefit of including advertisements supplied by local businesses so that more of the profit from the sale of the cookbook would be realized for their intended causes. Community cookbooks published throughout the state are sprinkled with advertisements for local businesses. *The Campbell Cook Book* includes an ad for E. E. Lownsdale's Rubber Tire Machine Blacksmith and Repair Shop detailing the services offered. "Have Barens' Shoeing Stocks. Don't fail to bring in your wild horses. Do all kinds of Blacksmith and Woodwork." The same cookbook promotes the J. M. Dunivan and Son Shaving Parlor on the south side. Of the several businesses advertising in the cookbook, only two establishments list phone numbers, the Gourley Brothers Livery, Feed and Sale Stable (phone 12) and the Hopper Planing Mill Company (phone 96). The First National Bank indicates in its ad that the bank holds a capital of $30,000 and a surplus of $1,500.

Churchwomen organizing *The Kitchen Oracle* offset their printing expenses with a variety of advertisements. An ad for Littell's Liquid Sulphur promises "It gives instant relief and cures for Burns, Scalds, Bites and Stings, Diphtheria, Sore Throat, Canker Mouth, Poison Oak, Hives, Nettle Rash, Tender Sweating Feet, Prickley Heat, Etc." Mound City Cereal Company in St. Louis promotes hominy for "Only 5c Per Package." S. Pfeiffer Manufacturing Company asks the cook to remember to try their old established

By advertising in the *Campbell Cook Book*, E. E. Lownsdale was able to support the community fund-raising effort and at the same time reach potential customers in their homes.

family remedies: Hosteter's Tonic Herbs to strengthen the nerves; Ru-bin-ade for colic, cramps and diarrhea; and Dr. Pepper's Chill Killers to be used instead of quinine, all for twenty-five cents each.

Two entertainment/travel companies promote services in the same cookbook. The Columbia Excursion Company indicates that the steamer *City of Providence* "can be chartered by Churches, Sunday Schools and Societies for day or evening Excursions during the coming Summer." The second, a rather elaborate full-page ad on the inside back cover, promotes the Iron Mountain Route. Readers learn that a train services Hot Springs, Arkansas (the Carlsbad of America), which, they are also informed, is owned and supervised by the United States government. Prospective travelers are further enticed by the numerous points of interest in the Southwest that may be accessed by the Iron Mountain Route: Austin, San Antonio, Galveston, Corpus Christi, Aransas Pass, Rockport, Dallas, Fort Worth, and Houston. The train also can take them to Mexico (the Egypt of the New World) and California (the

Golden Gate). Travel accommodations include "elegant Pullman Buffet Sleeping Cars, Reclining Chair Cars, Pullman Tourist Cars, and Elegant Day Coaches."

Few technological developments had a greater impact on Missouri's economy and the lifestyle of its citizens than the railroads. The state chartered the first railroads in the 1830s, but progress on construction was slow. Missouri sold bonds to generate start-up money for the railroads, and many local communities offered financial aid in order to secure the passage of a railway through their towns. By the 1850s, interest in railroad building had reached a feverish pitch.

Railroads brought great benefits to the state: farm products and manufactured items could be transferred around Missouri or to other states, and all sorts of items could be ordered by mail, and products would arrive to be picked up at local depots. Train travel also gave Missourians a new level of comfort and speed in transportation. With interconnecting routes, individuals could board a train in their town and travel to points of interest of their choice in other parts of the country in relative comfort. Dining and sleeping cars meant travelers could enjoy good food en route and arrive at their destination rested. Competition between lines led to additional amenities and special fares, possibly why the Iron Mountain Route ad mentions "tourist tickets at greatly reduced rates" in the ad placed in *The Kitchen Oracle*.

Advertisements supplied by national food-product companies likewise appear in Missouri's community cookbooks. Walter Baker and Company placed a one-page ad in *The Twentieth Century Cook Book* compiled by the Faithful Workers of the Presbyterian Church in Caruthersville in 1902, thus allowing the company to promote its product directly to Missouri cooks who were making candies, cookies, cakes, and pies. The ad announces that the company earned three gold medals at the Pan-American Exposition in Paris in 1900, and a third edition of the same cookbook includes a full-page ad promoting Igleheart Brothers Swans Down Cake Flour along with the company's popular cookbook, *Cake Secrets*. The colorful ad offers the only splash of color in the Caruthersville publication. The same ad indicates that readers may receive their own copy of *Cake Secrets* by sending a dime either in coin or stamps. The Ladies of the Good Will Circle of the Chaffee Methodist Church evidently enlisted the support of the Knox Gelatin Company for their 1926 cookbook since it included an advertisement line for this product on almost every page. As Missouri cooks searched for recipes, they

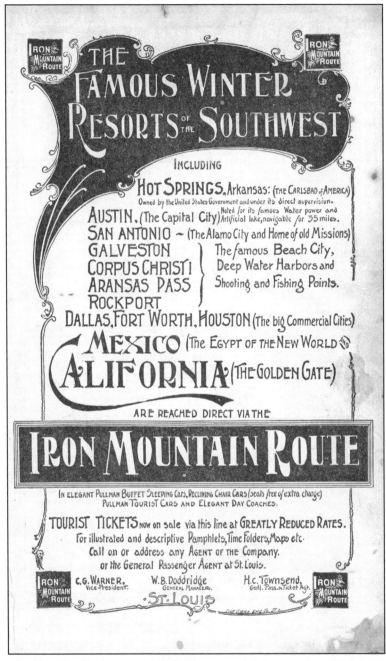

This advertisement for the Iron Mountain Route encouraged cookbook readers to take vacations.

Ads for Karo corn syrup and Kingsford's corn starch reminded experienced cooks and introduced new cooks to their products while their placement in the *Union Avenue Christian Church Cook Book* subtly suggested an endorsement by the book's compilers.

were reminded of Knox products and of the positive features of each. Royal Baking Powder supplied the only full-age color ad in this cookbook.

Once the recipes became a cookbook, the fine reputation of the cooks in the church would, it was hoped, make congregational membership and friends in the community eager to purchase it. Success of the book sometimes demanded that another cookbook be put out with popular recipes reappearing in successive editions. Two cookbooks organized by the Unionville Methodist Women demonstrate this practice in community cookbooks. *Favorite Recipes II,* published in 2000 after the original *Favorite Recipes* in 1975, acknowledges popular recipes by labeling each repeat as a "1st Edition Favorite." "Annie Webb's 24 Hour Cabbage Salad," "Jean Pratt's Spaghetti Sauce," and a recipe for pork chops and rice in memory of Mary Faye Spence along with directions for making Polish donuts make the cut for repetition in the second edition of the Unionville church cookbook.

During the '30s and '40s, several cookbook publishing companies in various states organized and became increasingly popular as they began to serve the needs of the community cookbook market. Their convenient package deals, including designs for covers and division pages as well as agreements to typeset recipes and to format the cookbooks attracted Missouri cookbook compilers then, and they still do today. At one time at least one company assisted groups with their ad-selling campaigns by contacting local businesses and by designing ads for companies choosing to support the project through advertisement. Very popular today, these cookbook publishers deliver attractive products. However, stock illustrations and photo options for covers and division pages and stock supplementary culinary, nutritional, and housekeeping hints sometimes result in uniformity among otherwise unconnected cookbooks. On the creative side, however, the publishers offer options for organizations to generate their own photos, illustrations, written pieces, and cover designs. Even though these options increase the price of the finished products, taking advantage of these choices results in more individualized cookbooks.

The development of community cookbooks by civic organizations and institutions generally follows the pattern implemented by church organizations, that of pooling favorite recipes and compiling a collection with the goal of selling it and using money raised to carry out the activities of the organization. One of the first recorded Missouri community cookbooks

Ella Park Lawrence, coauthor with her father, George S. Park, of *Industrial Lessons* or *Park College Cook Book,* published in 1883, one of the earliest fund-raising community cookbooks. (Courtesy Fishburn Archives, Park University, Parkville, Missouri)

originated in an educational institution. In the early 1880s, George S. Park and his daughter Ella Park Lawence compiled *Industrial Lessons,* also referred to as the *Park College Cook Book.* Lawrence developed recipes in a classroom format so that they could be used in the domestic science department at Park College. Money from cookbook sales was to be channeled into an endowment fund for the development of that department.

The author was very methodical in applying her recipe format. Each recipe opens with a list of ingredients that the cook is instructed to place on the table at the beginning. As in the recipe format found in many modern Missouri cookbooks, there follows a numbered list of steps for the preparation of the dish. Lawrence concludes each recipe with classroom review questions. Clearly written, it would seem that the recipes could have been used in the home as well as in the classroom. In addition to recipes, the author includes lessons designed to make sure that students will learn how to keep a kitchen range in good condition, understand how to clean kitchen utensils, and learn how to build a fire in the kitchen range.

In May 1875, George S. Park and John A. McAfee were instrumental in founding Park College in Parkville, Missouri. Four years later, after graduating the first class, they incorporated the school and created the original college charter, which included the vision that "the principles of the college shall be non-sectarian, but evangelical, imbued with the spirit of Christian liberty and charity."[12] Passages in the cookbook reinforce these principles with one of the lessons in the cookbook devoted to Bible views of domestic labor. The compilers open this lesson with a verse from Genesis, noting the price Adam and Eve paid for disobeying God, and then they move through the Bible, selecting verses that extol the values of work, truth, and wisdom. They follow each verse with an observation designed to deliver and to clarify the meaning of each scripture passage.

Beyond religious instruction, the original charter provided for both a male department, which included classes in agriculture, business management, skilled labor and practical wisdom, and a female department. Female students could take advantage of the religious, science, literature, and art studies, and they could also benefit from courses devoted to "household and domestic duties and management and culinary arts, accompanied with regular practical and skilled labor and wise arts required in American homes."[13] The practical work-study approach to learning was apparently advantageous to the college as well as to the students with the educational design allowing students who were unable to pay for their education to do so by contributing work hours at the college. "The young men farmed, constructed buildings, chopped wood, ran the printing press, and milked the cows; the young women cooked, cleaned, and did laundry among other types of typically female labor. Together, they performed nearly every task necessary to maintain the school."[14]

The *Park College Cook Book* (*Industrial Lessons*) earned discussion in early editions of the school's newspaper, *The Park College Record*. An article in an 1879 edition notes, "Col. Park and daughter are busily and earnestly engaged in preparing a book on Domestic Economy. This book, is soon to come forth from the College press." The book, slated for an 1880 publication, did not materialize until 1883. Student editor Lulu Boyd writes, "The first sheets were printed in 1880, but the failure in health of Miss Ella Park, (now Mrs. Lawrence), who has furnished the copy, and the many delays incident to a printing office run as this one is, has necessitated very slow work in publication." Boyd's article continues with the explanation that all stages of this work except the binding for this, their first bound work, were entirely accomplished by the students at the college. A sales receipt archived at Park College indicates that Ramsey, Millett and Hudson in Kansas City bound 1,446 cookbooks at a total expense of $235.43.[15]

Carolyn Elwess, Park University archivist, notes in a biography of the father-daughter team that in 1882, Ella married prominent attorney George A. Lawrence and settled in Galesburg, Illinois. Ella became actively involved in that community and was later honored by Knox College for her many contributions to worthwhile causes. At that event the Missouri cookbook was mentioned. "The fact that the book was mentioned in 1922 at such a prestigious event may demonstrate how precious it was to Ella and hints that she may have spoken of it often." Elwess indicates that college records do not reveal whether the cookbook was ever used in the classroom and concludes, "To my knowledge, the *Park College Cook Book* was never reprinted or updated and simply faded from memory into obscurity."[16]

From the Park project to current publications, cookbooks with connections to state educational institutions have been welcomed into Missouri kitchens. The 1980 collector's edition of *Kitchenology with Principia Friends*, compiled by the Principia Mothers' Club, shares historical information regarding the life of this Missouri cookbook. It was born out of a need to raise money for the building fund for Principia College. The project came to life when the mothers of five Principia students in St. Louis conceived the idea of a fund-raising cookbook. Each Principia family was asked to contribute three favorite recipes, and cookbook organizers received one thousand recipes, which were then tested, and six hundred were selected for the project. The book was ready to be marketed in 1933, and it went through two additional printings, one in 1935 followed by a facsimile collector's edition in 1980.[17]

Delightful illustrations by Rudolph Tandler, professor of art at the college, enhance the cookbook, making it one of Missouri's most visually appealing vintage cookbooks. Continuing their cookbook tradition, the Principia Mothers teamed with the Dad's Club in 2003 to develop *Cooking with Principia*. It features photographs of buildings on the St. Louis campus and the college campus. The original cookbook was printed by a St. Louis publisher, and the new publication saw a move to a cookbook publishing company.

Principia College, operated by Christian Scientists for Christian Scientists, overlooks the bluffs on the Mississippi River in Elsah, Illinois, and a campus for infants through high school-age students is located in West St. Louis County. The Principia educational concept began in 1897 with founder Mary Kimball Morgan, who set out to homeschool her sons. Interest in her concept grew as fellow Christian Scientist parents approved her methods and asked her to include their children in the homeschool process. Morgan opened a school the following year. As an independent school, Principia continued to grow, with the first high school class graduating in 1906, the first class graduating from junior college in 1917, and the first group of students receiving bachelor of arts degrees in 1934.[18]

With many schools in Missouri operating on tight budgets, priority lists must be made, and unfortunately, needed items often have to be cut. Community booster clubs and parent organizations across the state take an active part in helping school systems continue to meet the needs of students by raising money through various projects.

The Hillsboro PTA compiled *Town and Country Cookie Book* in 1953. This representative example of a Missouri specialty, or single-concept, cookbook takes readers on a nostalgic visit to the '50s with phone numbers in advertisements listed as Victor 3–4250 and Sunset 9–2033. The Hillsboro Café offers home-cooked food and fresh homemade pies. In addition to favorites from the '50s like coconut cuties, mint surprise cookies, Hawaiian coconut cookies, and tutti-frutti squares, the cookbook records recipes for reliable standards of the day: snickerdoodles, plain rolled cookies, hermits, drop gingersnaps, and rocks. Missouri's twenty-first-century "slice and bake" cookie fans benefit from a generous helping of recipes for "ice box," or "refrigerator, cookies," early versions of the modern packaged rolls of cookie dough picked up in supermarkets with the goal of delivering a quick plate of cookies. PTA members offer two dozen recipes for ice box cookies. It would seem from the popularity of this section of the cookbook that busy moms from the '50s might have wisely tucked batches of previously mixed cookie dough that had been formed into rolls and neatly covered with wax paper into their ice boxes for spur-of-the-moment use.

When new playground equipment was needed, community members and parents in one Missouri town stepped up to bat and produced a cookbook to help pay for these items. The Bucklin R-II School Playground Committee in 1999 delivered the message of their project in the cover design and through brief notes preceding the recipe collection featured in *Bucklin Alumni Cookbook*. The crisp black-and-white cover features drawings of assorted playground equipment. Including student recipes among other community contributions, the committee notes, "These recipes are from graduates of the 1920's to our future graduates." Marc Finney details a clever recipe for sidewalk chalk molded in toilet tissue tubes and allowed to dry for a couple of days. He directs at the end of his recipe, "Peel off the mold and chalk up a masterpiece!" Not to be outdone, Gracyn Hanson details her recipe for instant stickers. After cutting pictures from old magazines, comic books, or giftwrap, she brushes the backs with a mixture of water and flavored gelatin. She lets them dry and then, "The stickers are ready to lick and stick!" Charles Hughes closes the cookbook with his recipe for living in Bucklin: "First I sit in a comfortable chair, read my Bible and let God's love soak in. Then I open the front door and go out on the porch and let God's love pass on to anyone passing by."[19]

The Missouri State Teachers Association (MSTA) published their community cookbook in 2003. *Schoolhouse Treats* not only shares a wide array of Missouri recipes but also includes a brief history of the organization and takes cooks back in time with an image of the Woodland District II one-room school on the cover. The group originated in 1856 when a small group of Missouri educators met in Wyman's Hall in St. Louis. Information notes that 110 teachers from 22 counties in Missouri believed that they were ready to form a permanent organization. Adopted May 23, 1856, the constitution lined out the purposes of the organization, which were concerned with promoting "the sacred interests of education in uniting the different members, advancing their mutual improvement and elevating the profession to its just intellectual and moral influence on the community." Cooks learn that MSTA is the oldest and largest professional education association in Missouri and that the organization in its 150-year history continues to strive to "support educators as they work to shape the lives of children."[20]

The collection gathers recipes sent in from teachers throughout the state and offers an excellent representation of recipes for treats, old and new, being served and preserved in modern Missouri kitchens in the twenty-first century. Stephanie Wheeler (Stet R-XV) contributes a recipe for "Grandma William's Lime Pickles" and Sandra Gilkey (Lakeland R-III) details a more modern recipe for yam crisps and cajun dip. In keeping with modern diet-ing interests, Terrie Rose offers roast beef stir-fry including a notation that it is a "lo-carb" dish. Not to be forgotten are recipes for peanut brittle from Fred Wiktorek (Doniphan R-I), "Grandmother's Peach Cobbler" from Margaret Bangerter (District Office, St. Joseph), and homemade ice cream from Dorothy G. Bennett, a retired teacher. The cookbook also serves up recipes that represent dishes utilizing modern mix-and-match prepared food products. Judy Reed (Senath-Hornersville C-8) contributes a "modern mix it up recipe," death by chocolate trifle, a quick combination of a boxed brownie mix, boxes of vanilla pudding, and a container of Cool Whip. The dish to die for is topped of with crumbled Butterfinger or Heath candy bars.

Medical auxiliaries not only contribute hours to assist medical programs in Missouri hospitals, they also make significant additions to the state's com-munity cookbook buffet. In the introduction to *Cooking in Clover* (1977), David A. Gee, president of Jewish Hospital in St. Louis, offers words of praise for the Jewish Hospital Auxiliary, sponsors of the cookbook. After commenting on the irony of a hospital auxiliary publishing a cookbook, con-sidering "age old jokes about hospital food, with the unsalted peas and pureed carrots," he points out that the book "is aimed at the good times, when the digestive juices are flowing properly and the calorie counting is momentarily set aside." Discussing the value of hospital auxiliaries, he also associates the "good times" with auxiliary programs that "bring so many plus services to the Hospital and the patients which it serves" and mentions that the volunteers "provide services in over 30 different activities within the Hos-pital" thus delivering "added dimensions of support." Cookbook co-chairwomen Mrs. Richard W. Bazer and Mrs. John A. Isaacs point out one reward associated with this community-based fund-raising project, "the sat-isfaction of knowing that you have contributed to the continuing excellence of the Jewish Hospital of St. Louis."[21] During the cookbook project, forty-one women served as recipe testers, thus assuring quality recipes. On an interesting note, in this cookbook, in order to assist Missouri cooks, editors of the diverse recipe collection rank each recipe by degree of difficulty, from "easy" to "difficult," and include the time required to prepare dishes.

Committed to serving their communities through worthwhile service projects, Junior League members in Missouri donate their time and energies to raise money and then to channel it back into their communities. The devel-opment of stylish modern cookbooks has been only one of the successful projects organized by these civic-minded Missouri women. In 1975, in keeping with the popularity of entertaining during this decade, the Junior League of Kansas City published *Company's Coming: Foods for Entertaining*. Ann Lombardi sets the tone in the introduction, suggesting that cooking need not be a negative experience but can be a creative and dramatic event. The cookbook presents information focusing on the enjoyment of wine and includes a list of menus for special occasions. The use of fresh seasonal food products takes center stage in *The Roux We Do*, a St. Joseph Junior League 2001 publication. The St. Joseph Junior League also partnered with representatives of their local museum to deliver a second edition of the museum's cookbook *Palette to Palate*. This Missouri museum became a part of the community in 1913 when the St. Joseph Art League was founded. Under the direction of members of the community, the museum was designed to promote awareness and an understanding of the arts. A first major purchase for the museum was made in 1915 and growing interest and commitment led to the opening of the Albrecht Gallery in 1966. The museum underwent expansion in 1991 and at that time became the Albrecht-Kemper Museum of Art.[22] Missourians not only enjoy and appreciate the collection of art, they also benefit from cultural programs and special events staged regularly by the organization.

St. Louis and Springfield Junior Leagues also have developed cookbooks. St. Louis members share their favorite kitchen memories and recipes in *Meet Us in the Kitchen* and spotlight their city's cultural diversity in *Saint Louis Days... Saint Louis Nights*. A combination of recipes and delightful Ozarks humor blend to make the Springfield Junior League cookbook *Women Who Can Dish It Out—The Lighter Side of the Ozarks* a delightful culinary experience. The same group published *Sassafras! The Ozarks Cookbook*. Junior League cookbooks have sold millions of copies, raising considerable sums of money for causes in the organization's communities in Missouri.

Over the years, a mix of organizations have stirred up fund-raising cookbook projects that have taken their places on Missouri's cookbook buffet alongside church, educational, and medical community cookbooks. The Order of the Eastern Star in Grandin compiled *Best Cooking in Grandin* (nd). It drew ads from Grandin, Doniphan, Ellsinore, Hunter, and Van Buren. Readers learn in one ad in the cookbook that residents in the area can purchase their LP Gas, the "Modern Fuel," at Smith's and a Ford vehicle at Community Ford Sales in Doniphan and can buy a Chevrolet at Grassham Brothers in Van Buren. They might take in a movie at Hunt's Theater and pick up sundries at Ben Franklin, both in Doniphan. Numerous businesses keep area residents supplied with groceries for the table and feed products for farm animals in single-stop businesses. The Ellsinore Coffee Shop (then owned by Bill and Vi Skoggs) advertises that dinners are served on Sunday and that their establishment "Seats a thousand people—25 at a time!"

The Eastern Star women detail vintage recipes as well as those featuring modern food products. Ova Johnson offers a recipe for "14 Day Pickles" as well as one for Dutch cookies, which calls for three quarts of molasses and ten to twelve pounds of flour and produces a bushel of cookies that can be stored for several months. Among the more modern dishes is Dorothy Webb's "Latest Salad" utilizing packaged products straight from the grocery store. The last page of the cookbook includes recipes for "Supper Quantity Cooking." For a turkey dinner for 250 area residents, the ladies will purchase seven turkeys, seventy-five pounds of butternut squash, seventy-five pounds of potatoes, and ten bunches of celery. They indicate they will make twenty large cranberry rings and bake forty-four pies for the turkey event.

Missourians experience recipes selected by farm women of Missouri in their 1923 *Pure Food Cook Book,* compiled and published by the Women's Progressive Farmers' Association. The pie section becomes a culinary adventure. Obviously pie bakers, the ladies include over eighty-five recipes for pies. Mincemeat is a favorite, and they include eleven versions including a green tomato mincemeat version made by omitting meat from the recipe and substituting the popular garden vegetable.

Missouri farm women used green tomatoes picked just before fall frosts to make a batch of green tomato mincemeat to be used for pie baking during the winter months when fresh fruits were not as available. They stored jars of canned mincemeat in fruit cellars beside home-canned peaches, cherries, blackberries, and other fruits harvested in their gardens and the fields surrounding their homes. Farm housewives commonly included a clump or two of rhubarb in their large farm garden plots. Rural Missouri cooks baked at least two popular versions of rhubarb pie, both recorded in this cookbook, one made of fruit, sugar, and spices and the other a custard variation.

Even if times were hard and baking supplies were scarce, it appears that Missouri pie bakers needed only a few simple ingredients to make a delicious dessert for supper. In the *Pure Food Cook Book,* Mrs. Herman Klepper from Union contributes a recipe for prune pie made with prunes, egg whites, and sugar. Mrs. C. R. Ramsay from Bellflower shares details for preparing a vinegar pie. It appears that all she needs to place a pie on her table are a few simple ingredients: sugar, eggs, vinegar, water, flour, and lemon extract. Raisins, because they were readily available and easily stored, became a popular year-round pie ingredient, showing up in traditional pies as well as in unexpected combination pies. In the cookbook, Mrs. U. S. Braught from Cassville contributes a recipe for pumpkin raisin pie. When eggs were plentiful in the spring on Missouri farms, the cook might turn to a recipe sent in from Clarence by Mrs. Newt. Hodgin. Her recipe for "Amber Pie" called for seven egg yolks in each pie.

Today Missouri cooks can select and enjoy a variety of neatly packaged poultry products from the meat cases and frozen food sections of food marts for use in preparing their favorite chicken recipes found in the state's cookbooks. Until the advent of widespread commercially grown poultry, preparing a pot of chicken and dumplings or a pan of chicken and dressing oftentimes meant a short trip by the cook to the chicken yard to select her pick of the day from a flock of chickens she had raised from chicks. Two hatcheries placed ads in the *Pure Food Cook Book,* Smith Brothers Hatcheries in Mexico and Mrs. F. W. Spicer from Marshall. Spicer, a member of the American Poultry Association, enthusiastically features single comb white leghorns in her ad, pointing out that her birds are of "incomparable show quality" and are "bred for profitable egg production."

From the late 1800s through the early 1900s, poultry shows were popular in Missouri and throughout the country, thus the reference to "incomparable show quality." Apparently, Spicer marketed her poultry not only for egg production, but also for showing. At such events individuals displayed their poultry before judges with the winners receiving awards and prizes.

Chickens were an important part of the food supply beginning with the earliest settlers in Missouri. Settlers maintained small flocks to supply both meat and eggs for the family table. Farmers generally allowed chickens to range freely and thus to find most of their own food. Raising chickens in this manner meant it was necessary to search out the location of nests in order to retrieve the eggs, an activity often involving youngsters in the family. Poultry flocks weren't limited to farms; many residents of towns also kept a flock of chickens.

By the mid-1800s, farmers in Missouri had started using small sheds/houses in which chickens could be shut up at night for protection from predators. Protecting the flock meant that farmers often had extra poultry

Leghorns scramble for food at Booth Hatchery and Farms in Clinton. Clinton was once known as the "Baby Chick Capital of the World." (Massie Collection, reproduced courtesy Missouri State Archives)

that could be sold for cash. Both chickens and eggs could be sold or traded at local stores for needed supplies. By 1885, commercial poultry buyers had established locations at which farmers could sell surplus chickens and turkeys.[23] As markets developed for poultry, farmers increased the size of their flocks. With the development of the incubator after 1900,[24] large-scale hatcheries went into operation in Missouri to supply farmers with the baby chicks needed for their personal use on the table or for profit-making operations. In 1918, the U.S. Postal Service allowed chicks to be shipped, making it much easier for farmers to obtain the stock of chickens that they needed. Booth Hatchery and Farms, established by Royal Booth, became the first hatchery west of the Mississippi River.[25]

Missouri became a national leader in the production of baby chicks. Hatcheries were located in many parts of the state, but they became particularly numerous around Clinton in Henry County, causing Clinton at one time to be called the "Baby Chick Capital of the World."

Demonstrating their desire to contribute to solutions for recognized community problems, Harter House, a neighborhood market in Springfield, compiled recipes by their customers and employees. Proceeds from the *Harter House Cookbook* were donated to The Kitchen, Inc., in Springfield, following the lead of store owner Jerry Bettlach, who had supported The Kitchen in previous years. The Kitchen was started by Sister Lorraine Biebel as a soup kitchen in 1983. Committed to programs and services for the homeless, The Kitchen is supported by a force of volunteers who donated over thirty-nine thousand hours of labor to the project in 2000. The cookbook describes the numerous programs and services of the organization, among them the provision of housing, shelter, and meals; counseling, job-skills training, and health care for disadvantaged individuals in the community. A Nurturing Center addresses children's needs and a Youth Outreach Center provides a safe haven for street kids. The Kitchen also focuses on prevention of homelessness.[26]

People who have lived very long in Missouri are familiar with the old adage "If you don't like the weather, stick around, it will change." Missouri does have changeable weather, and these changes can occur rather quickly. Residents of the state enjoy four distinct seasons with significant variability within each season as well as differences north to south and east to west. Just as Missouri was a border state during the Civil War, it is also a border state from the standpoint of weather. Its location in the central part of the nation allows the state's weather to be influenced by several different air masses and frontal systems.

Western Missouri is in a position to receive winds and precipitation from storm systems moving across the Great Plains, and it is also far enough north to feel the impact of Canadian cold fronts. The state is also the recipient of warm moist air from the Gulf of Mexico, giving it rather hot, humid summers. Convergence of these air masses can sometimes cause stormy weather. Cool, dry air from the west sometimes causes turbulent weather when it meets warm moist air from the Gulf, making Missouri a part of "Tornado Alley," that part of the country experiencing a large number of tornadoes each year. Similarly, northern cold fronts clashing with Gulf moisture can bring significant snowfall to Missouri in the winter.

With weather a frequent topic of conversation, it isn't surprising that the subject of the seasons even makes it into a Missouri community cookbook. In their *1983 Show Me Missouri Four Seasons Cookbook,* the American Cancer Society, Missouri division, offers cooks an opportunity to "Share the cost of Living." Additionally the editors hope to "give the reader a 'taste' of the four seasons for which our state is well-known."[27] Compilers place symbols representing the seasons throughout the book to show the seasons in which cooks, relying on fresh seasonal produce from their gardens and markets, would normally prepare certain dishes. Thus a fresh strawberry pie recipe is tagged with a spring symbol while a recipe for blackberry cobbler earns a summer symbol. Apple pies are identified with summer and fall symbols.

Like cooks themselves, community cookbooks continue to be affected by societal changes. Replacing the made-from-scratch recipes that appeared in earlier projects, community cookbooks today are primarily filled with the types of recipes found in a steady flow of women's magazines, newspaper food columns, and food magazines designed to offer the cooks, albeit woman and men of the kitchen, the latest in cooking styles, techniques, and products. These cookbooks continue to define the foodways of the ever-changing Missouri kitchen even as they did in earlier days, documenting the foodstuffs available to cooks in the state, whether from a large farm garden or a modern super food mart. Even with all of these changes, a few of Grandma's recipes still find their way into modern fund-raising cookbooks offered by contributors who remember that great homemade taste, and who hold out to readers a reward for placing the prepackaged products back on the shelf or leaving them in the freezer and then taking the time to treat themselves to one of Grandma's favorites, a recipe she proudly contributed to her church or civic organization's cookbook decades ago.

Chapter 4

A Serving of Ethnic Cookbooks

We take the mundane act of eating and we raise it to the level of worship.
—*From Matzo Balls to Metrics: A Collection of Old and New Kosher Recipes,*
Shaare Zedek Sisterhood, 1976

Representative examples of Missouri's ethnic cookbooks demonstrate the cultural diversity of the state. In these projects, cooks stir up recipes reflecting specific cultural tastes, cooking styles, and food customs and traditions. Until the Louisiana Purchase in 1803, the French, the first to explore and settle the region of Missouri, dominated culture and language in the state. Their cultural influence was more persistent and pronounced in St. Louis, Old Mines, and Ste. Genevieve than elsewhere in the state. An influx of American settlers after this time brought new cultural influences to the area and to the dinner table. Some of these settlers were of English ethnicity, but even more were of Scotch-Irish descent. The 1830s brought large numbers of German immigrants who settled particularly in Cape Girardeau, Scott, Ste. Genevieve, and Perry counties and along the Missouri River in the area stretching from St. Louis westward into Lafayette County. The Germans exerted a strong cultural influence in these areas.

In the late 1800s and early 1900s, railroads brought numerous small groups of immigrants of German, Swiss, Italian, Hungarian, and Yugoslavian origins to Missouri to farmland owned by the railroads. Italians in Phelps County became known for their grape-growing and wine-making talents. Italians also built a significant community in the part of St. Louis known as the Hill, still famous today for its Italian restaurants. Other ethnic groups such as the Swedish, Irish, Dutch, Norwegian, and Polish were represented in small numbers scattered throughout the state.

Recipes of Old Ste. Genevieve, first published in 1959 by the Women's Club of Ste. Genevieve and in its eighth printing in 1997, takes cooks down the streets and into the kitchens of colonial Ste. Genevieve, Missouri's earliest permanent settlement. It is illustrated with pictures of notable historic colonial homes and historic eating establishments in the town, among them the Bolduc House (1770), the Jean Baptiste Vallé House (1782), the Ferdinand Rozier House (1814), Felix and Odille Pratte Vallé House (1814), the Old Brick Tavern and Restaurant (1785) and the Green Tree Tavern (1790). The text offers further information about the buildings.

Like cooks across the state, at the time of publication of this project, cooks in Ste. Genevieve were preparing popular dishes like "This 'Do-Ahead' Casserole A Complete Meal," tuna casserole, quick hamburger mix, and southern oven-fried chicken, dishes representative of modern-day Missouri kitchens, and they were included in the cookbook along with vintage recipes shared by cooks preserving their French and German culinary heritages. Old-time ethnic recipes sprinkled throughout the cookbook take readers back through the years: "Mrs. Vion Papin's Aubergine Farcie Creole (Stuffed Eggplant Creole)," "Mrs. L. J. Huber's Sauerbraten (German Pot Roast)," "Mrs. Harry Lidikay's Sauerkraut and Dumplings," "Mrs. Gilbert Flieg's Liver Dumplings," and "Mrs. Raymond J. Thomure's Creole Okra." The cookie and candy sections offer gateaux secs au gingembre from Mrs. Fred Steinkuhle, pfeffernusse from Bernetta Bader, and "Grandma Bader's 'Old World' Pecan Pralines." An old Ste. Genevieve French dish is documented in the recipe for chicken and bouillon dinner, prepared by stewing a hen in a gallon of water until tender and then adding and simmering chopped cabbage, onions, turnips, carrots, celery, and a few hot peppers.

The strong German influence in the Missouri kitchen is evidenced by notable cookbooks recording unique tastes. In *German-Missouri Cookbook of "Duden Country,"* material shared by the Augusta Historical Society, compilers of the project, includes the story of Gottfried Duden, a German explorer who spent several years on the Missouri frontier. His descriptive work *Report on a Journey to the Western States of North America* gives an account of his experiences, and at the time it stimulated German immigration to the area along the Missouri River. "Immigrants located around the east-central Missouri settlements of Augusta (Mt. Pleasant), Dutzow,

Femme Osage, Hermann, Marthasville, New Melle, Rhineland, Washington, etc."[1]

The cookbook explores the eating habits and favorite foods of the German immigrants who located there, "'hearty' dishes utilizing potatoes, peas, beans, and pork. . . . To their delight, and as Duden had written, Missouri offered those major ingredients in abundance." Editors of the cookbook point out, however, that adjustments had to be made in meal preparation as German cooks, new to Missouri, learned to adapt their Old World recipes and menus using new foods such as "sweet potatoes, various nuts, maple sugar and, of course, corn (maise)." The point is also made that German immigrants learned new ways of preparing foods from "their 'American' neighbors (early Anglo-American immigrants to Missouri from the U.S. South)."[2]

The collection says it includes "the traditional immigrant recipes that distinguish the 'Duden Country' area of Missouri and today make its church picnic menus, for example, distinctive." It not only includes "those of the old homeland but, second, also those which German Great-grandmothers had created to utilize the special products they found in their new Missouri homeland." For the collection, compilers selected distinctively German recipes from area community cookbooks as well as those from family recipe collections. Acknowledging that change is a part of the Missouri kitchen, they explain, "Modern dishes and new ways of preparing the traditional ones also have become part of 'Augusta cooking.'"[3] Therefore, they offer modern recipes in a final section of the project.

A brief informative culinary discussion opens each division of the cookbook (i.e., characteristics of German soups, why certain vegetables are so popular in German dishes, an explanation of "One Pot" [Eintopf] Dishes, and in the dessert section, an interesting discussion of the introduction of pies with crusts made of flour and shortening which they believe were unknown in German bakeries and to early German cooks in America).

Division introductions relate how Missouri's geography and agriculture affected German cooking. "On the Missouri frontier, corn bread was added to German menus." In Germany, cooks had commonly prepared pork and wild game dishes, and they continued to do so in Missouri where both were plentiful. German cooks, new to Missouri, learned to make and enjoy pies and also developed cake and cookie recipes using native nuts such as black walnuts and hickory nuts. In their homeland, Germans had become famous for beers made from grains and wines and liquors from fruits. "On the frontier the German immigrants made their own malt beer, corn whiskey, and fruit brandies, as well as wines. After some decades, Duden Country's grape wine would make Missouri famous."[4]

In 1981 the Senior Citizens of Freistatt published *Authentic German Recipes: Old Time Remedies and Historical Sketches of Freistatt.* The group devoted about half of the space in the cookbook to information other than recipes and dedicated the cookbook "to all who are interested in the beginning of the Freistatt community's way of living, customs and cooking habits."[5] Additionally, the dedication indicates the importance of the direct relationship and growth of the Trinity Church congregation with the community itself.

A discussion of home building, housekeeping details, farming practices, community development, social activities, and church life introduces a somewhat smaller collection of authentic German recipes than is found in the Duden cookbook. The first settlers in Freistatt "purchased land for $6.00 an acre from the Frisco Railroad" and built their homes. They covered their unpainted board floors with "rag rugs made by a blind rug weaver" padding under the rugs with "freshly thrashed straw, or newspapers or heavy wrapping paper" and made mattresses "from cornshucks or husks from the shucks close to the ear." An after-school snack, "Fettbrot," consisted of a slice of bread with lard spread on it topped off with sprinkles of sugar or if the family was "more well to do . . . a piece of butterbread with a molasses cookie on it."[6]

Introductory articles document the roles that family members played at harvest time and at butchering time on Freistatt farms when neighbors gathered at one another's farms to help with these events. Early in the morning on threshing day, chickens were butchered and made ready to be fried for the noon meal and pies were baked. "At about 9 a.m. sandwiches of home cured smoke sausage, fresh jelly-roll or cookies that were baked the day before, and coffee were taken out to the men, sometimes as many as 15 in number." The women then proceeded to prepare the hearty noon meal, which consisted of a familiar Missouri bill of fare: "fried chicken, mashed potatoes, two vegetables, gravy, sliced tomatoes, bread, butter and apple-butter, pie and lots of coffee cooked in the 3-gallon granite coffee pot that was brought from the attic and cleaned the day before." The cooking wasn't over yet. Once the dishes were cleared away, "A cake or two were baked for the afternoon 3:00 p.m. lunch, where another batch of sandwiches, cake and cookies, were packed in baskets and coffee was taken out to the men."[7]

Farmers in the Norborne area butchering hogs in the wintertime. (Courtesy State Historical Society of Missouri, Columbia)

Butchering day on a farm in Freistatt echoed a process which took place on farms across rural Missouri as temperatures dropped in the early winter. Depending upon the needs of the family, two or three hogs were butchered and worked up with the assistance of neighbors so that the job could be efficiently and quickly completed. Typically, every edible part of the hog that could be preserved was cured and smoked, canned, or sealed with hot lard in containers and stored in a cold place for winter use. The two-day butchering process produced hams, sides of bacon, cans of lard, and various kinds of sausages.

In addition to pooling their dishes of food for the gathering, the women cleaned and boiled the heads, hearts, and livers for use in head cheese, blood sausage, and liver sausage. One writer recalls in the cookbook the process of making blood sausage, a German delicacy. "After the hog was shot, it immediately was stuck in the throat to drain the blood, and the knife had to cut the jugular vein. Someone, usually one of the ladies, had to be there to 'catch the blood' and stir it until it was cold so it would not coagulate and become lumpy. It was saved for later for the blood sausage." The same writer also indicates that his uncle's "favorite delicacy was the brains and he expected them with his noon meal."[8]

The collection features, among others, recipes for schweine-knochel mit sauerkraut (pigs knuckles with sauerkraut), hassenfeffer (rabbit), ganse braten (roasted goose), sulze (head cheese) in memory of Mrs. Hy. Osterloh, blut wurst (blood sausage), and kartoffelkloese (German potato dumplings). The breads and cakes section includes a stollen recipe donated in memory of Mrs. Rudolph Lampe, pflaumen kuchen (prune dessert), and Bayerischer apfelstrudel (Bavarian apple strudel), and Schwarzwalder kirschtorte (Black Forest cherry cake), and the cookie section includes a traditional recipe for German springerle.

Compilers of *The Art of Hermann German Cooking* propose that "Missouri has aptly been described as 'A Bit of the Old World in the heart of the New.'" They believe the same to be true of Hermann, a "homey town ... [of] unusual and tasty eating." Like Missouri cooks across the state, Hermann cooks share their foodways as they dish up their favorite modern recipes but also include recipes for their traditional foods. Readers learn the story of fastnachts (doughnuts). "Fastnachts are a Shrove Tuesday Tradition. Hermann Children mask on the evening of Shrove Tuesday, run from house to house calling 'Fettkuechle' and are given Fastnachts and other goodies in their sacks."[9]

In keeping with their theme of the old and the new, Hermann cooks offer old-time recipes, often with a modern twist. The compilers include two apple butter recipes. The first, obviously a recipe for a "canning" reminiscent of "putting up" food for a large Missouri family, requires 55 crisp tart Jonathan apples, 2 quarts sweet cider, 5 cups sugar, 1/2 teaspoon salt, 3 large sticks cinnamon, and 1 teaspoon aniseed. After it is cooked down, the old-time biscuit topper is poured into hot sterilized jars and sealed. A second, more modern recipe titled "Easy Apple Butter," calls for 5 cups canned applesauce and additional ingredients in appropriate amounts for the smaller quantity. Delivering old-time flavor that in earlier years required several hours of stirring a copper kettle perched over a slow-burning fire in the backyard, both are conveniently cooked in a modern oven for several hours at a low temperature. Notes at the end of both recipes indicate that the apple butter can also be frozen, a more modern preserving adaptation.

In 1989 Novinger Planned Progress, Inc., published *Ethnic Cookbook*, dedicated to members of their community whose ancestors had immigrated to America and who had worked in the coal mining operations in their area of the state. The cookbook offers recipes reflecting foods prepared by Irish,

Scottish, German, Polish, Danish, Welch, Yugoslavian, Croatian, Austrian, Italian, French, English, Czechoslovakian, Canadian, and Anglo-American.

This smorgasbord of ethnic recipes offers Missouri cooks an international recipe feast. In the appetizer section, the Baiotto and Cima families contribute bagna cauda, an Italian butter dip, with instructions to "Dip vegetables in sauce, use bread as a napkin to catch the drips." They also explain that "It is against the 'rules' to dip bread until the bagna cauda is almost gone." Family members explain that "Northern Italians used this for a breakfast on special occasions."[10] The bread section features Finnish kropsua, Swedish hot cross buns, spice bread from Holland, pierogi from Polish cooks, and Croatian butter nut horns. Margaret Broseghini delivers a recipe for "Miners' Camp Cornmeal Pancakes." Cooks find an Italian recipe for fugaccio (onion bread), French bread, povitica (a Croatian contribution), and povetesa (a holiday raisin ring from Mrkope, Yugoslavia).

Main dish and vegetable recipes deliver possibilities for variety on the Missouri menu: "Flicky," a noodle-and-ham Bohemian recipe made with "a batch of noodles made of 4 eggs"; German buttermilk dumplings; bierocks from a Polish cook; braised ox tongue, a French dish; Belgian shrimp-filled tomatoes; corned beef brisket from an Irish cook; and "Coal Miner's True Cornish Pasties" from the *Novinger Miner*, the local newspaper. Likewise, cooks contributing to the Novinger cookbook add their culinary preferences to fresh vegetables grown in Missouri gardens: Hungarian stuffed cabbage, dandelion greens smothered (Italian), and red cabbage (Yugoslavia).

In the dessert section, Anna Stiglich willingly reveals her culinary secrets in a detailed explanation of "How to Make Golden Strudel Perfectly" which "can be worked right on a standard 40 x 24 inch kitchen table."[11] The compilers include recipes for Irish silk pie, kolaches (Bohemian), rozk (Polish), osta kaka (Swedish), Italian cheesecake, and Norwegian coffee cake. For the cookie jar, there are speculaas, a Belgian St. Nicholas cookie; Polish finger cookies; and Italian ribbons and bows.

Like the Freistatt and "Duden Country" cookbooks, *The Hill: Its History—Its Recipes,* by Eleanore Berra Marfisi, includes a generous serving of local history, this time St. Louis history, and a collection of fine Italian recipes. For Missourians preparing dishes for their own tables, the cookbook features a recipe that has been handed down through generations from each of twenty-four different families. The cookbook also includes recipes from four of the Hill's notable restaurants: Charlie Gitto's "On the Hill,"

Dominic's, Giovanni's, and Cunetto's. The mouthwatering recipes either will make Missouri cooks tie their aprons around their waists in order to spend more time in the kitchen or will encourage them to turn out their kitchen lights and head down to the Hill to enjoy a delectable Italian dinner.

Chapters interspersed with the recipes share the story of the Italian immigrants as they traveled to America, seeking a better way of life and hoping for improved working conditions and for opportunities for advancement in their lives in the neighborhood known as the Hill. These three sections of the cookbook track the development of a close-knit community of hardworking immigrants as they came to St. Louis and proudly built homes, businesses, churches, and schools. Chapters examine their social interactions, political contributions, and dedicated commitment to education as community members dealt with good times and bad times. The cookbook offers historical vignettes of businesses that became an integral part of the Hill. Missouri cooks learn about Italian food traditions such as those present during wedding occasions.

A generous photo collection in the cookbook ranges from modern glossy color "melt in your mouth" food photography to vintage black-and-white family and community snapshots. The images feature locals involved in family activities—Grandma Nunzi teaching her grandson, Charlie Gitto Jr., how to dry tomatoes in the sun for making sauce; the Tunesi, Bartoni, Amighetti, and Miriani families enjoying a backyard picnic; and Alessandro Fontana pouring wine for relatives sitting around his kitchen table. Photos document not only the importance of the family unit but also the emphasis on leisure activities—a local rabbit hunt, a game of pool, and a game of bowling, soccer, or bocce. In the photo collection, Marfisi notes that Baseball Hall of Fame members Joe Garagiola, Jack Buck, and Lawrence "Yogi" Berra all came from the Hill. "At one time Joe, Jack, and Yogi all lived on the same block in the Hill neighborhood."[12]

As part of a plan to finance the restoration of the only remaining building of their once-active community located eight miles south and two miles east of Marshall, concerned individuals under the leadership of Josephine R. Lawrence chose to spearhead a variety of fundraising projects to save the Pennytown Freewill Baptist Church. To help raise money for their project, the group published two editions of a church cookbook, the first in 1989 and a second in 1993. Lawrence served as chairman of the 1993 cookbook project, which not only brought in much-needed money for the restoration project, but also preserved the foodways from the kitchens of her small hometown. In *Sharing Recipes,* numerous contributions carry notations indicating that certain recipes are contributed "in memory of the older residents." Sue Hall, a descendent of a Pennytown family, notes, "Members of the congregation would likely have carried these foods to basket dinners at their church."[13]

The 1993 cookbook committee details a brief history of the African American community. "It is believed that Joe Penny came to Missouri from Kentucky and on March 30, 1871, purchased a little over eight acres of land . . . for $160.00 and divided it into 100 square feet plots and divided it amongst the people of his own race."[14] Small houses were then built on the plots. As a result of her study of Pennytown history and the Pennytown church restoration project, Karen Grace, editor of *Preservation Issues,* a publication of the Missouri Department of Natural Resources, believes this land transaction to be "a rare business transaction—possibly the only instance at this early period of legal transfer of land to a freedman."[15]

In the brief introduction to this edition, the cookbook committee recounts the story of the growth and demise of the small Missouri town. "For years Pennytown thrived with a store, a school, a recreation site, the Green Valley Methodist Church, the Freewill Baptist Church and a lodge." They point out, however, that "Although most of the people moved away in 1940, a tradition was started, the first Sunday in August would be observed."[16] The Pennytown Homecoming continues today with the first Sunday in August each year being reserved on the calendars of the Pennytown descendants who still gather in the yard of the now-restored Freewill Baptist Church for dinner on the ground followed by an afternoon church service.

Even though many contributors to the second cookbook share recipes typical of the last decade of the century, a significant number of the contributions take readers back to much earlier times in Pennytown kitchens. These old-time recipes reflect the cooking styles of rural Missouri cooks across the state, who were making dishes prepared with produce from their farms, gardens, and nearby fields. Bounty from streams and rivers and staple items purchased on occasional visits to the store rounded out the ingredient list in self-sufficient rural kitchens like those in Pennytown.

The cookbook finds early Pennytown cooks preserving sweet pickles and peach pickles, canning gooseberries, and making batches of watermelon preserves. Recipes for wilted lettuce and green onions, scrapple, fried frog legs, fried sweetbreads, and souse are reminiscent of early days in many Missouri homes where food was grown and produced close to the kitchen. Cooks find instructions for frying cured ham and making red-eye gravy to go with a variety of favorite side dishes: scalloped parsnips, homemade hominy, fried green tomatoes, and wild greens. In the baking section, recipes selected to honor early Pennytown cooks include those for sweet potato pie, sour cream pie, beaten biscuits, hot-water corn bread, old-fashioned gingerbread, southern fried pies, rhubarb cream pie, black walnut cookies, molasses cake, and bread pudding.

Recipes are not limited to those associated with women in the community. George H. Green details his way of cooking wild greens. "I gather approximately 1 gallon of crowfoot, 1/2 gallon of poke, lambsquarter; 1 pint of pepper grass, wild lettuce, black mustard, curly mustard, dandelion, wild beet, wild mustard and a handful of carpenter square." He then places a large iron pot on the stove with a quart of water and a pound and a half of smoked jowl. The greens are thoroughly washed, placed in the water, and seasoned with salt, garlic cloves, and red pepper pods and then cooked on moderate heat until they are tender and almost all juice is gone. Green serves his pot of greens with hard-boiled eggs, green onions, corn bread and potato salad.[17] Alfred Snoody contributes his recipe for stewed potatoes, Fred Robison provides his recipe for meat sugar cure, and a recipe for fried green tomatoes honors Frank D. Brown.

The cookbook includes Fannie Brown's recipe for corn cob jelly and her instructions for making taffy in memory of Eliza Alexander. One contributor honors Mrs. Joe Lawrence with a sweet potato pie recipe, and another remembers Annie (Babe) Lawrence, with directions for a sour cream pie with raisins. The committee closes their cookbook with a recipe for sassafras tea in memory of Florence Jackson.

Missouri cooks have an opportunity to experience the Jewish kitchen and the Jewish family table through a representative trio of Jewish cookbooks published in the state, two in St. Louis and one in Kansas City. Women sponsoring the projects express their attitudes and feelings about their religion as they share the connection of religious beliefs in the day-to-day selection, preparation, and serving of food in their homes. Likewise they detail special culinary activities and responsibilities associated with special religious celebrations in the home. Each cookbook demonstrates the kosher way of cooking.

As president of the women's organization, Marcia Slonim greets the cook in her "Forshpiece" of *From Matzo Balls to Metrics* compiled by the Shaare Zedek Sisterhood in St. Louis. Enthusiastic about the subject of food, she explains, "When it comes to using a happy occasion as an excuse to eat, the Jewish people are no different from other peoples of the world, only more so." She writes of the importance of family kosher meal preparation, a specific way of cooking which is guided by Jewish religious beliefs. "In the Jewish home, a kosher meal nourishes not only the body but also the spirit. For, traditionally, mealtime is an occasion for serious discussions, for learning the customs of our forefathers and mothers, and also for warm comraderie." Arnold Asher, Rabbi of the Shaare Zedek Synagogue, discusses the significance of the elements of symbolism included in festivals and also present at the family table. He explains that centerpieces on the table include specific objects and foods which serve as religious and traditional reminders. Regarding the association of food and religion, he explains, "We take the mundane act of eating and we raise it to the level of worship."[18]

In *From Generation to Generation: B'nai Amoona Sisterhood Cookbook,* also a St. Louis publication, by The Woman's Touch, B'nai Amoona Sisterhood, there is an article on "Keeping Kosher," which details kitchen strategies for preparing a traditional kosher dinner. As an example, one law of the kosher kitchen dictates that "Dairy (milchig) foods and meat (fleishig) foods may never be mixed or interchanged during the course of a meal." Details follow explaining how to follow this law. "The cook must have two sets of dishes, silverware, and utensils for each kind of cooking," and furthermore, "Separate colored, clearly marked dish cloths and towels are required for each set." The article concludes with this observation: "Establishing and maintaining the kosher kitchen provides the homemaker with challenge and creativity that lends a special charm, beauty and character to the Jewish home."[19]

Members of the Temple B'nai Jehudah in Kansas City in supplementary material in their recipe collection, *Memories Good Enough to Eat,* explain the concept of Jewish food. "That which is designated as Jewish food is seldom uniquely Jewish, since Jews have lived in every country of the world and learned to cook in the style of the land in which they resided." The discussion continues. "Yet, Jewish cookery differs from purely European, Mediterranean, or American cookery because the dishes were of Kashruth (Kosher)." They provide an example. A Jewish homemaker in Hungary simply "met the challenge of Hungarian Chicken Paprikash by omitting the sour cream, and the result was chicken Paprika, Jewish style."[20]

The same recipe collection includes a history of traditions for each of the Sabbath days with a menu and discussion of significant foods appearing on the bill of fares for these special days. The Rosh Hashanah (the New Year) menu includes "rich and sweet foods . . . symbolizing a wish for a prosperous and sweet new year." The first items on the menu—apple slices dipped in honey representing sweetness and gefelte fish symbolizing fruitfulness and plenty. They explain that "Gefelte Fish (literally, German for stuffed fish), may have originated in Holland, Russia or Poland."[21]

A final representative example of Missouri's ethnic cookbooks on the buffet focuses attention on the International Institute of Saint Louis. A timeline at the organization's current Web site indicates that the organization's history dates back to the national formation of the International Institute movement in 1916, which grew to the establishment of approximately fifty institutes over the next decade in major metropolitan areas in the East and Midwest. The focus of the International Institute of Saint Louis is "designed to move refugees and immigrants quickly from overwhelming dependence to productivity and self-sufficiency." In keeping with the goal of the national organization, this Missouri member also creates and supports programs designed to offer "public awareness of the important contribution ethnic diversity makes to the St. Louis area's economy and quality of life."[22] This philosophy developed in opposition to the thinking that refugees and immigrants should be "Americanized" by asking individuals to trade their ethnic heritage and traditions for a more "American" way of life.

The St. Louis organization opened its doors for service in 1919. Service activities in early decades included the sponsorship of its first International Folkfest in 1920, the Festival of Nations at the Municipal Auditorium (Kiel) as part of the dedication activities in 1934, and the organization in 1942 of the Women's Defense Group, a group of foreign-born women dedicated to assisting with the war effort. The St. Louis organization celebrated its eighty-fifth anniversary in 2004 and continues to offer services to the community.[23]

Under the supervision of Miss Elizabeth Hummel, a staff member at the time, the institute published *Menus and Recipes from Abroad* in 1927. Due to its popularity, a second revised edition, this time with Harriette F. Ryan as director, came out in 1932 under a new name, *Foreign Cookery*, with the cover design credited to Gisella-Loeffler. The small, softcover cookbook was "prepared by a group of women representing many nationalities." As well, those who worked on the project, send out a message of diversity and goodwill expressing the hope "that the friendliness and better understanding created during the preparation of this little book may spread to all who use these foreign recipes."[24] Recipes from thirty-three foreign countries are represented in the one hundred-page cookbook arranged alphabetically by country. Cooks then had and continue to have the means to produce a variety of ethnic dishes for their own kitchen tables in this unique early-twentieth-century Missouri cookbook. Albanian lamb stew, Bulgarian mousaka (eggplant), Hungarian vagas vescda (butter cookies), Japanese o-suimono (soup), Jugoslav sarma (sauerkraut balls), Swiss souffle au fromage (cheese soufflé), and Turkish turlu guvech (meat and vegetable hash) call attention to just a few.

As can be seen in the sampling of the state's ethnic cookbooks, Missouri has a rich ethnic food heritage waiting to be discovered and experienced in the kitchen. Missouri cooks tracking down these culinary jewels with the goal of adding international flair to their menus won't be disappointed.

Chapter 5

Missouri Cookbooks Record History

Since the foods people eat, the methods they employ in preparing them, and the ways they serve them are the quintessence of social history, the Missouri cuisine and related anecdotes featured in this book constitute a veritable portrait of Missouri in microcosm.—*Missouri History on the Table*, William E. Foley, 1985

Missouri cookbooks record for future generations the foodways of the past and the ever-changing culinary details of their time by revealing information about cooking practices, food products, kitchen appliances, cookware, and gadgets. Fortunately for modern readers of old cookbooks, authors and compilers also often stepped out of their kitchens and into their communities to collect for their books some community history.

Picking up a bit of Missouri history, *Lessons in Cooking* (1909) takes readers to turn-of-the-century seventh- and eighth-grade domestic science classrooms in the St. Louis Public Schools. Although many basic nutritional concepts, cooking techniques, kitchen practices, and food choices remain the same, kitchen technology of the early-twentieth-century domestic science class differs greatly from technology found in a modern consumer science class in the state. Students in the 1909 classroom learned how to build a coal fire, how to blacken a stove, and how to sterilize jars and can fruits and jellies. Today Missouri students learn how to cook using microwaves and convection ovens; how to use a food processor; and how to do cost, nutritional, and taste comparisons of ready-made foods, convenience foods, and homemade foods. As well, illustrations in the book document the type of clothing worn by stylish turn-of-the-century schoolgirls—quite a difference from the "hip" clothing styles of today's public school classroom cooks, both male and female.

Missouri cookbooks that record history come in a variety of formats, themes, and sizes. A small undated *Missouri Ozarks Commodity Cookbook*, mimeographed by an group identified only as a Community Action Agency, includes recipes using government commodities available at the time of publication. The cookbook serves as a reminder of the history associated with federal government food assistance programs in Missouri. Beginning during the depression era in the 1930s, the United States Department of Agriculture established programs to provide food assistance to qualifying institutions, individuals, and families through food commodity programs. The program accomplished two goals: aiding farmers in Missouri and other states by reducing surplus food products; and providing necessary food for needy families. Surplus agricultural food products referred to in the cookbook's recipes include cheese, honey, butter, dry milk, cornmeal, flour, and rice.

The enthusiastic response of southwest Missouri residents to a presentation made by McDonald County Home Economist Ardella Hixenbaugh sparked a 1969 cookbook project then sponsored by the McDonald County Homemakers Council, the *McDonald County Native Foods Cookbook*. Obvious interest at the time in her discussion of native foods led members to research not only the native foods prepared by the county's early settlers but also to explore their historic cooking styles, old home remedies, and housekeeping tips. Thus the recipe collection highlights a combination of the old and the new with an added bonus of a county settlement history. Hixenbaugh introduces the recipe collection, commenting on the challenging task faced by pioneer women as they headed out to the West.

> Pioneer wives moving westward gritted their teeth, rolled up their sleeves and cooked everything from Buffalo Tongue to Beaver Tail; their cuisine could be as adventurous as the life they led. They baked bread in makeshift ovens dug into hillsides, used buffalo chips as fuel, and learned to make use of anything that was available. They even discovered that the rocking of the covered wagon could be put to use in churning butter.[1]

The cookbook committee expresses the hope that interest "will be whetted to the extent that he or she will look more closely as some delicious foods

Illustrations from *Lessons in Cooking* provided readers with demonstrations of recommended techniques and show modern readers the uniforms and equipment common in the 1900s.

and drinks that may be obtained from some of the 'weeds' along the road-side, in the woods, or in the lawn and garden." Before the advent of super food marts, cooks in rural areas who were coming out of a cold Missouri winter, when fresh vegetables from the garden had not been available for several months, welcomed springtime when they could go green hunting. A committee member shared her recollection of such hunts: "Mrs. Opal Carden tells us that it is a native adage that there should be nine different kinds of wild plants in each mess of greens." Her list of available wild greens in the area includes mountain sprout, milk shawney (a form of dock), lamb's quarters (also called pigweed or goosefoot), square weed (white crown beard), wild beet, deer or adders tongue, wild lettuce, wild mustard, wild cabbage, coltsfoot, pokeweed, trillium, dock (both curly and sour), and dandelion.[2]

Carden's list of greens is just the beginning of an extensive list of edibles discussed in the cookbook that were used in dishes for the family table when Missouri women in rural areas went grocery shopping in the wild. A wide variety of wild fruits were "put up" as juices, jams, and jellies or made into pies and cobblers. McDonald County favorites include blackberries, strawberries, dewberries, grapes, plums, black cherries, gooseberries, currents, and raspberries. Cooks in the county dried and ground dandelion roots for use as a coffee substitute, and the flowers of the linden tree were collected to make a drink as were the red berries of the red sumac. Common nuts gathered include the black walnut, butternut, hickory nut, hazelnut, and the chinquapin. When noting harvest times, Hixenbaugh includes a discussion of mushrooms and the information that late May to early June is the time to gather cattail pollen to make cattail pollen pancakes.[3]

According to McDonald County cooks, ingredients for tasty main dishes were also to be found in the wild. Contributors offer recipes for fried eel, baked fish, and frog legs. Mrs. C. L. Fondoble of the Buzzard Glory Extension Club contributes a recipe for baked groundhog that she considers delicious and suggests stuffing the groundhog with slices of onion, chopped celery, and carrots before baking. The collection also benefits from her recipe for squirrel and chicken pie. County recipe files yield instructions for making groundhog pie and also venison mincemeat. Also of interest is a recipe for possum and sweet potatoes credited to Eliza Ann Montgomery Sims, born in 1833. The dish is spiced with red pepper and with a two- to three-inch sassafras stick.

Single recipes in Missouri cookbooks sometimes jog memories and take cooks and casual readers back to events of the past. Current and former residents of Unionville in northeast Missouri might recognize the historical significance of a recipe for "Calf Sale Chili" contributed by Neta Nowell to *Favorite Recipes,* compiled by the United Methodist Church Women in 1975. Not your typical family-size batch, this chili calls for five pounds of ground beef, a one-gallon can of chili beans, two onions, one gallon of tomato juice, and seasonings and yields three gallons of chili. According to former Unionville resident Jean Mowrer who remembers "Calf Sale Chili" from her childhood, "The recipe made enough chili that could be cooked in large pans used by the Unionville Methodist Church."[4] Mower recalls the Putnam County Feeder Calf Sale that was held annually for many years at the fairgrounds in her hometown. She says,

> The sale lasted one week and maybe longer for a sale such as a yearling sale. The activity ran 24 hours a day with sales held during the day. At night, trucks loaded sold cattle and brought in additional cattle to be sold the next day. Because there were not enough motel facilities, buyers stayed in the homes of Unionville residents with some buyers staying with the same family each year.[5]

Mower's hometown church became involved in manning a food stand to raise money during the yearly event.

> Two food stands served the buyers and truckers. They were both open twenty four seven. The Future Farmers of America ran one where the boys and their sponsor stayed all night, and the Unionville United Methodist Church members ran the other, also staying all night to prepare and sell food items. The Methodist group served breakfast, a daily special, and always chili, coffee, and pie.[6]

In a 2001 article for the *Unionville Republican,* reporter Duane Crawford recounts the statistical growth of the Putnam County Feeder Calf Sale: The first sale in 1941 was organized by the cooperative efforts of individuals in the county, lasted one day, and resulted in sales totaling $20,141.95 involving 426 head of cattle. In 1944 farmers sold 1,420 calves with sales ringing in at $70,248.65. Over the years, additional sale days were added. It became a two-day event in 1945, and in 1947 a third day was added as it continued to expand. Yearling steer sales had been added to the mix, and in 1958 sales topped a $1 million. "The million dollar mark was the first of many yet to come."[7]

The state's cookbooks also call attention to the historical significance of gristmills in the early development of towns in Missouri. Mills for grinding corn into meal or wheat into flour were vital to early settlement in Missouri and were one of the first businesses to locate in an area of settlement. Without them, families had to grind their grain by hand, a difficult, time-consuming task. A good site on a stream to build a mill sometimes led to the establishment of a town at the location. Gristmills dotted the landscape as settlement in the state increased. Settlers from miles around relied on the mill in their locale, and a trip to the mill also offered an opportunity to visit and learn area news.

During the Civil War, mills were of special importance since they could provide cornmeal or flour for troops on the move. A case in point involved the Hulston Mill located in Dade County and the Union soldiers under the command of Brig. Gen. Nathaniel Lyon.

> The Dade County Home Guard was called upon to furnish flour for Lyon's army which found itself one hundred twenty-five miles from the supply terminal encamped in Springfield, Missouri. Without food supplies from Huslton Mill and other area grist mills, Lyon's army might have been forced to retreat northward to the established supply lines; instead, Union troops engaged the Confederates at Wilson's Creek on August 10, 1861, and claimed victory to the second battle of the civil War.[8]

Some mills were damaged during the war by troops clashing or moving through areas of the state, which sometimes created hardships for local residents.

Local mills became less important as the railroad network developed after the Civil War. Owners of stores could buy meal and flour shipped in from larger mills and, consequently, did not have to depend on local mills as their primary suppliers. Residents preferred buying meal and flour from the store rather than taking grain to a local mill and waiting while it was ground. Missouri's mills, no longer essential, began to fall into disrepair, some disappearing and others remaining today as silent, nostalgic reminders of the state's agrarian history. Currently, however, Missourians are showing an increased interest in preserving, restoring, and even replicating these historic structures.

In 1987 the Dade County Historical Society published *Grandma's "Receets" from Missouri's Ozarks* with proceeds from the project earmarked for restoration and preservation of Hulston Mill. The cookbook calls it "the last remaining mill of at least ten that served pioneer Dade County" and goes on to say that the first mill was built at the location in 1838, but it was destroyed by floodwaters in 1839. The mill was rebuilt in 1840, and Chris Hulston later purchased it.[9]

Information at the mill Web site shows Hulston Mill passing through the hands of several owners in intervening years. "The operational history of Hulston Mill, spanning one hundred twenty-seven years, came to an end in 1967 as the result of the construction of a multi-purpose reservoir project on the Sac River." The mill was saved from "inundation by the waters of Stockton Lake" when steps were taken by the county court, historical society, the park board, and the citizens and the media of Dade County to move the mill to a safe site.[10]

The historical society, focusing on recipes with roots in pioneer times, opens the collection with directions for preparing sassafras mead. "Receets" lined up in the bread section include cooking details for preparing "water-ground cornmeal crackling cornbread," corn pone, and ash cake. Detailed instructions for the preparation, not often included in old Missouri recipes, show how ash cake was made: After cornmeal, water, and salt were mixed, "The dough is tossed backwards and forwards until taking an oblong shape, and then put in the clean place prepared on the rock and sprinkled with cold ashes, then hot embers on top of that. It stayed there until done (about half an hour), raking the coals occasionally, and tapping with the poker to see if it was hard enough. The cake being done it was removed and the ashes washed off with cold water."[11] Compilers indicate that the instructions were copied from an old cookbook belonging to Mrs. Ollie Williams.

Recipes take modern cooks back in time by evoking cooking styles of the past. A recipe for country pork sausage details two preservation techniques. The first involves either stuffing in "cleaned intestines of the hog," or "narrow bags of stout muslin large enough to contain in each enough sausage for a family dish." The bags are dipped in melted lard for preservation purposes and hung in a cool, dry, dark place. An alternative preservation technique directs the cook to pack sausage in jars and seal the tops with hot lard. When needed, the sausage was taken out "as wanted and made into small round cakes with the hands, then fried brown." Recipes for opossum and raccoon find their place beside instructions for making a chicken potpie and a pot roast. The hot biscuits served often in Ozark kitchens were made even tastier with a topping of home-preserved jams, jellies, or butters made from recipes in the cookbook. A pumpkin butter recipe instructs the cook to use one gallon of stewed pumpkin to one quart of molasses, and it also indicates that "sorghum is best." After cooking and adding spices, the recipe advises, "Put away in a cool place. This will keep a long time in cold weather." An elderberry jelly recipe combines elderberry juice and apple juice and reminds the cook, "In years of light fruit crops you will find this a splendid jelly."[12]

In *Albert E. Brumley's All-Day Singin' and Dinner on the Ground*, Missouri cooks find a unique nostalgic cookbook that doubles as a gospel songbook. To this unusual musical cookbook, Gene Gideon contributes a biographical sketch of Albert E. Brumley, a popular gospel songwriter from the Missouri Ozarks, discussing his longtime dedication to the music industry and noting awards bestowed upon him during his career. Brumley was inducted into two Hall of Fame associations—the Country Song Writers Association in Nashville in 1970 and the Gospel Music Association in Nashville in 1972. Children and grandchildren familiar with titles of their parents' or grandparents' favorite old church songs may recognize the gospel tunes included in the song section of the cookbook, two of which were written by Brumley. "Turn Your Radio On," his best-known song, published in 1938, became nationally and internationally popular when Ray Stevens recorded it in 1971.[13] Old-time gospel favorites found in the book include "Just over in the Glory Land," "Revive Us Again," "When I Reach That City," and "Life's Railway to Heaven."

Gideon also contributes a nostalgic article discussing dinner-on-the-ground church activities. "One of American's best traditions, we think, is her people's fondness for nostalgia. No worthwhile endeavor, it seems, will ever be completely forgotten, thanks to the generations of historians who have recorded so many of the noble deeds of the famous and not so famous people, and via paintings, drawings and books have allowed us to remember so many of the good times of the past." He believes that one old-time tradition "which hasn't been properly recorded which was immensely popular in the south and Midwest was the 'old time all-day singings and dinner on the ground.'" Typically, the schedule for dinner-on-the-ground Sundays included regular Sunday school and worship service followed by an impressive potluck dinner served out in the churchyard. Gideon points out that the singing usually started at 2:00 P.M. and continued until those attending had to go home to take care of farm chores. He also discusses variations of the Sunday event being held on Saturdays or sometimes in conjunction with weekend associational meetings during which there was "more emphasis on preaching than on singing." He explains, "These events produced three things hill people never tired of—good music, good food and good fellowship. This pleasure trio lured people from many miles around."[14]

Music at this church activity promised variety. Everyone shared in the group singing of old-time gospel songs. Additionally, attendees had an opportunity to sit back and enjoy their favorite church songs being performed as solos or in quartets, trios, and duos. Regarding instruments used to accompany the singers, Gideon indicates there might be "a piano or organ if the church had them," but fiddles usually were not used because "Many churches associated the fiddle with the work of the devil, since the fiddle was used at square dances where many people were hurt or even killed."[15]

Leon Howell includes the world-famous story of one of Missouri's most notorious citizens of all time in the *Jesse James Cookbook*. "Who would have guessed that the two sons of a Baptist minister and his wife were to become a legend in their own time?" Howell points out that Jesse's father was a devout minister giving "his money, time, and effort . . . to the Lord's work" and "was instrumental in the founding of William Jewell College" located in Liberty.[16] The author tracks the lives of Jesse and his older brother Frank, including their guerrilla activities during the Civil War and their days as outlaws afterward.

The author shares speculations related to events that may have influenced or contributed to the two brothers' notorious bandit life in later years, suggesting that "Jesse and Frank might have lived a peaceful existence, as many former Quantril men did, if they had not started a career in banditry." Jesse's bandit career ended in 1882 in St. Joseph when Robert Ford, one of the remaining members of the band, enticed by a $10,000 reward, shot James in the back of his head. The author speculates on why the James brothers were able to evade the law for so many years. "Many people condoned the robbery of banks and trains. It was difficult to get money from the bank. Interest charges were high. Many people did not trust the railroads and were afraid that they [the railroads] were exploiting them."[17]

Currently, a spot on the St. Joseph Web page ponders the popularity of the legend of Missouri's own Jesse James more than a century after the man's death. "Jesse James was a moral paradox. He was a good father and family man, and was religious in his own way. Whether he stole from the rich and gave to the poor, or just kept it all, has never been decided."[18] Information at the site proposes, "Today Jesse and Frank James are among the best-known Americans in the world."[19]

In recognition of their favorite son, Harry S. Truman, thirty-third president of the United States, the Junior Service League of Independence named their general modern cookbook *"If You Can't Stand the Heat, Get out of the Kitchen."* In taking readers back to the Truman years, the compilers acknowledge that numerous scholarly works document Truman's role in history, and so they have traded discussions of "the decision to drop the A-Bomb, the birth of the United Nations, the Truman Doctrine, the Marshall Plan, and the formation of NATO" for glimpses of Truman focusing on his "gentle humanity and wit."[20] Cooks find in the pages of this Missouri cookbook a generous serving of anecdotes, interesting facts, and quotes associated with President Truman.

At the time of his birth in Lamar, Missouri, in 1884, Truman's parents were unable to determine which of their fathers to name their son after with their choices being Solomon or Shipp. Their compromise? They chose to simply add an "S" to his name. Readers learn that Truman became an avid reader early in life and continued this practice when he returned from Washington to Independence in his retirement, reading five newspapers daily. Concerning his eating habits, the division page of the salad section includes a photo of Truman and his wife making selections from a table of food. In a quote below the photo, he explains his strategy for keeping his weight under control, a plan that includes walking "two miles most every morning at a hundred and twenty-eight steps a minute." Likewise, he proposes that with his healthy food choices, "I maintain my waistline and can wear suits I bought in 1935." The compilers indicate that at the time Truman was courting Bess, Virginia Wallace, his future mother-in-law "disapproved of the match, feeling Harry would never amount to anything."[21]

Photos in the cookbook portray historic moments in the life of President Truman, and quotes reflect his wit. In one photo he plays a tune with Jack Benny; in another he dines with dignitaries. The camera captures him as he proudly stands beside his hometown sign in Independence, and further on in the cookbook, there is a shot of him smiling over a candle-studded birthday cake. Speaking of his exalted political office, he is quoted as saying, "I am the hired man of one hundred and fifty million people, and it is a job that keeps me right busy" and "Criticism is something (a president) gets every day, just like breakfast."Paying tribute to the president from Missouri, the compilers of the cookbook express their belief that "He brought his Midwestern common sense, absolute honesty, and deep respect for and knowledge of history to the office of the presidency."[22]

The same women's group featured Bess Truman in *The Bess Collection*. Junior Service League of Independence members not only selected their own favorite recipes for the collection but also highlighted several of Mrs. Truman's recipes and included biographic information about the first lady. The authors note that she was known as "a reluctant politician's wife." "Bess Wallace Truman never wanted to be our nation's first lady." However, when she became the first lady, "She put aside her own feelings and filled her new role."[23]

Recalling her years in the White House, the compilers express their view that "Bess's pleasant demeanor and concern for others made her a favorite among politicians and White House regulars," and they also note that her husband "took to calling her 'the boss,' but she didn't like it when people made a fuss over her." They go on to say, "She often told the servants to stop working so hard. She dressed simply and never was pretentious."[24] The first lady's recipes, which include those for punch, bran rolls, bing cherry mould, meatloaf, turkey stuffing, tuna noodle casserole, and frozen lemon pie, seem to reflect her no-nonsense attitude about food and life.

In 1946 Sir Winston Churchill delivered his historic "Sinews of Peace" speech, now popularly remembered as the "Iron Curtain" speech, in the gymnasium at Westminster College in Fulton. Churchill voiced concerns regarding the division of powers following World War II, on one side the Western powers and on the other side the countries controlled by the Soviet Union. On this occasion, accompanied by President Harry S. Truman, Churchill focused his words on his desire for peace. Kurt Jefferson, a professor of political science at Westminster, indicates that the "Iron Curtain" speech "is remembered as one of history's most significant orations." Jefferson also explains why he believes Fulton, Missouri, was chosen as the location for the speech. "The context, a small Midwestern town and venerable college, had historical significance given that the U.S. President, Harry S. Truman, felt it was important to have the former British prime minister visit his (Truman's) home state as a sign of friendship and symbol of Anglo-American harmony."[25]

In 1961, a discussion involving "the College President, a visiting English architect and two representatives of the St. Louis Branch of the English-Speaking Union" led to a conclusion that a "condemned [Westminster] College chapel might be replaced with a London Church as a memorial to the historic event." Professor Patrick Horsbrugh, then a visiting professor of architecture, traveled to England to discuss this possibility with government and church officials which became a reality after the meeting. "To commemorate that historic visit the British people gave the Church of St. Mary, Aldermanbury, London to Westminster College for the people of the United States."[26]

The St. Louis Friends of the Winston Churchill Memorial record this historic event, the history of the church, and the chronology of the delivery and reconstruction of the church at Westminster College in the pages of *The Cookery Book* (1977). Noting that English cookbooks are typically called cookery books, the group found it a fitting name for their project. The noteworthy recipe collection is enhanced by the historical element of the project. Portraits of Sir Winston Churchill and The Right Honorable The Baroness Spencer-Churchill open the book. Line drawings by James R. Riddle and architectural renderings by students of Patrick Horsbrugh offer a visual history of the progression of the Winston Churchill Memorial and Library project, thus allowing Missouri cooks to visit the historic site through the pages of the cookbook.

Recipes by St. Louis cooks as well as others from around the state and country blend with cookery instructions sent by cooks from England for the publication. The collection starts with a recipe for English potted shrimp contributed by Marshall Sisson, architect for the removal and reconstruction of St. Mary Aldermanbury Church. Mrs. Neal S. Wood, wife of the Missouri cookbook committee chair, contributes her instructions for mushroom soup. That is followed by directions for making cream of green pea soup offered by Mrs. Noel Mander, wife of the organmaker for St. Mary Aldermanbury Church, London, England.

Following a major renovation of the museum and library at the memorial site, Westminster College hosted a celebration of the reopening of the Winston S. Churchill: A Life of Leadership Gallery on March 5, 2006. The event commemorated the sixtieth anniversary of Churchill's speech. Special guests included Churchill's daughter, Lady Mary Soames; his granddaughter, Edwina Sandys; Truman's grandnephew, John Truman; and Dwight Eisenhower's granddaughter, Mary Eisenhower. Sandys's sculpture "Break-through," which was created from eight sections of the Berlin Wall, is located near the church as part of the memorial.[27]

The Old Tavern Book of Recipes published in 1927 and sponsored by the Arrow Rock Chapter of the Missouri Society Daughters of the American Revolution contains over seven hundred recipes compiled by Don F. Pealer. Pealer notes that the recipes were "secured from every section of Missouri and wholly from Missourians" and explains that in addition to the recipes "There are given various items and illustrations of fact and fiction, which in a measure explain the Old Tavern and Arrow Rock." This additional material is given "as a means of preserving these items, but also, with the hope that it will arouse still greater interest in this old historic building and community."[28]

One of the "various items" included in the cookbook concerns the naming of Arrow Rock. On Friday, February 25, 1927, J. Paul Biggs delivered an address on Arrow Rock and the Old Tavern located there over radio station WOS at Jefferson City. The text of the radio show is included in the cookbook. According to Biggs, "The name, The Arrow Rock, is first mentioned by Lewis and Clark in the account of their expedition in 1804 and is derived from an old Indian legend." Biggs sets the stage for the legend by first detailing Arrow Rock's geographic location. "At this point the river is very narrow, running north and south. On the Saline County side there is a high white limestone bluff; on the eastern side of the river opposite this bluff was a large Indian camp." In the legend, the fate of a beautiful Indian daughter is to be decided in a contest designed by her chieftain father. The father announces that after a day of feasting, he will award his daughter to the young man in the tribe "that could stand on the eastern bank of the river and strike with an arrow shot from a bow, the white rock bluff on the western bank." All of the Indian braves see their arrows "fall short of the mark and splash in the waters of the Big Muddy." Then comes the final brave, the beloved of the chieftain's daughter. "His bow was twice the strength of any other in the contest" and "His arrow was a straight reed, barbed with a slender flint and headed with a feather from an eagle's wing." When his arrow landed on the white bluff on the western shore, "The happy Indian maiden cried out to her father in broken English, 'Arrow rock.'"[29] Today, historians believe the town got its name from the Native American practice of making arrowheads from rocks in the nearby bluffs along the Missouri River.

In an address in 1927, Biggs, speaking of Arrow Rock history, places the French explorers there prospecting for gold and silver in the second decade of the eighteenth century. He believes the area became a trading point between the Indians and the white men significant enough to warrant the establishment of a trading post in the first decade of the nineteenth century with Maj. George S. Sibley arriving to oversee the post. Sibley stayed at the post for a year. Biggs tracks the evolving settlement of the area. At one point in his historical narrative, he notes the movement of settlers from Virginia, Kentucky, and Tennessee, "families, in search of new homes and finally settling at or near Arrow Rock." This group includes settlers who would leave their mark on Missouri history. "Among those later families were the Jacksons, Marmadukes, Sappingtons, Prices, Hustons and Binghams. Names destined to become famous in war, politics, art, medicine, business and the social life in Missouri."[30]

Biggs also points out the significance of Arrow Rock to settlers headed West. In 1829, as wagon trains continued to roll to the West, "It was then that the town of Arrow Rock was incorporated and laid out in town lots." Meredith M. Marmaduke, later a governor of Missouri, served as the surveyor on the project originally named Philadelphia (also referred to as New Philadelphia by some) and later changed to Arrow Rock. Biggs points out, "The increase in travel and trade brought with it the need for an inn or hostelry." That need was filled in the 1830s when Joseph Huston, one of the original town commissioners, built the Old Tavern, which still stands today identified and managed as a Missouri historic site. About the construction of the building, Biggs explains, "Of the material used in the building, the bricks were fashioned and burned on the present site of the building by slaves belonging to Huston; the wood, entirely black walnut, was gotten out by hand on his farm; and the old bell, still used to call the guests to meals, was given by a steamboat captain."[31]

The list of notables connected with Arrow Rock and mentioned by Biggs reads like a Missouri History Hall of Fame: Dr. John Sappington developed quinine fever pills, an alternative treatment for malaria, and four of his daughters married Missouri governors. Three Missouri governors called Arrow Rock their home—Meredith M. Marmaduke, Claiborne Fox Jackson, and John S. Marmaduke. Governor M. M. Marmaduke married one of Sappington's daughters and Governor Jackson married three of Sappington's daughters in succession. Gen. George C. Bingham, Missouri's famous artist, lived in Arrow Rock during part of his life.[32]

Time markers have been the impetus for the development of cookbook projects that record Missouri history. Numerous organizations around the state celebrated their communities' histories in conjunction with the nation's bicentennial year, and Missouri's cookbook buffet also includes culinary publications celebrating Missouri's sesquicentennial, the history of the governor's mansion, and community centennials.

The First State Capitol Restoration and Sesquicentennial Commission published the *Missouri Sesquicentennial Cook Book,* dedicated to Mrs. Warren G. Hearnes, then Missouri's first lady. Proceeds from the 1971 cookbook were designated for expenses related to the promotion of the celebration of Missouri's sesquicentennial. Historical pieces included in the cookbook enhance the project. Jerena East Giffen, author of *First Ladies of Missouri* writes about "Cooking in Missouri's Mansions." Exploring early food preparation she notes, "State planners must have been aware of the importance of food preparation, but they forgot one very important part of the first living quarters provided the governor in Jefferson City. The first 'mansion' did not have a kitchen." She points out that soon after the completion of the first building in 1825, "Money was voted for two outbuildings—one a kitchen and the other a stable." The stable was built, but the kitchen was not. She speculates that this may have been because the governor was a bachelor.[33]

The governor's residence built in 1834 was the first constructed as a separate home. The kitchen for this residence was located in a building in the backyard, which was not unusual at the time. Noting that Governor Daniel Dunklin and his wife, Emily, were the first family to live in the residence, Giffen points out, "There certainly must have been a great deal of cooking in the backyard kitchen to feed the Dunklin family of seven children."[34]

Articles about Missouri's past are sprinkled throughout the cookbook with photographic illustrations by R. C. Holmes. Historian Floyd C. Shoemaker discusses Alexander McNair, the first governor of Missouri, and cooks learn about the different regions of the state through articles written by regional and state historians. Mrs. Nelson B. Tinnin delivers the story of Bollinger Mill and the Burfordsville Covered Bridge, which, she claims, is one of five covered bridges in the state. Cooks who believe Harry S. Truman to be the only president of the United States from Missouri learn otherwise in the cookbook. According to one historical piece, David Rice Atchison, as president pro tem of the Senate, "served as President from noon on Sunday, March 4, 1849 until 11:30, Monday, March 5." The reason? "In 1849 the terms of President James K. Polk and George Dallas, vice-president, officially expired at noon, Sunday, March 4. President-elect Zachary Taylor, a very religious man, refused to take the oath of President on Sunday and waited until the following day."[35]

Walter C. Daniel of Lincoln University details a history of African Americans in Missouri in "A Sketch of the Negro in Missouri." He begins his article with information relating to the introduction of 219 Negroes in 1719 by Philip Renault, who brought them with him from Santo Domingo to work in Missouri's lead mines. Daniel calls attention to two significant legal cases that began in Missouri and went on to be heard by the Supreme Court: the Dred Scott case in 1857, "which brought to a Missouri Negro international prominence and which became a factor in bringing on the Civil War" and the case in 1936 involving Lloyd Gaines, a Lincoln University student who "sought admission to the Law School at the University of Missouri." These cases were significant not just for Missouri, but for the entire country. In the Gaines case, the Court ruled in his favor, leading to a 1954 decision "outlawing segregation in education in the United States."[36]

Daniel notes the successful involvement of black Missourians in politics, mentioning, among others, Walthall M. Moore, the first black Missouri legislator in 1920, and Representative William L. Clay, elected in 1968 as the first black Missourian to be sent to Congress.[37] He discusses numerous black Missourians who have made literary and artistic contributions to the state and nation, including Langston Hughes, Chester Himes, Grace Bumbry, Eugene Haynes, "Blind" Boone, W. C. Handy, Dick Gregory, and Sarah Vaughn.

The recipe collection features a generous helping of introductory and side notes relating to the history of selected submitted recipes. Out-of-state cooks invited to submit recipes include wives of national political dignitaries. Mrs. Nelson A. Rockefeller offers a recipe for "Executive Mansion Butter Cookies" which yields 350 tea-size cookies; Mrs. Richard Nixon, then wife of the president, provides a recipe for raspberry pie; and Mrs. Spiro Theodore Agnew, wife of the vice president, contributes a recipe for lemon log cookies. In state cooks also contribute their favorites to the collection. Of course, not all the contributors are as well known. From Mrs. August Begeman comes a recipe for German applesauce cake with a note indicating that the recipe was brought by the family from Germany in 1890 when they settled in Hartsburg. Mrs. Dan Devine in Columbia gives readers her recipe for peanut butter squares, and there are recipes for "blarney stones" from Mrs. Bernard Pratt from Festus and beef short ribs from Mrs. Ferd Goeltz from Lodi.

A second significant Missouri cookbook focuses specifically on the history and hospitality of the Missouri governor's mansion. *Past and Repast*, first published in 1983, found Carolyn Bond, wife of the governor at that time, serving as editor-in-chief of the project. As the cookbook opens, the stage is set, signaling the official opening of the new executive mansion hosted by Governor B. Gratz Brown and his wife, Mary:

> A cold wind whipped across the river and swept against the treeless bluff where the tall red brick mansion stood. The windows on the north side rattled, but inside the sound was muffled by the lilting strains of a popular waltz performed by Professor Mahler's orchestra. The house already was filled with guests and more were arriving every minute, alighting from carriages and clutching tightly to their hats and cloaks as they hurried toward the huge front doors.[38]

The date? January 24, 1872.

Over one hundred years later, in 1974, Mrs. Bond, together with a group of concerned individuals, encouraged continued efforts to preserve the historic governor's mansion through the development of Missouri Mansion Preservation, Inc. (MMPI). *Past and Repast* became a part of this effort, a project designed not only to share the history of the building, but also to provide a way for Missourians, through the purchase of the cookbook, to have a part in financially supporting the preservation effort with proceeds from the cookbook being channeled into the project. The significant historical narrative in the first section of the cookbook takes readers back to governors' residences prior to the building of the present governor's mansion in 1871. Alexander McNair, Missouri's first elected governor, traveled to St. Charles, the temporary seat of the new Missouri government "on horseback from his home in St. Louis to meet with the legislature, living in rented rooms in a rock house near the buildings that served as the first state capitol." In the first executive residence/capitol building in Jefferson City, built in 1826, "The

Senate met on the second story of the new brick building, the House of Representatives on the ground floor, and the bachelor Governor, John Miller, lived in two rooms in the northwest corner." A second governor's residence, more suited to family living, was built in 1834, but by 1868 it was showing its age. The historical narrative includes information concerning its condition referring to an 1868 editorial that declared, "That old rookery, known as the Governor's mansion, presents such a slushy appearance that a gentleman mistook it for a soap and candle manufactory a few days since."[39]

After B. Gratz Brown became governor in 1871, "On February 10 a reception was held in the old house which many city residents declined to attend, fearing a disaster might result from overcrowding on the upper floors." Thus made aware of the negative conditions existing in the residence, the legislature authorized "$50,000 for a new Executive Mansion to be constructed on the same location where the first residence/capitol had been built nearly 50 years before." Governor Brown and his family moved into the new residence in January 1872, and during the same month they hosted the "first official function . . . a luncheon for Grand Duke Alexis of Russia who was on a hunting expedition to the West—and on the following evening, the grand ball."[40]

The historical section, which precedes the recipe collection, includes a wide array of information relating to the mansion and its past residents. Of interest is the diversity found in the families' daily lives and in the activities hosted by ever-changing administrations. Jennie Woodson gave many dances and masquerade balls while her successor, Mary Barr Hardin, a devout Baptist, convinced her husband to call for a "special day of fasting and prayer . . . held on June 3, 1875, at the height of a grasshopper plague that was destroying Missouri's crops; the next day rain fell, and shortly thereafter the grasshoppers disappeared." In 1889, First Lady Martha McFadden Morehouse adopted a custom popular at the time and gave as her first entertainment a "Pink Reception," with decorations and refreshments planned around a single color, and Governor William Joel Stone and his wife, Sara (1893–1897), "began the tradition of the New Year's Day Military Ball." After the United States declared war on Germany in 1917, "First Lady Jeanette Vosburgh Gardner became very involved in the war effort, planting the state's first 'war Garden' on the Mansion grounds."[41]

Like any other Missouri home, the governor's mansion requires funding for maintenance and improvement, and that funding hasn't always been appropriated. During the Great Depression, World Wars I and II, and the Korean War, there was reduced funding for its care. Around the middle of the twentieth century, consideration was even given to moving the first family into a "more modest and efficient home." However, the decision was made to keep the building, and a research committee recommended restoring it to its original appearance at "an estimated cost of $500,000 for repairs." The legislature voted to appropriate $40,000, and improvements began with renovation and redecoration continuing in the '60s during the John M. Dalton years (1961–1965) and during the Warren Hearnes years (1969–1973).[42]

Governor and Mrs. "Kit" Bond focused on historic preservation of the mansion. Realizing that the mansion had been a victim of years of "a crisis-correction approach to maintenance," Mrs. Bond, during her husband's years as governor, studied the problem and determined that "careful restoration and long-range planning were necessary" leading to a "'living restoration'— a restoration that was authentic to the 1871 period when the Mansion was built, yet adaptable to today's functions." The cookbook notes that the statewide, nonpartisan, not-for-profit corporation founded in 1974 had raised at the time of the publication of the cookbook over $1,500,000 in donations of cash and furnishings for the mansion.[43]

Past and Repast includes before and after photos of the restoration process as well as comments by the first lady about recipes in the collection. She shares a recipe for dove in wine used by her husband and her father-in-law following their traditional September 1 Missouri dove hunt each year. Reflecting on apple-picking time in the state, she includes a recipe for apple mousse with apricot sauce. For Missouri home gardeners dealing with rows of prolific squash plants, she suggests a zucchini chocolate cake and follows that recipe with one for Current River chocolate sheet cake, a cake her family took along each spring on their annual float trip down the Current River (safely packed in a cooler).

Published in 1978, the *Odessa Centennial Edition Cookbook* is a representative example of a Missouri cookbook organized as a part of a community centennial celebration. Citizens of Odessa, like those of other communities in the state, use cookbook projects as a way to celebrate their past. Mrs. Robert Keyserling opens the book with a history of Odessa, first detailing how her community "owes its name and existence to the Chicago and Alton Railroad." She explains, "When the railroad tracks were being laid in 1878, people from the communities of Mt. Hope and Greeton began to gravitate to the area." Keyserling also believes the name of the town came to be when "According to accepted accounts, T. B. Blacksone, president of Chicago and Alton Railroad, suggested that the land around the new settlement reminded him of land around Odessa, Russia."[44]

Her account offers a picture of the early development of the community. "The new town grew rapidly. Many structures were moved from Mt. Hope. The first train came through in 1878. People came, often living in tents until homes were built. The 1880 census listed a population of 100 persons. In 1881, a county history estimated 800 persons were living in Odessa."[45]

Documenting landmarks still standing and some that are gone, Keyserling shares moments and images from her community's past. She mentions the Phoenix Opera House, where traveling companies performed, and notes that "On July 22, 1913, the opera house burned shortly after a performance of 'Custer's Last Stand.'" She documents the location in Odessa of the Western Bible and Literary College (no longer in existence) and explains the popularity of Lake Venita, originally named Mulvill Lake. The location of civic events, including a July 4 fireworks display, dancing, boating, and bathing along the beaches, the lake was considered "the most popular resort on the highway between Kansas City and St. Louis."[46]

Missouri historian William E. Foley enthusiastically introduces *Missouri History on the Table: 250 Years of Good Cooking and Good Eating*, a cookbook originating from Ste. Genevieve, the state's first permanent settlement. Commenting on the significance of Missouri cooking, he explains, "Since the foods people eat, the methods they employ in preparing them, and the ways they serve them are the quintessence of social history, the Missouri cuisine and related anecdotes featured in this book constitute a veritable portrait of Missouri in microcosm."[47] Packed with history from cover to cover and in recipe after recipe, this cookbook is, the editors write, "a 'different' cookbook in many respects. Mostly it is unusual because it arises out of an unusual state—Missouri." Project organizers associated with the Ste. Genevieve 250th Celebration Commission state, "It was our intention that this recipe collection reflect the growth and development of our state's 250 years of white settlement coming on top of centuries of Indian residency. We thought the best way to accomplish this was to solicit the collaboration of people throughout the state. This we did by way of an historic cooking con-

The cover for *Missouri History on the Table*, edited and illustrated by Jean Rissover, depicts equipment used by Missouri cooks through the years.

test, open to all Missourians." Thus, they explain, "the same people who made this state—native-born and immigrant, rural and urban, 'down-home' and high-toned—made this cookbook."[48]

Individuals submitting recipes for the contest included stories associated with their historic recipes. According to the editors, "In our judgment the stories were as important as the food. Indeed, some of the yarns behind the dishes might be more interesting than the food described."[49] The editors also include introductory narratives to familiarize cooks with each historic time period tracking back to Missouri's early Indian cooks and moving forward to the early French explorers and then on to the campsites of those who worked in the mines of Missouri's first permanent town, Ste. Genevieve. The cook's historical journey continues through the 250-year period.

Of all the recipes submitted, six winners stand in the spotlight. Margee Andrews contributed the first-place recipe in the contest, and she remembers visits to her German grandmother's farm in Frona in the summertime with its vegetable garden. There she helped tend the garden and enjoyed picking produce for the kitchen table. One of her favorite cooking lessons with her grandmother resulted in a recipe for zucchini pancakes made with zucchini, a blend of cheeses, and seasonings.[50]

Ida Elizabeth Hunter from Columbia took second place with her "Queen of Puddings" recipe. The editors believe this recipe to be representative of "elegant Missouri cuisine": "The glorified bread pudding originated in Ida's mother's family over a hundred years ago." Hunter notes that it became her favorite dessert when her grandmother "made it with a layer of homemade tart jelly between the baked pudding and the meringue topping" and remembers it being "baked in a graniteware pan in the oven of a wood-burning stove."[51]

Dorothy Conquest Allen's recipe for "Palomar," or pigs in a blanket, earned third place in the statewide recipe contest. Her recipe passed through generations of cooks in her family of Swedish origin. A mixture of ground beef and pork added to cooked rice, an egg, and spices is rolled into cabbage leaves and baked for a tasty main dish.[52]

The contest produced three fourth-place winners. Catfish à la Francaise, from Estelle Powers of St. Louis, demonstrates the ability of French cooks to adapt native foods to French tastes. Catfish fillets are dipped in lightly beaten egg and rolled in dried whole wheat bread crumbs and sautéed in equal amounts of lard and butter in a heavy skillet. "The very American catfish is given the same gallic treatment as a denizen of the Mediterranean Sea or the River Loire." A recipe from one of Missouri's German kitchens demonstrates creativity in the kitchen. This family recipe passed down from Mildred Stumph of Ste. Genevieve delivers instructions for preparing "Falsche Vogelen" (fake birds). In this recipe, one that tracks back to family cooks in Kandel-Ahein, Germany, the "birds" are strips of round steak with savory stuffing. Geraldine Savage, operator of the Hillcrest Cooking School in Ste. Genevieve at the time of the cookbook's publication, contributed a recipe for floating island, a French custard-and-meringue dessert prepared for her by her French-Irish grandmother.[53]

The editors sum up their thoughts on Missouri and propose the benefit of the cookbook project to Missouri cooks. "In our 'Show Me' state, no good cook is likely to accept anything on blind faith. So the editors of this unique cookbook encourage you to use any or all of these historic concoctions as the basis for your own creative contributions to any future attempt to put Missouri history on the table."[54]

Missouri's cookbooks offer readers a vehicle ready to take them on a cook's tour through over a century of the state's history, where readers can discover Missouri's heritage of foods and facts.

Chapter 6

Individually Authored and Edited Cookbooks

With the 1943 edition, it became the nation's most popular cookbook . . .
The Joy of Cooking became a fixture in America's kitchens.—St. Louis Walk
of Fame tribute to Irma Rombauer and her famous cookbook

Missouri's twentieth-century cookbook authors and editors deliver variety in their projects. Selections on this part of the buffet include a cocktail
cookbook authored by an African American in St. Louis, a company-
sponsored cookbook edited by a domestic science expert, general cookbooks,
homemade recipe notebooks, "a cookbook Bible," a Bible cookbook, softcover "little cookbooks," "sampler collections," a specialty recipe collection,
health-focused cookbooks, and cookbooks supplemented with personal
experiences, family heritage, and Missouri history.

Thomas Bullock's *The Ideal Bartender,* published in St. Louis in 1917,
stands out among Missouri's early-twentieth-century cookbooks, which
were typically authored by white females. Bullock, an African American,
was employed as a bartender at the prestigious St. Louis Country Club, one
of the first clubs of its kind in the country. One of the club's noted members,
a wealthy St. Louis banker and golfer, evidently knew Thomas Bullock and
appreciated his recipes.

George Herbert Walker, grandfather of George Herbert Walker Bush (41st
president) and great-grandfather of George Walker Bush (43rd president),
contributes an introduction to the Bullock collection of cocktail recipes.

For the past quarter of a century he has refreshed and delighted the
members and their friends of the Pendennis Club of Louisville and the

In 1917, Thomas Bullock, a popular bartender at the prestigious St. Louis Country Club, authored *The Ideal Bartender,* a collection of cocktail recipes. (Courtesy Michigan State University Libraries)

St. Louis Country Club of St. Louis. In all that time I doubt if he has erred in even one of his concoctions. Thus if there is "many a slip twixt the cup and the lip" it has been none of his doing, but rather the fault of those who have appreciated his art so highly. But why go on! His work is before you. It is the best to be had. Follow on, and as you sip the nectar of his schemings tell your friends, to the end that both they and he may be benefited.[1]

The information preceding the cocktail recipes in Bullock's book is also interesting. It includes an editorial piece originally printed in the *St. Louis Post-Dispatch* on May 28, 1913. The author of the editorial has fun regarding a situation in the news at the time "when Col. Roosevelt was vindicating, by a libel suit, his reputation of sobriety and temperance." Supposedly, Roosevelt had admitted that he drank "just a part of one julep at the St. Louis Country Club."[2]

The author of the piece objects. "Who was ever known to drink just a part of one of Tom's whom there is no greater mixologist of any race, color or condition of servitude, was taught the art of the julep by no less than Marse Lilburn G. McNair, the father of the julep. In fact, the very cup that Col. Roosevelt drank it from belonged to Governor McNair, Governor of Missouri, the great-grandfather of Marse Lilburn and the great-great-grandfather of the julep." The writer continues, "To believe that a red-blooded man, and a true Colonel at that, ever stopped with just a part of one of those refreshments which have made St. Louis hospitality and become one of our most distinctive genre institutions, is to strain credulity too far. Are the colonel's powers of self restraint altogether transcendent? Have we found the living superman at last?" He concludes, "When the Colonel says that he consumed just a part of one he doubtless meant that he did not swallow the mint itself, munch the ice and devour the very cup."[3]

Bullock organizes over 170 recipes alphabetically in his fifty-page project. He includes instructions for mixing apple jack cocktail, blood hound cocktail, bizzy izzi high ball, and blue blazer. The blue blazer is mixed in two pewter or two silver mugs. The ingredients: one teaspoonful bar sugar dissolved in a little hot water and one wine glass or jigger of Scotch whiskey. He instructs, "Ignite the mixture, and while blazing pour it several times from one mug to the other. Serve with a piece of twisted lemon Peel on top."[4] Moving down the alphabet, mixing instructions follow for how to stir up chocolate punch, diarrhea draught, free love cocktail (club style), and horse thief cocktail. The list goes on: leaping frog, stinger, twilight cocktail, and whiskey Irish hot and not to be overlooked, two recipes for Mint Julep—Kentucky style and overall julep-St. Louis style.

Lulu Thompson Silvernail worked for the Southwestern Milling Company in Kansas City. Her cookbook, *Nine Hundred Successful Recipes* (1923), is an example of a Missouri cookbook published under the instruction of an individual trained in domestic science, a field of women's studies developed in the nineteenth century and the forerunner of the public schools' home economics, now consumer science. Women trained in this field worked for companies developing product recipes and were sometimes given author credit for the project as in this case. Silvernail conducted domestic science classes in the use of hard winter wheat short patent flour for the company.

The centerpiece of Missouri's cookbook buffet most assuredly is *The Joy of Cooking*, later shortened to *Joy of Cooking*, by Irma Rombauer. The cookbook that became well known around the world started out as a self-published project in St. Louis in 1931, a time when middle-class women were finding that they could not afford help in the kitchen. A complete kitchen guide was just what they needed, and Missouri's own Irma Rombauer delivered it. Encouragement by friends to publish her recipe collection and changes in her financial status after the death of her husband moved her to organize her recipes for self-publication. A proposal for a revised version of the cookbook netted a contract with Bobbs-Merrill in 1936, and the company brought out the first edition of *The Joy of Cooking* the same year.

The project with such a humble beginning racked up phenomenal sales over the years and is considered, based on sales figures, to be the most popular American cookbook of all time. After the first edition, Rombauer and members of her family continued to revise. Marion Becker, Rombauer's daughter, who had worked with her on several updated editions of the book, continued the revision processes after her mother's death. When Becker died, one of her sons, Ethan, became the family representative on the cookbook. He is acknowledged as a coauthor with his mother and grandmother in the 1997 Scribner edition. Edgar Becker, also Marion's son, provides an introduction to a facsimile edition of the original 1931 publication. The seventy-fifth anniversary edition in 2006, a revision of the best-selling 1975 edition, brought Ira Rombauer and the *Joy of Cooking* into the twenty-first century. For *Joy* enthusiasts, it appears that a 2008 edition is in the wings.

What made this Missouri cookbook so popular and so enduring? When Rombauer sent the manuscript off to be published, her personality "traveled" with it. Ever-present in the pages of the project, she offers a suggestion here or there and occasionally stops the flow of recipes to take time to share a meaningful story. Her cooking tips are presented in a warm, chatty manner, definitely encouraging for cooks unfamiliar with their kitchens and with the diverse aspects of meal preparation. A new cook faced with preparing her first breakfast could find a detailed recipe for a culinary task as simple as a boiled, fried, or poached egg; a more confident cook might try a

Irma Rombauer authored the best-selling all-time favorite cookbook *The Joy of Cooking*, first published privately in 1931 in St. Louis. Here she is in 1933. (Courtesy *St. Louis Globe-Democrat* Archives, Mercantile Library, University of Missouri–St. Louis)

challenging recipe for a special occasion, such as one for poached eggs on tomatoes with hollandaise sauce (eggs Blackstone). Rombauer puts cooks at ease with her unpretentious honesty. For example, about Jerusalem artichokes, she says in the 1936 edition, "It is a relief to hear that everybody is ignorant, only on different subjects. This was one of my subjects."[5]

In 1998 Rombauer was inducted into the St. Louis Walk of Fame. A notation about *The Joy of Cooking* at the Walk of Fame Web site indicates, "With the 1943 edition, it became the nation's most popular cookbook . . . Comprehensible, comprehensive and fun . . . *The Joy of Cooking* became a fixture in America's kitchens."[6] Rombauer's popular cookbook, oftentimes referred to as a "kitchen Bible" and described as an "all-purpose cookbook," certainly has put Missouri on the map with millions of copies sold. The cookbook underwent extensive revisions in 1997 following the previous update in 1975. *The Joy of Cooking* earned a place on the New York Public Library's list of 175 Books of the Century in 1995. It has shown up on lists of most influential cookbooks, keeping company with famous American cookbook authors Julia Child, James Beard, Fannie Farmer, and Craig Claiborne, as well as other famous cookbooks, such as General Mills's *Betty Crocker's Picture Cook Book*.

Published in Kansas City in 1943, *Rhythm in Foods* combines the cooking expertise of Lamora Sauvinet Gary and the nutritional analysis of a team of experts. Their combined efforts deliver a cookbook that not only presents a tasty collection of recipes to Missouri cooks but also includes a calorie count as well as a mineral and vitamin analysis per portion. Dr. Nils Larsen, introducing the project, addresses the emphasis then being placed on the nutritional study of food. "Those who believe in taste and flavor have been scorned by those who have analyzed food only from the health standpoint. There has been development of the thought that anything that is very tasty cannot be healthful." He points out that Gary expresses the hope that "Before the art of tastefully flavored recipes is entirely lost, it would be worthwhile attempting a union of these two schools of thought." Working with the team of experts, Larsen believes that the author "has succeeded in the effort to maintain the harmony, or, as she calls it, the beautiful rhythm of food combinations that are most pleasing to the palate and at the same time understandable and analyzable from the health standpoint."[7] Gary offers recipes with flair—veal baked with white wine, spaghetti Caruso, and avocado and crabmeat salad. Far from tasteless culinary creations, she includes recipes for eggs suzette, feather coconut cake, and caramel pie.

The cookbook includes a variety of informative, health-related sections. An article explains how to preserve vitamin and mineral values during cooking, and there are tables of ideal weight and height for men and women. One chart maps out average daily energy requirements (calories based on degree of activity) while another lists daily dietary requirements for good health.

The pool of Missouri cookbooks written and edited as individual projects expanded during the second half of the century. In his introductory remarks to Mary Schroeder Hosford's *The Missouri Traveler Cookbook* (1958), Max Leif, a Hollywood and New York author, informs readers that the author is not only a good cook but also an actress, realtor, international hostess, and mother of four. Hosford, a native of Kansas City, landed a role in *Missouri Traveler,* a movie starring Paul Ford, Lee Marvin, Gary Merrill, and Brandon de Wilde. Leif fittingly refers to this delightful Missouri cookbook as an "autogastronomy" and believes that it is "a singular and unique cookbook" in that it blends "significant episodes in the author's life with some of her favorite recipes" which seems to offer a "mixed grill to delight mind and palate alike."[8] Commenting on the organization of the project, Hosford indicates at the beginning of her book that the project isn't a typical cookbook that travels from appetizers to desserts. Instead she shares brief life memories followed by recipes suited to each story.

One memory details an account of her Grandmother Carr making the trek from northern Illinois to Missouri "in that hot-rod of the prairies—the covered wagon." Before a recipe for homemade bread, she recounts stories about the trip told by her grandmother. "I do remember her telling me that her party of 'tourists' were accorded great hospitality in the farmhouses enroute. They all slept between clean-smelling sheets and devoured the fresh, wholesome bread—the staff of life of those weary pioneers."[9]

Hosford presents a delightful collection of personal narratives in the cookbook. She recalls a family trip to the Arrow Rock Inn, where she first slept in a four-poster bed and spent the night dreaming of a delicious dessert she had eaten at dinner. The author remembers long walks and fishing trips with her father in the Lake of the Ozarks area, a section of the state where much of the action of the movie takes place. She re-creates the dessert recipe from the Arrow Rock Inn and also includes a recipe for southern corn puddin', an item she considers a necessity on the menu of a fish fry following an afternoon of fishing.[10] Hosford includes a hamburger recipe that she created and named after Franklin Studebaker Riley Jr., an early boyfriend who picked her up for dates, often in a different car than the time before.

In the cookbook, the author explains how she was "discovered." While dining with a friend, she met Cornelius Vanderbilt Whitney, the Hollywood movie magnate who, according to Hosford, had been searching over two years for an actress to play the role of Anna Love Price in *Missouri Traveler.* After the couple had been invited to join Whitney and his group at their table, Hosford suggested the coq au vin as a dinner entree for the group.[11] The dinner ended up being quite a success for this Missouri girl . . . good food and a part in a movie. The author documents this significant "food memory" with her recipe for the entree she suggested at the chance dinner.

That same year, a cookbook written by Marian Maeve O'Brien, food editor for the *St. Louis Globe-Democrat* and popular speaker, came to Missouri kitchens. O'Brien opens the cookbook with an interesting premise. "Two things, our faith and our food, are more closely bound up with our daily living than any others. And since this book was conceived, I have marveled over and over at the strength of the link between food for the body and food for the soul."[12] The author discusses the importance of the element of food in the Bible. In *The Bible Cookbook,* O'Brien blends biblical history, including information in recipe introductions and on section division pages, with a general collection of recipes. She introduces each recipe section with ten commandments relating to the section (i.e., "Ten Commandments for Making Pies") and also includes a chapter on feeding the multitudes, where Missouri cooks will find recipes for dishes designed to serve fifty.

Werner Nagel brought humor to Missouri kitchens with *Cy Littlebee's Guide to Cooking Fish and Game* (in its fourth printing in 1964). In the cookbook, conservationist Nagel teams up with a Missouri wild game connoisseur, Cy Littlebee, a character created by Nagel. The project first stresses the importance of knowing how to select and handle the state's abundant supply of wild game before bringing it to the kitchen. Nagel comments on the wealth of meats available in the state. "With over 30 kinds of fish, 18 kinds of birds and mammals and five miscellaneous edible creatures (frogs, eels, turtles, mussels and crayfish) there are more that 50 possibilities even if we lump the ducks and geese together and ignore the protected species." Cy Littlebee casts the lure—chatting about the many tasty ways to introduce wild game dishes to the table—and Nagel reels his readers in. "Before we get down to cases about how to cook this and that, they's a few things everybody ought to keep in mind about cooking wildlife. Let's get them things cleared away right off, before we get to talking about the recipes themselves."[13] Littlebee's straightforward cooking strategies and techniques follow.

Nagel circles the state in selecting recipes. He believes many of the recipes have been developed by cooks who personally enjoy wild game cooking. The collection opens with a recipe for all-game dressing appropriately introduced by Littlebee. "Now, before we go into the recipes for each kind of game and fish and such, let's start out with one that's good for all kinds of game they is in the State of Missouri. It was worked out by Mary (Miz. John) Hughes of Jefferson City." Introducing the recipes in the rabbit section, Littlebee explains, "You take a state where from four to six million rabbits is eat in a year, not counting tame rabbits nor any shipped in, all you can figger is that either a lot of folks likes some rabbit, or some folks like lots of rabbit." Moving on to the recipes, he points out that in her recipe, "Miz. W. D. Coffin, from down near Cabool, don't go so heavy on extra flavoring, but depends on baking the rabbit in its own gravy for a fine dish."[14] This cookbook, a project of the Missouri Department of Conservation, spiced throughout with the flavor of Cy Littlebee, proves to be an outstanding entree on Missouri's cookbook buffet.

Ella Mae Tucker, from Walnut Grove, opens her collection of recipes, *Dear Daughter Cookbook* (1965), with a letter written in 1865 by Nancy Henderson to her daughter, Adelyn Henderson Coppenbarger. The author explains that many of the recipes in the collection passed through several generations. Additions by the author and her immediate family members complete the project with recipes being selected from the last one hundred years. Tucker shares an interesting custom in her family relating to the transfer of recipes from generation to generation in the "old days." Unlike modern cooks who enthusiastically pass recipes from one Missouri kitchen to another and from computer to computer, she recalls that many recipes passed from her own mother "were carefully kept secret, for the table a woman set and the food she served were a merit badge of her success as a housewife, and therefore not to be shared with those with whom she must compete in this field of honor." Tucker, however, willingly shares several family heirloom recipes from the mid-1800s, among them instructions for making peach leather, hoarhound candy, lemon drops, old-fashioned ginger cookies, cornmeal mush, and Grandma's gingerbread. She includes her grandmother's recipe for making homemade yeast and her instructions for a technique used in 1850 to make dried yeast cakes from homemade yeast. The author includes several recipes just as they were written by her grandmother. "Grandma's Salt-Raising Bread" (1850) begins, "Early morning, as soon as the tea-kettle reaches a boil, take a quart earthen jug or milk pitcher, scald it, and fill one-third full of hater hot enough that you can just bear to hold a finger in it."[15]

Dorothy Ross, wife of the founder of Beta Sigma Phi, a women's organization focusing on social, civic, and cultural activities designed to meet the needs of the stay-at-home housewife of the early '30s, authored *Dorothy Ross' Cookbook* in 1969. The women's organization was founded in Abilene, Kansas, on April 30, 1931,[16] and has achieved international status. Its headquarters are currently located in Kansas City.

Not a rural Missouri cookbook with typical country recipes, this collection seems to meet the needs of hostesses who are searching for more sophisticated dishes for entertaining. Ross includes a generous section of recipes on party fare, an informative section on preparing sauces, and a significant section on low-calorie fare. Unlike many Missouri cookbooks which have large dessert and pie sections, this cookbook offers a simple sampling of recipes for cakes and cookies. The author includes a variety of hostess-friendly soup recipes, including those for cream of crab soup, Americana bouillabaisse, and herb and spinach soup.

Springfield author/editor Pauline E. Pullen created and edited *The Missouri Sampler: A Collection of Favorite Recipes from All Counties* (1971). After sending out letters to the state's cooks asking for recipes from all counties, she received thousands of recipes from men and women cooks in the state, thus creating a pool of recipes representative of all areas of the state.[17] This generous collection shows Missourians still cooking from scratch and also taking advantage of prepackaged food items. Cooks seeking old-time rural and regional cooking instructions will not be disappointed in Pullen's selection of some old favorites: egg butter, johnny cakes, homemade egg noodles, scrapple, country salt-cured pork, ash hominy, peanut brittle, and buttermilk pie. Missouri's ethnic heritage also surfaces in the culinary collection with recipes for rivel soup, Swedish bread, Irish soda bread, schnitzbrodt, and lebkuchen.

Eula Mae Stratton, according to the publisher of her cookbook, is known in southwest Missouri as "Aunt Nan of the Ozarks." Stratton preserves a collection of recipes typical of kitchens during pioneer days in Missouri and explains the source of many of her recipes in *Ozarks Cookery: A Collection of Pioneer Recipes* (1976). "During the Roaring Twenties it was my good fortune to inherit my little Scotch-Irish Grandmother's cardboard shoe boxes. Each was filled with old-time 'receipts' (handwritten data for cookin')." She believes some of the recipes date back to "Colonial time, Indian relatives, and pioneer settlers of Pittsylvania County, Virginia." Others are reminiscent of "covered wagon crossing into Missouri," and still others are from the Civil War era. The editor of the *Ozarks Mountaineer* notes that the magazine "has been publishing recipes as part of our effort to preserve and promulgate the heritage and culture of the Ozarks region" and that the author "has conducted the 'Ozarks Cookery' column for most of those years" receiving "recognition by the Smithsonian Institution and the Ozark Arts & Crafts Fair Association."[18]

The collection of bread recipes takes modern readers back to pioneer days. Stratton opens her collection of recipes with Cherokee fried bread, shuck bread, and Indian bread and points out that her grandmother made light bread three times a week, four loaves at a time. She includes recipes for cracklin' bread and persimmon bread. Interspersing Ozark food stories, she moves from recipe to recipe. Readers learn how to prepare frog legs, sweetbreads, chine (hog backbone), "Washbiler" eggs, kraut, fried corn, squaw corn, fresh blackberry pie, vinegar cobbler, and wild strawberry preserves.

In a note before her final recipe, she indicates, "No pioneer cookbook should end without a 'receipt' for making soap as early settlers made it." Before detailing this process, she determines that it is too complicated for the modern generation so she includes instructions for modern-day lye soap, which was used by her mother until 1908. "This is truly a fine soap like that bought in French shops for my mother learned it from the early French settlers. Grandma always made hers the hard way as she didn't hold with 'modern fool things!'"[19]

A Little Fur in the Meringue Never Really Hurts the Filling (1979) mixes servings of everyday housewife and "mom humor" with a batch of the author's favorite recipes, delivering a "good read" through the entertaining text by Cherie Blanton combined with the delightful illustrations of Anne B. Rowe. Rowe's whimsical illustrations keep the upbeat theme of the cookbook moving through the final recipe. Both women graduated from Stephens College in Columbia and settled in southeast Missouri after marrying "Sikeston boys." Blanton, writing from Sikeston, tosses in tips for successful theme parties, one of which includes a recipe for "Blanton's Bombshell," a drink mixed by the gallon for large parties of adults. She explains, "By the time the party's over, everyone can hula, the host included."[20]

Two Missouri cookbooks published in the '80s offered cooks recipe variety. The *St. Louis Post-Dispatch: The Best Recipes Cookbook* (1983) treats Missouri cooks to a twenty-one-year collection of favorite recipes from the food column of the *St. Louis Post-Dispatch*. Barbara Gibbs Ostmann, food editor for the newspaper at the time of publication, also serves as editor for the project. She indicates that the idea of featuring the "year's favorite" recipes originated with Dorothy Brainerd, the food editor in the '60s, and that it became a yearly tradition.[21] Ostmann provides the original introductions to the recipes in order to preserve "the flavor of the times." Cookbook enthusiasts will recognize recipes for potato skins, Herman starter, and pizza spaghetti pie from the '80s. The '70s offered recipes for beer bread, and the Watergate foods . . . Watergate cake with cover-up icing, Watergate salad, and chocolate Watergate cake. The '70s food columns brought the gooey butter cake to Missouri cooks as well as the recipe for the popular Famous-Barr French onion soup that shoppers enjoyed while taking a break from their shopping at the popular St. Louis department store. The '60s food articles deliver pineapple love dove cake, old-fashioned beef pot roast, salmon croquettes, and key lime frozen pie.

In 1986 Sandy Buege packed the pages of her cookbook, *Recipes from Missouri . . . with Love,* full of information about the state. Each chapter division features an illustration of a Missouri heritage quilt pattern. Additionally, the page includes the name of each quilt's maker as well as historical details relating to the pattern and to the date of construction in addition to comments concerning fabrics used in making the original quilt. Throughout the cookbook, the author mixes recipes with bits of Missouri history. Information about Col. Alexander Doniphan's regiment of Missouri volunteers who served in the war with Mexico follows a recipe for hot chili dip. As they search for recipes, cooks are briefly introduced to such Missouri personalities as Tom Sawyer, Jim the Wonder Dog, Rose O'Neill (designer of Kewpie Dolls), Belle

Starr, the Younger gang, Daniel Boone, and Martha Canary (Calamity Jane). They are reminded of Missourians who made significant contributions in the areas of politics, science, business, and technology through notes about Gen. John J. Pershing, George Washington Carver, Charles Lindbergh, and James Cash Penny. Likewise, notables in the fields of journalism, literature, and entertainment are served up in the cookbook. Along with favorite recipes, readers find information on Mark Twain, Joseph Pulitzer, Molly Brown, Harold Bell Wright, Scott Joplin, and Walt Disney. Other additions to the table include facts on Missouri's Civil War battles, vacation spots, historic events, and Missouri landmarks.

Missouri authors produced a variety of cookbooks in the final decade of the century. Charlie and Ruthie Knote, writing from Cape Girardeau in 1992, share years of culinary expertise in their contribution to Missouri's cookbook buffet. In defense of the style of eating promoted in the cookbook, the authors open *Barbecuing and Sausage-Making Secrets* by addressing "food panicked Americans." "This unusual cookbook has been written because we found a big American food need. People like more flavorful, zestful, and tastier foods. However, thousands of Americans are 'food-panicked' and millions are now afraid of America's food!" They discuss concerns about fat content, cholesterol, calories, salmonella, and trichinosis. Hoping to dispel food myths and uncover food truths, they deliver information focusing on healthy selection and safe handling of beef, pork, poultry, seafood, lamb, and wild game. They also provide extensive sections on outdoor cooking equipment and grilling and smoking techniques that will benefit the outdoor cook. Speaking as an experienced sausage maker, Charlie Knote shares his expertise in hopes of reviving a disappearing culinary art form. Discussing sausage recipes, he prefers a lower-fat mix that he created and has used successfully as compared to an older higher-fat sausage mix found in a seventy-five-year-old USDA butchering bulletin. Following the instructions for his homemade sausage, fat can be reduced from the 40 percent found in much sausage to 15 percent.[22]

W. J. Walkley pays tribute to Ruth Walkley, the "Grandma" in his cookbook, recounting her baking expertise in *Grandma's Pie Pantry Cookbook* (1992). A narrative in the cookbook shares her early training in the family kitchen in Kansas City where she learned to bake pies on an open hearth as well as in a wood stove. She began her baking career at Bruns Cafeteria in the 1920s when she was seventeen. She continued working at various restaurant locations during most of the '30s. In 1938 she and her husband opened their own restaurant, Wally's. She later sold pies wholesale to restaurants and cafeterias in the Kansas City area, including Crane's Cafeteria. Family members calculated that she baked well over 1,000,000 pies in her lifetime.[23] The back cover of the cookbook displays a photo of Walkley alongside Spencer Christian when she appeared on *Good Morning America* in May 1991. The book includes recipes for many of her creations, including recipes for standard fruit and cream pies as well as recipes for specialty pies such as caramel nut, cheese chess, lemon velvet, and chocolate satin pies.

Dianne Mayes and Dorothy Stafford from Carthage authored *It's Christmas* (1994). This cookbook takes cooks from a "Do-It-Ahead Buffet" planned for tree-trimming day through a variety of holiday food events to a wrap-up of the holiday food festivities with recipes using leftovers and then on to foods for New Year's events. A final chapter offers decorating tips for the holidays.

In the first section of *Drop Dumplin's and Pan-Fried Memories . . . along the Mississippi* (1997), Angie Thompson Holtzhouser, writing from Lilbourn, includes a collection of family recipes, anecdotes, and photos representing six generations of an Irish family and their food heritage. The author not only offers instructions for preparing but also specific directions for eating her great-great-grandfather's favorite bread, Irish soda bread. She notes that St. Patrick's Day in the Old Country would not be complete without boiled bacon and cabbage. "But, when Irish settlers, like my great-great-grandparents came to America, bacon was too expensive to use as a main dish, so most families used corned beef instead."[24] Holtzhouser contributes her family's St. Patrick's Day menu, complete with recipes for corned beef and cabbage, sour cream rolls, oatmeal lace cookies, and Irish coffee. The second section of the cookbook combines additional family favorites with recipes contributed by eating establishments along the Mississippi River.

At the turn of the century, Shirleen Sando explores cancer-fighting foods for the millennium in *Beyond Low-Fat Baking* (2000), a cookbook dedicated to delivering low-fat, low-cholesterol, high-energy recipes to the Missouri kitchen. Sando experiments with traditional and modern recipes and incorporates soy products, encourages the use of foods rich in phytochemicals and isoflavones in healthy recipes, and includes a discussion of fiber and whole grains in healthy food preparation. Determined to bring variety to the table, she includes recipes for such healthy culinary creations as sun-dried tomato whole-wheat pizza, herb-cheese focaccia, amaretto cheesecake, cran-apple strudel, and devil's food muffins as well as reworked versions of favorites like sweet potato biscuits, snickerdoodles, peach cobbler, and banana nut bread.

Generations of Missouri cooks have taken a creative approach to fashioning the formats that house their personal collections of recipes. Grandmas' red or green plastic recipe boxes have served them well, and similar decorative models have now replaced them on modern kitchen countertops. Binders are convenient and become cookbook friendly when combined with pages of recipes designed by using desktop publishing programs. Cut-and-paste scrapbook/notebook types of cookbooks have also been used to solve the problem of the organization of collections of recipes clipped from newspapers and magazines and handwritten recipes. Various types of folders offer a way to "contain" personal homemade "cookbooks." One such example in recent years was discovered in the Missouri home, now a museum, of one of America's favorite and best-known authors. A reprinting of the book has allowed cooks in twenty-first-century Missouri kitchens to share some of the author's favorites.

When she was twenty-seven, Laura Ingalls Wilder began her life in Missouri on a farm near Mansfield with her daughter, Rose, and husband, Almanzo. They arrived in 1894 in a covered wagon. Not until she was in her sixties did she start recording memories from her growing-up pioneer days. These writings became the popular Little House books. Wilder named their farm Rocky Ridge, and she stayed there until she died in 1957 at the age of ninety.[25] The Mansfield family home, open to the public, is now the Laura Ingalls Wilder–Rose Wilder Lane Home and Museum.

The Laura Ingalls Wilder Country Cookbook, based on Wilder's personal scrapbook recipe collection, was published by the museum association in 2003. Throughout the cookbook, Wilder historian William Anderson provides generous commentary relating to the farm life and foodways of the Wilder family. He points out, "Until recently, the key to Laura's cooking—her recipes—lay lost among reams of the yellowed papers that are witness to her writing life. But when her home-made cookbook appeared, waterlogged and wrinkled, the pages conjured up the smell, taste, and texture of her legendary meals."[26]

He describes the cookbook. "The cookbook she compiled was actually a scrapbook. Recipes were pasted over pages of a cardboard-covered invoice book used by Almonzo while he was a fuel oil deliveryman [in Mansfield] in the early 1900s." Judging from the material in the cookbook, Anderson believes that it was compiled primarily in the '30s and '40s. Continuing his discussion of the book he explains, "On some pages, Laura carefully penned ingredients and cooking instructions. On others she pasted clippings from newspaper food columns, or from magazines like *The Country Gentleman*." Typical of so many Missouri cooks, she used the white space on various household papers to jot down recipes and kitchen information for storage in her recipe collection. Anderson mentions examples—"meal plans on the reverse of letter from her New York literary agent" and "A bread recipe was penciled over an August 1942 calendar leaf," and he also notes that Wilder recorded "cooking advice gathered from her mother, Caroline Ingalls, and her daughter, Rose Wilder Lane."[27] Recipes in the 2003 edition were tested and updated for modern use by Mary Kate Morgan. Photographs by Leslie A. Kelley take cooks into Laura's kitchen and around the farm while vintage photos visually introduce the Wilder family.

The recipe lineup includes family favorites, many representative of the Missouri table of Wilder's time as well as present-day tables. In the main dish section, cooks find recipes for "Almonzo's Favorite Swiss Steak," macaroni casserole, "Rose's Famous Chicken Pie," and one of Laura's favorites—old-fashioned chicken and dumplings. The vegetable and side dishes section includes Missouri succotash, glazed beets, potato pancakes, and dandelion soup.

It isn't surprising that Laura's cookbook spotlights several apple recipes since she and her husband developed a productive apple orchard on their farm. She used the harvest in such homey desserts as apple upside-down cake, applesauce cake, charlotte de pommes, apple tart, apple slump, and apple pudding. The dessert section also shares the recipe for one of Laura's favorite baked items, gingerbread.

Editors Gwen McKee and Barbara Moseley offer Missouri cooks *Best of the Best from Missouri: Selected Recipes from Missouri's Favorite Cookbooks* (2001). The cookbook, a part of Quail Ridge Press's Best of the Best State Cookbook Series, features recipes selected from sixty-five Missouri cookbooks. Traveling across Missouri in search of Missouri cookbooks, when all was said and done, how did they answer the question "What do people in Missouri like to eat?" They say, "Missouri's cooking heritage is as Mid-American as its locale. It's a wonderful culinary mixture with a solid base of simple country, a touch of elegantly fancy, a generous helping of ethnic cuisine, a few dashes of flavorful barbeque, and lots of modern and healthy dishes mingled in . . . the variety of Missouri cooking seems endless."[28]

With their pens and their mixing bowls, Missouri's cookbook authors and editors have earned counter and shelf space in the state's kitchens. They have featured favorite recipes, explored ways to improve fare placed on the table, shared family culinary styles and techniques, and preserved foodways and culinary skills, both those common to Missouri kitchens and those unique to a mix of heritages and regions.

Chapter 7

Producer and Festival Cookbooks

If you are concerned about your health and want to eat food that is good for you—and yet not sacrifice taste and flavor for better nutrition—then buffalo is the meat for you.—*Cooking with American Buffalo,* Missouri Bison Association, 2003

Farmers moving into Missouri in the early nineteenth century sought to establish farms on land fertile enough to allow them to grow crops and raise livestock they could then sell at a profit. Often this required several years of hard work, including building a house and clearing land. For a few years, new settlers farmed at a subsistence level, but most gradually succeeded with crops and livestock, producing more than they needed for the family table. They then could sell part of what they produced for cash, which they could use to buy needed supplies.

Because there was a chronic shortage of money in early-nineteenth-century Missouri, farmers also bartered for items such as coffee, sugar, cloth, and tools. Butter and eggs in particular were sometimes abundant on farms during certain times of the year. Merchants frequently accepted them in lieu of cash. Missouri became known for its cured meats, particularly ham and bacon, during the French colonial period in the late 1700s. Merchants also accepted these items in trade.

In larger towns, farmers' markets developed, giving farmers another outlet for selling or trading items they had produced. On one day of the week, usually a Saturday, farmers brought whatever they had in excess to open-air markets. The variety of products found at these markets included live poultry, eggs, seasonal fruits and vegetables, canned jellies and jams, cured and fresh meats, and handcrafted items.

The tradition continues today in rural roadside stands and farmers' markets in town and city locations. In rural areas, farmers dust off their produce signs and place them where they can be easily seen from the road. In urban areas, Missouri residents frequent farmers' markets in a quest for fresh tasting produce as it arrives from home and truck gardens. Modern Missourians' desire to experience homegrown taste delivered from the state's gardens and fields is evident throughout the growing season wherever towns and individuals host well-attended markets.

One very successful example is Soulard Market, a St. Louis historic site, which continues the long tradition of bringing area farm-fresh produce and food items to the neighborhood for community shoppers. In his history of the concept of the public market, historian Jay Gibb begins his discussion of Soulard in the time before a single stall was built: "Space for the city's first market was set aside by Pierre Laclede in his 1764 plan for the new village" and he also points out that this original market site "survived in various capacities for almost a century."[1] Offering additional history of the St. Louis site, he explains,

> Originally part of the common fields of the City of St. Louis, some of what is now Soulard was given to Antoine Soulard, surveyor general of Upper Louisiana, by the Spanish governor in the 1790's as payment for his services. Soulard's widow, Julia, stipulated in her will that two city blocks be given to the City of St. Louis for use as a public market. She died on May 9, 1845. Her bequest survives today in the form of the Soulard Market.[2]

Generations of St. Louisians have looked forward to weekend trips to Soulard Market to purchase fresh foodstuffs for their next week's meals. Items grown and produced by area farmers continue to be available as do products from farther away resold by vendors. On a typical day shoppers can find both the expected—vegetables and fruits suited to the table—and the unexpected—fresh trapped and dressed raccoons, rabbits, and beavers. A turn around the stalls also nets pickled quail eggs, chicken feet, live turkeys, and freshly fried pork skins.

Taking Missouri cooks back to the early days of the market, Suzanne Corbett shares the story of St. Louis's historic public market in *Pushcarts and Stalls: The Soulard Market History Cookbook.* Her collection of recipes includes those contributed by "Soulard vendors, area farm families and personal heirloom 'receipts' my family prepared on our South St. Louis truck farm." According to Corbett, recipes in the project "celebrate the joys of cooking fresh seasonal ingredients, meats, cheeses, and spices from one of America's unique public markets." She says that "Soulard market is the oldest, continually operated public market in Missouri. One of the oldest West of the Mississippi."[3]

Corbett's recipes deliver instructions for the preparation of fresh food items purchased seasonally at the market. For the spring menu, cooks find instructions for barnyard chicken soup, field potato soup, wild asparagus and spring mushroom soup. Fresh cuts of beef purchased become beef birds with roasted vegetables and gravy, a kitchen pot roast, or horseradish kettle beef. Freshly picked and prepared green beans find their way to the table in the form of sweet and sour green beans. If St. Louis shoppers tire of simple corn on the cob, they might try recipes contributed for baked creamed corn and fried corn on the cob.

Modern-day producers not only continue to fill Missouri's shopping baskets with the "makings" for great meals, but in some cases they opt to deliver preparation instructions for the use of these products in handy promotional cookbooks. Additionally, produce-themed cookbooks, published by community organizations, serve as promotional tools. Cookbooks in the state also document festivals that celebrate production in various areas of the state.

Campbell, located in the southeast Missouri and today referred to as the Peach Capital of Missouri, held its first Peach Festival in 1944. Ten years earlier the State Agricultural Experiment Station had established a peach research orchard that increased interest and aided peach growers in the Campbell area. Campbell's Web site details the history of the Peach Festival. The one-day event in 1944, sponsored by the C. Dolph Gehrig American Legion Post 109, local peach growers, and area businessmen, included an all-day picnic and barbecue. At the event, prizes were awarded for the best peaches. Over the years, sponsorship and organization of the Peach Festival passed from one organization to another. In 1981 the Peach Festival, through reorganization, became the Missouri Peach Fair.[4]

The Campbell Business and Professional Women's Club published *Peach Recipes from the Peach Capital of Missouri* in 1975. Recipes range from cakes and the ever-popular cobblers to other desserts, jams, and jellies, and the collection includes a section of recipes designed to yield banquet-size amounts. In that section, a fruited macaroni salad and an oatmeal peach bread pudding both yield one hundred servings. All recipes in the cookbook include the Campbell peach as an ingredient.

This cookbook quite possibly inspired locals and fresh peach enthusiasts from surrounding towns to make more than one trip to a roadside fruit stand or to one of the peach orchards as they attempted to select the fruit for their favorite peach recipes, perhaps strawberry-peach cream cheese pie, peach skillet pie, peacheesy pie, fried peach pies, peach delight, or peachy keen. And for area residents willing to "put up peaches" in order to enjoy Campbell's bounty year round, the cookbook includes recipes for skillet peach preserves, peach jam, spiced peaches, freezer bag peaches, and spiced brandied peaches. Commonly, cooks in the area purchased Campbell peaches by the bushel for freezing and canning purposes.

Information in the cookbook offers a map pinpointing thirty-five orchards in the immediate area of Campbell at the time the cookbook was published. The orchards' owners are listed as well. Current statistics on the city Web site indicate a prospering peach market in Campbell today: "The three thousand acres of peach orchards begin within the Campbell City limits and almost surround the town. Approximately two hundred thousand trees produce more than one million bushels of fruit annually, bringing in a gross income of six to eight Million dollars."[5] The current number of orchards is significantly fewer than that listed in the 1975 cookbook, and most of the peach crop comes out of the Bader production operation.

Not only does Missouri have a peach capital, it also has, in the northwest section of the state, a self-proclaimed mushroom capital. The *Richmond Chamber of Commerce Mushroom Cookbook*, published in 2000, commemorates the twentieth anniversary of the annual Richmond Mushroom Festival and includes an important resolution by the city council. Each recipe in the cookbook includes morel mushrooms in keeping with the resolution adopted for the very first Richmond Mushroom Festival. Resolution No. 228–80, declared by Mayor C. B. Thompson Jr., attested by Sam Freel, city clerk, and recorded in the cookbook, acknowledges the proliferation of mushrooms in and around Richmond during the spring each year. It points out that "Richmond residents and Ray

Countians take to the woods and fields every spring in search of mushrooms," and furthermore, "Many other mushroom lovers from elsewhere converge on Richmond and Ray County for their chance at finding the delectable gift of the wild, the incomparable Ray County mushroom." The resolution continues, "The passion that so many people have for Ray County mushrooms makes it self-evident that this creation of nature should be honored." It concludes, "BE IT RESOLVED that the City Council of Richmond, Missouri with the assent of the Mayor of Richmond on this day, April 16, 1980, does declare Richmond, Missouri, to be The Mushroom Capital of the World."[6]

The selection of recipes collected under the direction of Jean Hamacher goes beyond old-time Missouri country cooking. For meal starters, the author's suggestions include paprika morels, morels with shallots and garlic, sautéed morels, and cheese-stuffed morels. Several recipes produce tasty sauces. Hamacher includes recipes for morels and asparagus pasta, wild mushroom lasagna, and mini sausage/morel pizzas. She features a variety of recipes designed to put international dishes on the table, and Missouri deer hunters will find among them dishes to their liking—deer hunter's surprise and another for venison bourguignon.

The cookbook provides tips for the mushroom hunt with the text first advising readers regarding proper attire followed by information relating to collection containers. Ray County hunters share their site identification tips, although it seems that they are not willing to give away specific directions to these secret locations. To determine whether discovered mushrooms are edible or poisonous, novice morel hunters are advised to contact their local Extension office or the Missouri Department of Conservation for necessary additional information so that they will have a safe mushroom hunt.

Within the bright orange pages of the *Pumpkin Festival Cookbook*, Mayor Nancy Grant shares the history of Hartsburg, a small central Missouri town. Although settled by the Hart brothers in the 1870s, the town was not incorporated until 1901. At that time the original name of the town was changed from Hart City to Hartsburg.[7]

The cookbook celebrates Hartsburg as Mid-Missouri's pumpkin patch where, each year, the population of fewer than two hundred citizens welcomes over forty thousand visitors on Pumpkin Festival weekend, the second weekend in October. According to Grant, during the 2005 festival there were fifty-five thousand visitors to the patch.

A unique recipe for pumpkin with soup inside, in which a delightful soup is baked and served in a fresh pumpkin, opens the pumpkin recipe collection. In the bread section, Hartsburg cooks deliver recipes for pumpkin yeast bread and one for pumpkin cornbread. Also of interest is a recipe for slow cooker pumpkin cake. And what better way to celebrate the harvest season than with a ginger crisp pumpkin cheesecake? For the cookie jar, Hartsburg cooks offer such pleasing fare as pumpkin chocolate chip cookies and pumpkin face cookies. In the pie section, beyond the old standard, there are pumpkin chiffon, pumpkin-almond, and maple pumpkin pies. A recipe for pumpkin empanadas wraps up the collection.

The editors of the *Pumpkin Festival Cookbook* speak fondly and enthusiastically of the star of their cookbook. "While pumpkins are a colorful symbol of our fall celebrations, they are also a delicious and very nutritious source of food that can be enjoyed any time of the year." Should the reader need convincing, they elaborate, "One cup of Pumpkin contains 80 calories, 20 grams of Carbohydrate, 3 grams of Protein and virtually no fat. One 1/2 cup serving of Pumpkin contains 34000 international units of Vitamin A, which easily meets the recommended dietary allowance for men and women of all ages. In addition, 1/2 cup Pumpkin also provides 37 Milligrams of Vitamin C."[8]

When temperatures begin to drop in the fall, shoppers' thoughts turn not only to pumpkin pie and jack-o-lanterns but also to tasty memories of apple pies, fresh apple cakes, and skillets of fried apples. A quick trip to one of the state's orchards or farmers' markets nets a tasty selection of apples complete with helpful labels to explain which are best for eating, baking, or preserving.

A visit to the University of Missouri's online Missouri Apple Site offers an assortment of apple-related facts. "Early records state that 'Genetin' apples were produced and shipped by rail car in Missouri to Cheyenne, Wyoming and then transported by wagon to gold miners in Central City, Colorado in 1869" and in 1897 "9 million barrels (30 million bushels) were grown in Missouri, which is the largest crop on record in the state." The site also indicates that "By 1900, Missouri was the center of activity for growing apples in the U.S. as production shifted from the eastern states to the Midwest." Consequently, "Apples were transported in wooden barrels by rail cars and boats to such destinations as Sioux City, Minneapolis, Detroit, Buffalo, Philadelphia, Baltimore, Birmingham, Mobile, New Orleans, Galveston, as well as European ports." Four years later, "There were 25 million apple trees planted in Missouri that produced a crop worth $30 million (worth about 501 million in today's dollars)." Also of interest is the fact that the 1913 crop census shows "nearly 15,000 apple growers with most of them producing their crop on less than 10 acres of land." Problems related to insects and diseases developed in the state's apple orchards in the '20s and the '30s, and Missouri's unpredictable weather conditions negatively affected apple production at about the same time. For these reasons "Apple production moved westward to states with less erratic climatic conditions and lower pest populations."[9]

Two Missouri cookbooks, *Home Cookin' Apple Recipes from Missouri Apple Growers,* compiled by Kathy Beckner, and *The Fayette Apple Festival Cookbook* (1994), by Sylvia Forbes, serve as representative examples of apple-themed recipe collections that bring dishes to the table prepared with Missouri apples. The first cookbook includes a Missouri map pinpointing forty Missouri orchards in 1990. Forbes's cookbook details a brief history of apples in Howard County, noting that apple trees were listed for sale in the *Missouri Intelligencer* as early as 1823.[10] The same cookbook includes recipes from early cookbooks in the area: dried apples from the Fayette *Methodist Cook Book* (1904), apple preserves from the First Christian Church's *The Best Yet Cookbook* (1907), and a recipe for cider cake from an untitled cookbook from the 1880s. Together the cookbooks deliver over fifty different favorite recipes for apple pie as well as recipes for crisps, dumplings, grunts, fritters, and streusels. Demonstrating the culinary creativity of Missouri cooks, apples even find their way into recipes for catsup, barbecue sauce, chutney, punch, pancakes, and doughnuts.

Corn, first grown in Missouri by Native Americans, was also the first crop put in by early Missouri settlers because it could be planted in rough ground not completely cleared and because of its multiple uses. It could be fed to livestock or shelled and ground into meal for making a variety of breads and puddings. Corn's versatility and adaptability made it a vital yearly crop essential to the survival of settlers in most parts of the state.

Acreage designated for corn expanded steadily through the nineteenth and early twentieth centuries. For most of this time, it remained the number one crop in Missouri and still is a major crop for the state, now outdistanced only by soybeans. Corn production received a boost with the introduction, in 1923, of the first commercial hybrid corn seed, which dramatically increased yields.[11] With continued improvements in corn varieties, some farmers have exceeded two hundred bushels per acre. The Missouri Corn Growers Association indicates that the state "produces nearly 300 million

The *Fayette Apple Festival Cookbook* cover shows readers how community cookbooks use art to help them stand out from more slickly produced mass-market publications.

bushels of corn annually" and "In the average supermarket, more than 4,200 products contain corn."[12]

In Northeast Missouri the Knox County Promotional Council sponsored several cookbooks in conjunction with the county's Corn Fests held in the late '80s and into the '90s. The *Knox County Corn Fest Second Annual Cookbook* opens with a concise history of corn and highlights a section of "corn-related" recipes in an otherwise general cookbook. Compilers include a page devoted to the uses of corn in addition to the usual human and livestock consumption. Readers might be surprised to learn that corn is used in making numerous everyday products, among them fireworks, plastics, printing inks, photographic film, brake fluid, batteries, explosives, and artificial silk. Knox County hosted its twentieth Corn Fest in 2006.

Soybeans came to Missouri in 1909 when the U.S. Department of Agriculture sent seeds to the Missouri Agricultural Experiment Station in Columbia. Until the mid-1930s, the station recommended that farmers grow soybeans for a hay crop. After this date, soybeans began to be farmed for seeds.[13] Early in the twentieth century, George Washington Carver, a native Missourian from Diamond Grove, began his experiments on the soybean at Tuskegee Institute, which led to the discovery of additional uses. Because of his research and that of other scientists, soybeans came to the Missouri dinner table. *The Best of Soy* is a compilation of recipes submitted over a five-year period to the Missouri Soybean Merchandising Council. Each recipe includes products from soybeans, the number one crop now grown in the state.

Today health-conscious Missourians who carefully read labels on processed foods realize that soy products are in many of the packaged foods purchased at food marts. Information in the cookbook notes, "Every man, woman and child in America consumes, on average, 260 pounds of soy each year." In recent years, interest has increased in Missouri's number one crop as significant health benefits have been attributed to it. Cooks have become interested in discovering how they can add more of these healthful benefits to dishes prepared in their own kitchens. Missourians may submit recipes using soy products to encourage consumers to incorporate soyfoods in their diets.[14]

After listing the top ten health benefits of eating soy, the cookbook offers recipes for everyday meals or for social occasions. Missouri contest cooks certainly seem to be taking steps to enhance their breakfast foods nutritionally with soy products. A recipe for apple pancakes includes soy flour and soy oil, and one for blueberry oatmeal pancakes includes soy milk and soy flour. Locating recipes for healthy appetizers and snacks is no longer a problem. The cookbook presents recipes for numerous tasty party treats: artichoke and spinach tofu dip, Mighty Mo munchies, Popeye pesto, and not-so-devilish eggs. Missouri cooks show equally successful results in their salad, main dish, and dessert healthful recipe creations and recipe modifications. The cookbook includes recipes for calico soybean salad, ginger tofu stir-fry, dern good meatballs, and veggie calzones, all using Missouri's top crop. Determined to have their sweets and their nutrition too, the cooks create and adjust healthful recipes for soy doughnuts, Midwestern Mississippi mud cake, chewy gooey tofu cake, chocolate chippers, and coconut cream pie.

Honeybees, brought here by early European settlers, were not a favorite of Native Americans, who referred to them as "white man's flies." Recognized today for their industriousness, these diligent workers not only provide a versatile sweetener in the form of honey, but also pay an added value through the pollination of Missouri's cultivated crops. Crops such as watermelons rely on insect pollination to produce an abundant yield. In honor of the value of the honeybee to the state's agriculture, the legislature named the honeybee Missouri's state insect in 1985.

In 2001, after compiling their favorite honey recipes, the Missouri State Bee Keepers Auxiliary delivered *Missouri Honey Recipes,* a general cookbook to encourage the use of Missouri honey in cooking. They include a history of honey which notes among other historical details that, "For 10 to 20 million years, bees have been producing a miraculous sweetener from the nectar of flowering plants." Missouri cooks might be amazed to learn from the cookbook that "A hive of honeybees must fly over 55,000 miles and must tap 2 million flowers to make 1 pound of honey" and that "The average bee visits thousands of flower blooms every day."[15] Cooks probably expect recipes for desserts, cookies, and candy, and they are here, but honey also serves as an ingredient in appetizers, soups, salads, vegetable dishes, and entrees. A section called "This and That" offers recipes for banana moisture mask, corn relish, bread and butter pickles, chapped lip balm, and wax pastel crayons.

Pork and beef have been welcome items on the Missouri menu since the state's earliest settlers began to clear land for farms. Most settlers brought some livestock with them. The hog was one of the most versatile types of livestock. Generally, hogs could find most of their own food, and they produced large litters while farmers were busy clearing land in preparation for planting crops. Pork was often the first product of early farms. It was much in demand and was also relatively easy to preserve through curing and salting. Cattle, likewise, proved adaptable for early settlers providing meat, milk, and power to pull farm equipment. On their Web site, the Missouri Beef Industry Council cites Missouri's climate as a positive contributing factor to the development of successful livestock production in the state. "The climate of Missouri is such that livestock are not subjected to the higher temperatures of the more southerly states and the disease and pest problems associated with them. Yet it is not so far north as to require livestock to endure extremely harsh winters."[16] The council also points out that Missouri climate allows "a long growing season for native grasses and improved pastures" and notes that "The Southeastern sections of the state provide feed grains while the hilly Ozark plateau is only suitable for animal agriculture."[17]

The state has historically been a leader in developing improved lines in both cattle and hogs, and Missouri-produced stock regularly took top honors at livestock shows across the country. Under the leadership of the Missouri Beef Industry Council and the Missouri Pork Association, the state continues to be a national leader in livestock production. Both the Missouri Beef Industry Council and the Missouri Pork Association promote beef and pork consumption through alternative format "cookbooks" located on their Web sites.

The Missouri Beef Industry Council delivers to Missouri cooks a recipe archive packed with recipes for special occasions and features recipes specific to particular cuts of beef or to ground beef as well as offering categories for types of dishes or methods of preparation. In the same vein as slick modern hard- and softcover cookbooks, the online alternative format "cookbook" is enhanced with color photography and provides nutritional information. Cooks find tips related to food safety and to the selection of beef and its preparation for the family table.

The Missouri Pork Association offers an online newsletter, *The Daily Pork*, on their Web site, which features "*The Daily Pork* recipe finder" allowing cooks to search a collection of over fifteen hundred recipes using their product. They explain, "*The Daily Pork* recipe finder can pinpoint the perfect pork dish in seconds, based on criteria important to you."[18] Visitors to the site key in specifics to locate recipes to suit their needs and tastes. The recipe finder locates in a flash recipes that can be prepared in, say, less than thirty minutes or recipes that include certain requested ingredients. The site encourages the cook to start searching and to take advantage of the onsite "My Recipe Box." Missouri cooks simply locate recipes of their choice and file them in their online recipe boxes or print the recipes out in either in standard format or in a 3 x 5 recipe card format. The recipes also can be emailed easily. This convenient method efficiently stores recipes and saves kitchen shelf space.

Information in *Cooking with the American Buffalo* spotlights a Missouri product developed in recent years.

> Bison numbering in the hundreds of millions once roamed freely across our prairies. As the American culture expanded westward, it collided with these great herds, resulting in their near extermination. A century ago, fewer than a thousand of these magnificent animals remained. Thanks to the efforts of dedicated individuals, Native Americans, private ranchers, and conservationists, these animals have returned from the brink of extinction and are no longer endangered.[19]

Additionally, "The buffalo has found its place in modern agriculture."[20]

Commenting on buffalo in Missouri, the cookbook editors indicate that "Missouri is in the heart of America. Fertile fields across the state produce food for Americans and the world. Lands not suitable for field crops are a source of rich timber and pasture for livestock. The patchwork of farms that covers the state is as diverse as the farmers themselves. More than 3,000 bison, usually called buffalo, have found a home here in Missouri." They also note that on a buffalo farm "Grass can provide the only food needed for the survival of these huge beasts," "Antibiotics are unnecessary," and "Hormones and steroids are never used." They point out that buffalo farms in Missouri tend to be small with herds of fewer than thirty animals. Consequently, because of smaller amounts, "Meat is usually sold at the farm gate or at local farmers' markets." Buffalo is tapped as "America's original health food" because of its lower level of fat, calories, and cholesterol when compared with chicken, beef, and pork.[21]

Cooking with American Buffalo focuses on the easy and pleasurable aspect of adding buffalo to Missouri menus. In tips for cooking with buffalo, the

While buffalo meat has become increasingly available in the last few years, this cover, produced by the Missouri Bison Association, uses an out-of-the-ordinary image to draw readers' attention to the book about a sometimes-uncommon main ingredient. (Drawing by M. Shannon)

book notes that the meat can be substituted for beef in any recipe, but it cooks much faster than other meats, and slow cooking plus the use of a meat thermometer produces the best results.[22]

The collection of recipes delivers tasty dishes easily prepared. Among the recipes cooks will discover instructions for preparing buffa-nacho casserole, Mexican buffalo cornbread, bison breakfast sausage, low-fat bison lasagna, and bison Cajun jambalaya as well as the more gourmet pecan-crusted bison medallions with bourbon mash, and, of course, best bison chili. To get a party started, Missouri cooks might decide to try buffalo chip dip, drunken buff dogs, buffalo cheesy bean dip, or mini buffalo quiches.

With health and nutrition and fresh foods becoming modern-day requirements, roadside fruit and vegetable stands, local producers, farmers' markets, and alternative agriculture operations have become popular sources for healthy food options. Numerous producer and festival organizations throughout the state illustrate the diversity of Missouri's agricultural products. From honey and hogs to peach cobbler and pork chops, traditional cookbooks and in more recent years high-tech online recipe collections show cooks how to take Missouri-grown products to the table.

Chapter 8

Company/Product Cookbooks

Good tools contribute much to the performance of any task. Many new wrinkles have been introduced in recent years, and great strides have been made in improved household equipment and methods.—*Home Comfort Cook Book,* Wrought Iron Range Company, 1952

Some of Missouri's most kitchen-friendly cookbooks were originally published by companies as advertising tools to promote new products. Companies introduce the products to consumers, pass along tips and general information discovered in their research, and deliver tasty recipes to encourage consumers to try products and then to continue to use them. Aristos Flour, fancy cast iron Majestic Ranges, Crock-Pots, Hammons Recipe-Ready Black Walnuts, and Stone Hill Wine have all been promoted in this way.

The introduction of Turkey Red wheat, a hard red winter wheat, also called Red Turkey wheat in advertising, to Kansas in the 1880s by the German Mennonites created an increasingly reliable supply of wheat to be milled. Kansas City, in an ideal location to receive wheat from Kansas, milled wheat and distributed flour across the country. The development of railroads following the Civil War and into the twentieth century also stimulated the growth of the Kansas City milling industry. These factors helped Kansas City to become Missouri's most significant milling area, although not the only important site.

Missouri milling companies promoted their flour products through cookbooks. In 1911 the Southwestern Milling Company in Kansas City offered the *Aristos Flour Cook Book,* an attractive softcover cookbook featuring a bright red turkey on the cover. In the "Wise Words" section, cooks learn about the positive features of Turkey Red hard winter wheat in an informative comparison of the kinds of wheat available for baking. The text explains that pastry flour is made from soft winter wheat, which has a "sticky" quality. Spring wheat, when used for making cake and pastry, requires the addition of more shortening. Turkey Red hard winter wheat used in making Aristos Flour combines the qualities of soft winter wheat and spring wheat. Therefore, the cook learns, Aristos Flour is suitable for making bread and biscuits, cakes, and pastries.[1] In *Town Crier Ready Mixed Flour Recipes,* Town Crier Food Products explains that their flour "already contains soda, salt, phosphate, and etc."[2] This colorful miniature cookbook, a mere inch and a half wide and three inches tall, contains recipes printed in four languages: English, Polish, Spanish, and Italian.

An essential item in Missouri kitchens has been and continues to be a good cookstove, and stove manufacturers in the state have delivered the goods in this respect. Statistics in the online version of the "Polk-Gould St. Louis Directory-1925 indicate that St. Louis, as a stove center, shows stove and range production three times greater than in any other city in the world."[3] Missouri stove company cookbooks offer modern cooks a view of the ever-changing stove technology.

The Majestic Manufacturing Company, founded in the 1890s by L. L. Culver and Robert Henry Stockton, grew to be a prosperous St. Louis stove manufacturing company.[4] *The Great Majestic Range Cook Book* includes numerous testimonials from satisfied customers from around the country as to the baking qualities, durability, and fuel efficiency of their product. Some customers point out that as Majestic Range owners, they have spent very little for repairs; others comment on the water-heating capacity of the range. Mrs. A. G. Mussler of St. Louis writes that she has enough coal left for another year. From Paris, Illinois, Jessie Scott explains that she had "Fifteen gallons of steaming hot water in my Majestic Range reservoir while cooking breakfast." Another owner says, "It [the Magestic Range] is to be depended upon to supply a bath room with all the hot water needed."[5] Cookstoves equipped with various types of water reservoirs did double duty as water heaters for the home in Missouri kitchens.

A page with the heading "How to Obtain Best Results from the Great Majestic Range" offers quite a contrast to directions arriving with Missouri's more modern stovetops and smart ovens. The cookbook instructs the cook.

This trio of flour company cookbooks represents both promotional and educational efforts by Missouri companies to get their products in the hands of the state's cooks.

"When starting a fire in the Great majestic Range, use plenty of kindling.... When using coal, break it in fine lumps and never put on more than a fire-shovel-ful at a time.... No matter what kind of fuel is used, always keep the ashes well shaken out of fire box, as dead ashes not only check the draft, but burn out the linings and grates."[6]

Before temperature controls came to Missouri kitchens, regulating oven heat required expertise, which experienced cooks had no doubt honed by daily practice preparing three meals each day. The cookbooks offer novices some suggestions.

> When baking, open the oven door as little as possible. Every time the oven door is opened, it cools the bottom of the oven. When more heat is desired on bottom of oven, close the draft door above ash pan, and draw out the ash pan about two inches. When more heat is desired at top of range for cooking, and at the same time the usual amount around the oven for baking, open the draft door and draw out the ash pan about

two inches. When oven is too hot, close both draft door and ash pan, and open check draft in first joint of pipe. When you desire to heat the kitchen, open the oven door. Always keep the damper pulled forward and heat going around oven, after fire is started.[7]

Illustrations of Majestic Ranges show wood, coal, combination coal and gas, and gas models with large combination gas and coal ranges weighing in at one thousand pounds.

Production of these stoves ceased in the years following World War II, but the Majestic buildings have remained a part of the urban St. Louis landscape. The company's name is still evident in the city as the manufacturing buildings are currently being converted to residential lofts under the name Majestic Stove Lofts. The names of the two St. Louis businessmen are also remembered today in another area of the state. Stockton along with Culver's widow, Mary, were philanthropically inclined, and they turned their attention to Christian University in Canton. In 1917, Christian University's name was changed to Culver-Stockton College to honor Mary Culver and Robert Stockton for their generous donations to the college.[8]

Two promotional cookbooks, *Magic Chef Cooking* and *Lorain Cooking*, were published in the 1920s and 1930s by American Stove Company, which was also located in St. Louis. In the early 1880s, stove makers Charles and Louis Stockstrom joined John Ringen and George August Kahle's St. Louis business, which manufactured household items, among them a cooking stove they called "quick meals." The successful venture of the four businessmen then led to the formation, at the turn of the century, of the American Stove Company. In 1919, the company introduced the first oven temperature-control device labeled the Lorain Oven Heat Regulator, and in 1929, it introduced another first, a brand name stove. The Magic Chef brand name became so popular in America's kitchens that the American Stove Company changed its company name to Magic Chef in the early '50s.[9]

As early as 1925, editions of American Stove Company publications such as the *Lorain* cookbook and *Magic Chef* cookbook, developed by Dorothy E. Shank, were instructing cooks in the use of their oven temperature-control device. The Lorain Oven Heat Regulator, the first thermostatic control to be placed on a gas range, automatically controlled the flow of gas to the oven burner, maintaining any desired baking temperature. The Red Wheel, a temperature regulator located on the side of the oven, allowed the cook to set the

"Quick Meal" ranges offered readers of 1910's *Union Avenue Christian Church Cook Book* the latest in modern cooking technology.

desired baking temperature. Prior to this device, cooks had to regulate the temperature of the oven by adjusting the gas cocks by hand, a process not always successful in maintaining the desired temperature for baking. These advancements in cookstoves represented one more step toward the technological ease now enjoyed by twenty-first-century cooks in Missouri kitchens. With the development of this new device on their cookstove ovens, busy cooks eliminated much of the guesswork when it came to baking their favorite breads, pies, and cakes. Information in the *Magic Chef* cookbook explains that the cookstove will deliver fewer burned baked goods and reduce the need to check on baking items, thus allowing more time to attend to other kitchen and household duties. The publication explains, "It [the cake or pie] can be forgotten from the time it goes into the oven until the time for it to be removed."[10] Since temperature control was such a new option, the cookbook provides cooks with reminders of time and temperature needed at the beginning and end of each recipe.

The promotional cookbooks were not all about cooking. Of interest is the marketing plan included in the also-successful St. Louis based Wrought Iron Range Company discussed in the *Home Comfort Cook Book*. "Since the founding of the Company, its Sales Department has placed more than a million 'Home Comfort' ranges in American homes." Apparently, an army of traveling salespersons fanned out across Missouri and on to "every county of every state in the Union." The well-trained, salaried sales force, specifically selling Home Comfort Ranges, operated under the direction of sales managers located in the St. Louis home office and under district managers placed throughout the United States. Focusing on quality control and customer satisfaction based on moral company policies of honesty and integrity, the company took their Home Comfort Range to the cook.[11]

"Salesmen traveled throughout the country in large wagons which carried four cookstoves, making a house-to-house canvass and delivering these cook-stoves as they were sold." In the 1890s, the peddling wagons were replaced by the sample wagon, which carried a single range for demonstration. "These wagons were drawn by fine teams of matched horses or mules, and the men took great pride in keeping team, wagon, harness and sample range in apple-pie order." Within the first decade of the twentieth century, the sample wagon was replaced by small model ranges, miniatures of the real Home Comfort and "correct to the last detail" to be used by company salesmen. Salesman carried their small models in horse-drawn buggies until improved roads allowed them to deliver their goods by automobile to cooks in Missouri and in other states. Representatives of the company believed that this personal contact helped the company stay in tune with the "tastes, needs, and preferences" of their customers, thus encouraging sales.[12] The 1952 cookbook includes historical illustrations of the peddling wagons, the sample wagon, and the small model ranges used by the sales force.

The Rival Crock-Pot took its place on Missouri kitchen counters in 1971. A history of the company claims that the appliance "redefined how many Americans cooked their meals, and at the height of its phenomenal growth, the company reported receiving letters claiming saved marriages, meals salvaged, and inspirations of poetry—all due to this revolutionary method of cooking." This newfangled small kitchen appliance assisted working cooks and busy homemakers by simmering their soups and stews while the owners were at work or while mothers tended to the children and to other tasks around the home. Before introducing the Crock-Pot, the Rival Company, founded in Kansas City in 1932, produced a line of kitchen aids, including the Juice-O-Mat Juice Extractor, an ice crusher, the Can-O-Mat, and the first electric can opener.[13]

The company's catchy slogan certainly must have caught the attention of busy Missouri cooks. As it said in the cookbook, it "cooks all day while the cook's away." *Rival Crock-Pot Slow Electric Stoneware Cooker Cookbook,* published in Kansas City, features photos of several models in popular '70s colors—harvest gold, avocado green, and tangerine. To encourage cooks to go beyond cooking soups and stews in their new kitchen appliance, the collection of recipes includes instructions for such dishes as spareribs-cabbage'n'kraut, down south barbecue, and veal scallopini. In the seafood section, the introduction to a jiffy lobster newburg recipe suggests, "This Gourmet dish may be assembled in minutes . . . let the Crock-Pot be the chef."[14] Cooks learn that packaged cake mixes can be mixed according to box directions and baked in two- to three-pound coffee cans in the Crock-Pot.

Preceding the recipe section is an introduction to slow cooking, including several articles designed to help cooks get ready for this new era of meal preparation. Readers are also informed that a two-volume Braille edition of the cookbook, including all 150 recipes, is available. The cookbook published in Kansas City explains that the company believes their product will benefit the blind homemaker since it does not require open flames or exposed range-top elements. Likewise, the book reminds readers that the exterior is safe to touch, and no stirring, watching, or careful timing is necessary.

Over the years, Crock-Pot designs of the '70s have been replaced with styles more likely to fit changing modern kitchen décor and advancing technology in the state's kitchens. Companion cookbooks also reflect changing tastes and advancing technology. For example, in *Rival Crock-Pot Cooking* (1975), recipes for tongue and stuffed heart included in the original cookbook are nowhere to be found. A section labeled "Dieter's Fare" shows up in the later publication. Cooks learn that coffee cans, initially used for baking cakes in Crock-Pots, can be replaced with specifically designed Bread'n'Cake Bake pans. Missouri cooks may now use high-tech programmable Crock-Pots, and those who are computer savvy will enjoy the Rival *New Creative Cooking Cookbook* available in a very modern CD version. One Crock-Pot in the company's special edition line features a design by the successful St. Louis artist and businesswoman Mary Engelbreit.

In 1960 Theodore R. Gamble, president of the Pet Milk Company, discussed the history of the company in a speech delivered in St. Louis. "The founding of our Company was actually the culmination of a century-long quest for a safe and palatable method of preserving milk so that it could be transported and stored for use where fresh milk was unavailable." He mentions the work of Nicholas Appert, who won 12,000 francs from the French government in 1810 for successfully developing a process for preserving milk that could be used at home and by France's distant armies, and he points out that milk-preservation efforts moved forward in the United States as well. "In the middle of the nineteenth century, Gail Borden successfully marketed sweetened condensed milk which was widely used during the Civil War."[15]

A Missouri connection relating to Appert's historic food-preservation discovery developed years later when John Meyenberg, after working for an American-owned company in Switzerland, moved to St. Louis. Meyenberg's work focused on the preservation of milk without the use of sugar. He became associated with a group of farmers in Highland, Illinois, about thirty-five miles from St. Louis. In 1885 the Helvetia Milk Condensing Company was formed with plans to market their first product, Highland Brand Condensed Milk. The product went through several name changes in the years that followed. The final name for Meyenberg's product was Pet Evaporated Milk and the company name, Pet Milk Company. Although the Pet Milk Company was founded in St. Louis in 1923, the company under its previous name had moved its headquarters to St. Louis two years earlier.[16]

Cookbooks published by the St. Louis company provide information about the importance of milk and instruct Missouri cooks in the use of its products. *Pet Recipes* (1930) promotes milk as "The Most Nearly Perfect Food," assures cooks that "No human being ever contracted an infectious disease from Pet Milk," and offers an explanation of the production and sterilization processes. Readers are reminded of an additional positive feature of the product: it has a long shelf life. Although the recipes in the cookbook are designed for the use of Pet Milk, the editors also explain how Pet Milk may be modified for used in regular recipes.

Through the decades, additional Pet Milk cookbooks came off the press in St. Louis. Erma Proetz tested recipes for Pet Milk Company and developed the radio personality Mary Lee Taylor. The "Mary Lee Taylor Program," a fifteen-minute radio show for the homemaker, "featured Pet recipes and meal plans, promoted cookbooks and offered household hints" with the first show airing just before Thanksgiving in 1933. Her first recipe was pumpkin pie filling using Pet Milk.[17]

Like the pie filling, which still occupies a place in Missouri Thanksgiving traditions, the Pet Milk Building remains a part of the St. Louis downtown scene. Although no longer in use by the Pet Milk Company, "After a short period of vacancy, the tower is being renovated into apartments."[18] At a cost of forty-nine million dollars, 118 luxury apartments called Pointe 400 will be developed in the former Pet Milk building. Located at 400 South Fourth Street, the sixteen-story building is directly east of the new Cardinal Stadium.[19]

Not until 1988 did the Milnot Company locate its headquarters in St. Louis. Current owner Eagle Family Foods outlines the company history. The company originated as Litchfield Creamery Company in Litchfield, Illinois, in 1912. Charles Hauser became a part of the company in 1915, and during the '20s, he began actively promoting one of the company's new products, Milnut. The "nut" in the name referred to the use of coconut oil in the product. In 1939, cotton seed oil replaced coconut oil in the formula, and the name was changed to Milnot. The oil changed again in 1953 when a new formula was developed with soybean oil.[20]

Milnot was slow to catch on with consumers in some part due to federal legislation. Legislation enacted during Milnut's early years "prevented the selling of the product across the state lines" because "The product was considered a threat to the industry since its uses were 'milk-like' but the product itself was not considered a 'pure' milk product." Consequently, Milnot could only be sold in the state it in which it was produced, so Hauser continued to expand the operation by adding a plant in Indiana. The Milnot operation came to Missouri in the 1940s when Hauser "came to Seneca Missouri and purchased land lying on the Missouri-Oklahoma line."[21]

In an interesting and strategic move, Hauser was able to sell the product to two states from one plant. "The Seneca plant was constructed straddling the state line, thus allowing it to market to both Oklahoma and Missouri." "Two sets of equipment were installed in the plant and two warehouses were built—one for Missouri and one for Oklahoma." As the company history notes, "A brass floor marker running through the plant denotes the division of the states to this day." In the mid-seventies, the company began selling Milnot products throughout the country when the law prohibiting sales across state lines was rescinded.[22] Eagle Family Food currently operates a plant in Seneca.

In the second edition of *Tested and Tasted Economical Recipes* (nd), a Milnot company cookbook, the company defines the product and supplies hints for its use in kitchen. The product is made by blending "highly refined vegetable fats" with "pure, whole milk from which the fat and part of the water are removed." Missouri cooks reading about the product learn that one of the "exclusives" highlighted is that "Milnot has 24% fewer fat calories than evaporated milk" and that it costs "far less than evaporated milk."[23] Cooks are encouraged to use Milnot in their favorite recipes for baked cheesecake, fudge, and pumpkin pie as well as in chilled and frozen desserts, soups, sauces, salads, and main dishes. The Milnot company now includes a selection of recipes at their Web site, including some for kids such as no-cook chocolate pie, strawberry smoothie, and kool freeze.

Cooking with Black Walnuts, published by Hammons Pantry in southwest Missouri, treats Missouri cooks to a collection of recipes featuring one of the state's wild nuts, the walnut. In 1990 in recognition of Missouri's leadership in black walnut production, the state legislature designated the "Eastern" American black walnut the state tree nut. The Hammons family's black walnut operation headquartered in Stockton has significantly contributed to the success of the production of this native Missouri food product.

At midcentury, Ralph Hammons, grandfather of Brian Hammons, now Hammons Products Company president, owned a small grocery store in Stockton. In 1945 he started buying black walnuts from local people and shipping them to a company in Virginia. A year later, aware of the abundance of black walnuts in the Ozarks, he determined to market his own brand of walnut nut meats. In 1946, he purchased a cracking machine and started selling "Missouri Dandy" walnut nut meats. Now operating under the Hammons brand, this Missouri company has become the world's premier supplier of black walnut nut products. Each fall walnuts that grow in the wild are hand harvested and brought to 250 buying locations in a 16-state area. Millions of pounds of nuts are then delivered to the Hammons Company in Stockton for processing.[24]

With the increasing popularity and public awareness of the health benefits of this Missouri product, the Hammons Products Company is wisely looking to the future to assure a continuing supply of walnuts harvested in the wild as well as in managed orchards. The company has created Sho-Neff Black Walnut Farm for research and educational purposes in conjunction with the University of Missouri, the Missouri Nut Growers Association, the USDA Forest Service, Forrest Keeling Nursery, and the Center for Advancement of the American Black Walnut.[25]

In the Hammons cookbook, Missouri cooks are advised that Eastern American black walnuts contain riboflavin, calcium, and iron, healthy editions to recipes used by Missouri cooks. Walnuts find their way into enticing recipes such as sunshine spinach salad and tropical chicken salad. Adventurous cooks might want to try the recipe for black walnutburgers, a lean ground beef double burger stuffed with spices, walnuts, and bacon. The cookbook offers instructions for preparing Missouri pesto made with walnuts, a recipe for walnut wheat bread for health-conscious cooks, and for special occasions, a recipe for caramel lover's fudge cake flavored with walnuts. The final recipe in the cookbook is Show Me preserves with the Missouri ingredient being black walnuts.

With the advent of home computers, online recipe collections developed by Missouri companies have supplemented, or in some cases replaced, the traditional promotional cookbook. Today's connected cooks locate food company Web sites, and with a few clicks of the mouse select and print the recipes they want. They may revisit the site to repeat a recipe, or if it becomes a favorite, they can save the hard copy, storing it just as Missouri cooks for decades have clipped and saved recipes from local newspapers and magazines. Some Web sites allow the cook to "drop" the recipe into the online "recipe box feature."

Ott's Foods, located in Carthage, in southwest Missouri, at one time provided Missouri cooks with a promotional cookbook featuring recipes that included salad dressings produced by the company, which was established with "the original Ott's Famous Dressing" in 1947. Not having the recipe for a favorite family salad dressing, Walter Ott put his chemistry and engineering skills to work. During his research, Ott successfully reproduced the taste of his mother's homemade salad dressing enjoyed at the family table. He and his wife served his mother's "ruby-red" dressing on their salads at a family café in Carthage in the 1940s. As his dressing became popular, customers began to request take-home bottles. Travelers who stopped at the café began to spread the word about "Ott's Famous Salad Dressing," the label attached to the bottles being sold out of the restaurant. "Even celebrities like Clark Gable and Gene Autry went out of their way to stop at the restaurant to buy bottles 'to go.'"[26] Numerous requests for bottles of the dressing led Ott to move from the restaurant business into the salad dressing business. Ott's Dressing and other products are still produced in Carthage and are distributed throughout Missouri and several surrounding states. Products can also be purchased online. Recipes are now available in an online collection.

Meat companies have long promoted their products with recipe collections. As production of both cattle and hogs flourished in Missouri, two major packing centers emerged, the first in St. Louis and the second in Kansas City. Additionally, until after the Civil War, Missouri was the end point of numerous cattle drives from Texas and Kansas. Thus, the state became the center for shipment of livestock and processed meat to eastern markets. Evidently not a cookbook for home use but one to be used in professional meat processing facilities, *Modern Practice of Canning Meats*, by G. T. Hamel, was published in 1911 by the Brecht Company, a butchers supply company established in St. Louis in 1853. On the final page of the cookbook, the publisher provides an image of its main offices and factories in St. Louis, explaining that the main plant is "equipped throughout with the most modern machinery, and devoted to the manufacture of machinery and appliances used in the meat industry and the working up of its by-products."[27]

Hamel, evidently dedicated to safe processing practices, makes note of books being published by noted bacteriologists regarding this issue but believes that "Packers and their foremen in charge, have seldom gone through all the pages of those most valuable scientific works." The purpose of his book is twofold: to explain healthful meat-packing processes to companies in the preserving and canning industry and secondly, "to make the great consuming public understand that canned meats, when properly packed up, are just as wholesome as any other article of food on the market." He predicts that since the "consumption of canned foods is increasing all over the world," "their manufacture is now, or will be, everywhere under the inspection of skilled Government appointed inspectors."[28] Hamel includes numerous illustrations of equipment in use in the meat-packing industry in the first decade of the century.

The author explains why he places recipes in the book. "Although this book is only intended to be a summary of the modern practice of canning meats in the large packing houses, I have not been able to resist the temptation of giving the recipes of a few products of higher class."[29] He details recipes for corned beef, roast beef, tongues (ox, pig, and lamb), dried beef, bacon, and fowl (chicken and turkey) and shares recipes for potted and

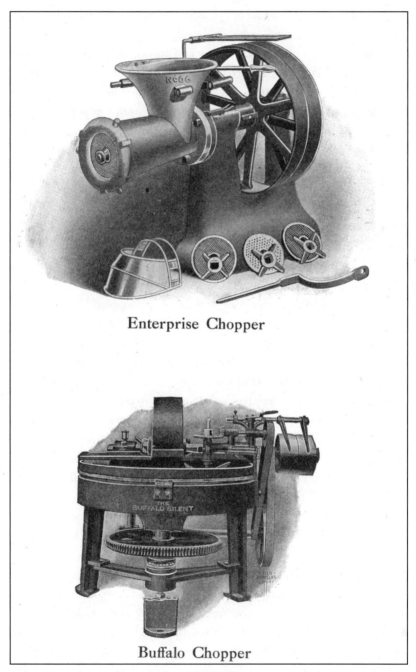

Enterprise Chopper

Buffalo Chopper

In *Modern Practice of Canning Meats*, G. T. Hamel showed readers commercial meat packing equipment.

deviled meat products and for soups as well as recipes for stewed kidneys, mincemeat, chile con carne, pork and beans.

Hamel addresses his concern that packers are not including enough meat in one very popular item—canned pork and beans. Understanding the viewpoint of the meat packer, he admits that "the competition in selling prices has induced the packers to cut down, more and more, the proportion of pork in the product, so that the buyer is sometimes disappointed in what he buys."[30] His ingredient list for a number one can of pork and beans includes one ounce of pork, six ounces of beans, and four ounces of soup.

Missouri has a long reputation of producing fine country cured hams. Even before statehood, the French colonists became noted for the quality of their hams, which were always in demand in New Orleans. As settlers populated the farmland along the Missouri River west from St. Charles toward Kansas City, an area known as Boone's Lick Country became one of the first areas in the state where pork products were produced. Farmers in this region, skilled at curing hams and bacon, found ready markets in St. Louis and in other cities. At their location near the river, they could easily pack these products in barrels and ship them downstream. Competitions developed between individuals for the best ham as evidenced by ham-judging contests at county fairs in Missouri. Boone County became particularly noted for its cured hams.

Burgers' Smokehouse, located near California, in central Missouri, carries on the tradition of country cured hams. Burgers' processes and delivers 750,000 hams each year to market (E. M. Burger sold 6 hams off his farm in 1927).[31] The company uses an online cookbook to promote their products. Missouri cooks may choose from a variety of recipes located on the company Web site. At the Burger's Smokehouse Visitors Center, visitors learn about "the natural curing, drying, and aging of a properly prepared country cured ham."[32] California is also the site of the annual Ozark Ham and Turkey Festival. On the first day of the yearly event, festival attendees enjoy ham sandwiches and roasted turkey legs among other food offerings.

Favorites from Farmland, a slick, heavily illustrated promotional cookbook published by Farmland Foods, founded in 1959 and headquartered in Kansas City, quite possibly is being out-distanced by the company's own high-tech nontraditional alternative—a recipe box currently on its Web site. The box is filled with recipes featuring company products. Conveniently organized, the recipe box allows cooks to search the collection by ingredient, product, course, or cooking method or view an alphabetical list of all recipes. It also allows a cook to generate a shopping list to be printed out with selected recipes.

Barbecuing, slowly cooking meat over glowing coals, has long been a part of Missouri's food heritage. In fact, the seventeenth- and eighteenth-century explorers were cooking this way but without sophisticated equipment and barbecue jargon. The practice of barbecuing emerged as a culinary artform midcentury as increasing numbers of Missouri men armed themselves with long-handled forks and burger flippers and headed out to grills positioned in their backyards alongside picnic tables loaded with coleslaw, potato salad, baked beans, and fruit cobblers or layer cakes prepared by women and girls in the kitchen.

Originally a "pit barbecue" was just that, a shallow pit dug in the ground to hold fire. Instead of charcoal from a bag, early barbecue chefs made their coals by burning down oak and hickory logs. The coals were then shoveled into the pit and topped with wire mesh to hold the meat. Over the years, barbecuing equipment in backyards has evolved from simple charcoal grills to stainless steel behemoths featuring bottles of propane gas, temperature controls, rotisseries, and multiple grilling sections, some side dressed with drink wells to keep favorite beverages cool and side burners designed to prepare side items on the menu while the barbecue is progressing on grill. Aside from the bevy of barbecue cookers available, Missouri outdoor chefs express their creativity by designing equipment to suit their specific styles of barbecuing.

Not only is there friendly disagreement over the best equipment for the job, decisions must also be made regarding types of heat. As well, spirited debates regarding the choice of sauces and rubs and the matter of selection of "secret seasoning ingredients" to be used must be addressed. Generally two types of favorite sauces are associated with Missouri barbecue. In the southern part of the state, particularly in the Bootheel, barbecue means pork and it requires a vinegar-based sauce containing black pepper, paprika, and other spices, although chicken is also favored on the grill. In contrast, the sauce associated with the widely acclaimed Kansas City–style barbecue is thicker and tomato-based with beef and mutton being included in the mix of items to be barbecued. An assortment of commercially packaged rubs, marinades, and sauces are produced in the state. Wickers and KC Masterpiece serve as examples of Missouri barbecue products.

Wicker's barbecue sauce, representative of the southern style, currently promoted as "The Great American Barbecue Sauce from the Little Missouri Town," was "born and raised" in the Missouri Bootheel in Hornersville and currently is being produced a few blocks down the street from where it got its start. Marketed by word of mouth and by a presence on the Internet, the original barbecue sauce now is often referred to as a marinade. Even though the company markets a number of versions, the original mix continues to be popular among barbecue enthusiasts.

Wicker's Food Products shares the history of the sauce at their Web site. Because of his pranks when a youngster, Walter Wicker earned for himself the nickname "Peck" (an abbreviation of "Pecks Bad Boy"). He inherited his lifelong enjoyment of preparing food from his mother as he tagged along when she cooked in her café in Hornersville. In 1940, Peck developed a sauce recipe for barbecuing meat. "He would dig an open earthen pit for the fire, fasten wire over it to hold the meat, then baste it with his special sauce throughout the cooking process." Word of the sauce spread, and barbecue seekers in the area wanted more of his barbecue than they might sample at church dinners and at lodge groups. By 1947, he was selling his product in gallon jugs from a small building, the first Wicker's barbecue sauce manufacturing facility, constructed near his home. Area individuals attending the Farmers and Merchants Watermelon Festival purchased his barbecue by the pound at his stand on Main Street each year. Customer suggestions to sell barbecue sandwiches inspired Peck to enclose an area behind his manufacturing facility for that purpose. "The sides were covered with screen wire and the ground was covered with sawdust for the floor," and Peck was open for business at "The Pit" on weekends from May through October with waiting lines not uncommon.[33]

Strictly by word of mouth, the popularity of his barbecue made it to New York. Historical information at the Web site indicates that Craig Claiborne, restaurant reviewer for the *New York Times*, once visited "The Pit." "After his visit, over the years Peck would pull out his wallet and carefully unfold a yellow scrap of newspaper and announce in conversation, 'This is what The New York Times wrote about Wicker's,' he'd say, beaming with pride."[34] Instead of developing a traditional promotional cookbook, Wicker's Food Products chooses to offer its promotional recipes and tips for the use of their products online, thus extending its message far beyond Hornersville.

A little over four hundred miles northwest across the state, barbecue takes on a different flavor and style. In *Bar-B-Q Kansas City Style*, Shifra Stein and Rich Davis say that barbecue's "most distinguishing feature is its variety." Explaining its diversity, they continue, "Throughout its early history it has drawn upon many types of woods, meats and sauces to become the most eclectic barbecue in the United States." They suggest that "Kansas City has both barbecued pork and brisket, as well as chicken and lamb of equal caliber."[35] Barbecue experts developing sauces following the Kansas City style, create or modify recipes or add their ingredients of choice to a Kansas City–style commercially bottled sauce with the end result in most cases being a spicy, sweet, tomato-based creation to dress their barbecue items.

KC Masterpiece Barbecue Sauce is the creation of Dr. Rich Davis who "began barbecuing back in the 30s, learning from his father on a homemade grill and smoker." His love of barbecuing led to successful barbecue competitions, including a first-place award at the American Royal Barbecue Contest in Kansas City, and to the development of his own sauce and the founding of his own company. "A man of many talents, he has also been a family physician, Dean of a medical school, and a successful family and child psychiatrist."[36] Like Wicker Food Products, the HV Food Products Company, current owners of KC Masterpiece sauces, offers its collection of product recipes featuring chicken, beef, and pork, seafood, and meatless dishes at its Web site. The versatility of the online collection allows Missouri cooks to select by barbecue product or by recipe. Like traditional company cookbooks, the online site promotes the company's featured barbecue sauces as well as its additional products—in this case a group of KC Masterpiece marinades, a BBQ seasoning, and a steak seasoning. Cooks also benefit from tips related to marinating, seasoning, grilling, and food safety.

Arguments and discussions over whose barbecue is best have spawned numerous contests in communities across the state. Depending upon the location of the contest, featured categories generally include various cuts of pork, beef, mutton, and poultry. Kansas City's American Royal/Oklahoma Joe's Open Barbecue Contest in its 28th year and promoted as the world's largest barbecue contest even offers a "Side Dish Contest" and a "Dessert Contest" where competitors have an opportunity to enter their baked beans, potatoes and other vegetables, and sweet creations in competition. While the question of who makes the best barbecue in Missouri may never be answered, many of the state's barbecue cooks have established outstanding barbecue restaurants around the state to accommodate the hankering for a pig sandwich, a side of ribs, a hefty pork steak, a brisket sandwich, or a half chicken if the kitchen has been closed for the day.

One of Missouri's growing industries, the grape and wine industry, owes its presence to the mid-1800s German settlers. Much of the better agricultural land along the Missouri River valley was already taken when they arrived. However, they could obtain what was considered less productive land on the bluffs south of the river. Because of their hillside horticultural experience in Germany, they were able to establish orchards and especially vineyards. Wine production developed especially in the areas around Hermann and Augusta.

The growth of this industry benefited greatly from the work of George Hussman, a German immigrant who educated himself in all aspects of grape growing and wine-making. Of particular benefit was Hussman's work with native grapes. These were much better adapted to Missouri's climate than European grapes, and Hussman learned how to make exceptional wines from these grapes.

By the end of the nineteenth century, Missouri ranked second in the United States in wine production. However, when Prohibition went into effect in 1920, it destroyed Missouri's wine industry for several decades. Vineyards were abandoned, and wineries fell into disrepair. Even after the repeal of Prohibition, Missouri's wine industry was slow to make a come-back. The renaissance began in the 1960s with the rebuilding of old wineries. Today, Missouri's grape and wine industry has become a bustling business with the state establishing the Grape and Wine Advisory Board to aid promotion. A breeding and production research program has been established by Missouri State University at its Mountain Grove research facility. Missouri now boasts over fifty wineries, and their wine consistently wins national and international competitions. Many of these wineries have added restaurants, and they feature tours and wine-tasting events, making tourism an important part of the wine and grape industry. Also, to help promote this growing industry, in 2003 the Missouri legislature named the Norton/Cynthiana variety the official state grape. This native purple grape has become a staple of Missouri's wine production.

Jim and Betty Held, who lived on their farm in the Hermann area, were instrumental in helping to bring the wine industry in Missouri back by focusing on their self-assigned task—"producing and marketing the finest wines that can be made and putting Hermann back on the map as a world-class wine producing area." In 1965, the Helds purchased Stone Hill, which had been established in 1847 and later become the second largest winery in the United States. Producing award-winning wines known worldwide, "By the turn of the century, the winery was shipping 1,250,000 gallons of wine per year." One of Missouri's many success stories, the Stone Hill Winery, which had been a victim of Prohibition and later put to use as a mushroom-growing facility, "has been carefully restored under the direction and management of the Helds, producing 215,000 gallons of wine" in 2005. The Stone Hill Winery has earned more than 2,850 awards since 1993.[37]

Betty Held originally published her collection of recipes in *Wine and Dine with Frau Held*. In this family cookbook, favorite recipes benefit from the addition of wines developed at the winery: wine cake (Golden Rhine), glazed baked ham (Stone Hill Rose), harvest grape pie (Stone Hill Concord), hasenpfeffer (a dry red wine), German sauerkraut (Vidal Blanc), and venison sauerbraten (a dry red wine). Currently the company Web site includes the family's favorite recipes, with Stone Hill wine being "a common ingredient among many of the recipes," and the Helds plan to add a new recipe each month to the popular cooking section of their e-newsletter. The collection of recipes includes Frau Held's traditional family recipes for hot mulled wine, German potato salad, Stone Hill wine cake, and Concord wine punch as well as newer recipes created by the chef for Stone Hill's Vintage Restaurant.[38]

Jim and Patricia Hofherr opened the St. James Winery for business in 1970. The winery, under the management of the Hofherrs' sons, John and Andrew, currently offers a slick promotional mini-cookbook, *Our Favorite Recipes*, showcasing the company's favorite recipes. In the main dish section, company wines make appearances in Missouri recipes: steak-topper mushrooms, skillet chicken stew, and country red beef roast. Although the collection includes made-from-scratch recipes, several recipes for the Missouri cook on the run can be stirred up in a hurry with the use of prepackaged cake mixes and canned or dried soups. A more extensive collection of online recipes supplements the company's small promotional cookbook.

The St. James grape industry history in Missouri dates back to the arrival of Italian immigrants, who first planted grapes in the area.

Officially recognized as the Ozark Highlands, our region is fondly known as 'Little Italy of the Ozarks' thanks to the establishment of an

Italian settlement in the areas more than 100 years ago. The Italians who settled here planted vineyards, and by 1922 over 2000 acres of grapes on about 200 vineyards dotted the landscape. Over the years a strong Italian heritage and influence has remained in the St. James area.[39]

The St. James Winery recognizes "the hard work and determination of the Italian settlers" by including School House labels in their wine stock,[40] which recall the schoolhouse used to educate the children of the early Italian immigrants. It is still located near the winery. As cooks shop for the wines called for in recipes in the cookbook and on the Web site, they learn not only the characteristics of each wine but also the awards credited to each selection.

The final cookbook featured in this chapter certainly deserves its place on Missouri's cookbook buffet. *The Never Ending Season: The Cookbook of Missouri* became a collaborative project of the Missouri 4-H Foundation, the Missouri Department of Agriculture, the Missouri Food Processors Association, and Leisure Time Publishing. Throughout the book, the text successfully blends details about Missouri history with information about numerous Missouri food companies while featuring recipes that use company products. Compilers also detail a history and discussion of Missouri's 4-H program, a program organized to contribute to the development of youth in the state.

In 1914 the passage of the Smith-Lever Act created the Cooperative Extension Service, and youth programs across the state became a part of the service. "Missouri girls and boys, in primarily rural areas, were enrolled in the State Extension youth program known as Boys and Girls Club Work. It wasn't until 1927 that the name was changed to 4-H Club Work."[41]

Iron County, through the actions of B. P. Burnham, became the birthplace of Missouri 4-H. Burnham is recognized as organizing "the first corn clubs in the old school on Knob Street in Ironton and then in the small community of Annapolis." He developed the clubs based on concepts distributed by R. H. Emberson, the state club leader from 1914 to 1923. The club concept "required members to grow one acre of corn, applying bone meal and barnyard manure, and measuring the yields" with "teachers and leaders working with young men to teach them how to grow corn." The cookbook indicates that "These successful corn clubs were the embryos from which 4-H was born, patterning 4-H work after Burnham's work in Iron County." In the decades that followed, 4-H members stayed true to their motto, which pledges service "for my club, my community, my country and my world."

They planted victory gardens in the '40s, urban gardens in the '60s, and covered open wells in the '80s. Information in the cookbook spotlights individual member and club accomplishments. For example, two of those mentioned are "Larry Hicks produced 20 tons of watermelons in Ray county in 1957" and "Eight 4-H clubs planted 8,000 trees along road sides and around ponds in Cape Girardeau County in 1952."[42]

Even though early local clubs focused on agriculture and home economics, "4-H projects are now structured for youths in urban areas as well." Current 4-H programs include, among other worthwhile goals, those to develop effective decision-making, problem-solving, communication, leadership, and self-expression skills.[43]

When it comes to selecting food products and kitchen appliances and gadgets, Missourians, now more that ever before, are staying true to their Show Me reputation. As members of a high-tech, health-conscious society, cooks are reading labels on food products with an eye toward nutrition and healthy eating. They continue to investigate equipment that will help them save time in the kitchen. Before TV and the Internet, product and company cookbooks served as the primary means of delivering pertinent information to the cook. Company and product cookbooks have guided cooks from wood and coal cookstoves through the decades to smart kitchens that Missouri cooks now enjoy. Now in traditional and online formats, they continue to assist cooks in putting dinner on the table.

Chapter 9

Cookbooks from Restaurants Past and Present

Indians, early settlers, Mormons and the James boys came and went,
but it took Virginia McDonald's Tea Room to put Gallatin on the map
permanently.—*How I Cook It,* Virginia McDonald, 1949

Missourians enjoying a meal at their favorite eating establishments have often been able to take home cookbooks so that they can prepare favorite menu items in their own kitchens. *The Unity Inn Vegetarian Cook Book,* published in 1923 by the Unity School of Christianity in Kansas City, offers a collection of recipes for the preparation of vegetarian dishes like those served at the Unity Inn. This publication wasn't the first offered by the establishment, nor was it the last with additional cookbooks recording Unity Inn recipes in 1910, 1955, 1966, and 2004.

Charles and Myrtle Fillmore cofounded the Unity School of Christianity in 1889. In 1939 Dana Gatlin discussed Unity's early history, explaining that one way the Fillmores chose to deliver their spiritual message was through the printed word with Charles beginning to deliver his ideas in the first issue of *Modern Thought* in 1889. Wishing to expand their publications to a growing audience, Charles, in an ad the same year, sought "a young man or woman who can set type, and who is interested in the reforms we advocate." According to Gatlin, response to the ad resulted in the hiring of Harry Church.[1]

Eric Page, archivist at Unity Library and Archives, believes that "Harry Church, a Seventh-day Adventist, a vegetarian, and the first printer for Unity—is the first source for vegetarianism in Unity. With Church's urging, Charles and Myrtle Fillmore began non-meat diets in the 1890s and wrote

The Unity Inn Dining Room at Ninth and Tracy, Kansas City (ca. 1921–1925), featured a variety of vegetarian dishes. (Courtesy Unity, www.unityonline.org and Unity Archives)

often about the practice."[2] An article by the editor of *Restoration News* discusses several of these writings. *Weekly Unity* ran a column titled "The Vegetarian" starting in 1911 and continuing for several years, and in the same publication, in 1916, Charles Fillmore delivered his objections to eating meat. The next year an article signed by "Veg," the pen name for Royal Fillmore, Charles and Myrtle's youngest son, offered a discussion of the issue of eating meat as related to environmental concerns. The editor also includes comments noted in a *Kansas City Star* story in which the author advocates that "meat eating is the cause . . . for uncontrollable liquor drinking and many diseases."[3]

Royal Fillmore, in a 1915 edition of *Weekly Unity*, shares a history of the Unity Inn.

> The Unity Inn idea dates back to the early days when the Unity Center consisted of a dingy little brick house perched upon a lonely hill. The few who handled the work at that time felt the usual twitches of hunger twice a day. The cold lunches which they brought were not comforting so a stove was provided for the workers to prepare their

meals. These meals were kept from burning by the printer's devil—now known to us as the managing editor of this magazine. As the delicious odors filtered through the house the hungry came and were fed.[4]

Vegetarian dishes stirred up at the printing office became popular with visitors as well as with the workers, and the the idea of a meatless diet was launched in the magazine *Unity*. In 1904 the house located on the lot at 913 Tracy that had been used for Unity purposes and business was moved to the back section of the property, and a new facility was built for the church and publishing services. The old house at its new location was put to use to serve vegetarian meals to Unity workers and to offer rooms for visitors.[5] Archivist Page finds that the inn's first registered guest entered in 1906.

The Unity Inn, at various locations, has continued to serve vegetarian meals to Unity workers and members, Kansas City residents, and visitors to the city for over one hundred years. It hasn't remained strictly vegetarian. A 1966 article in *The Voice of Unity* announces the addition of meat dishes to the menu, but it reminds readers, "Long one of America's famous vegetarian cafeterias, Unity Inn will continue to feature the delicious vegetable specialties upon which its reputation was built."[6] Unity Inn is now located at Unity Village in Jackson County with vegetarian menu options still present on the menu.

The 1923 cookbook showcases "receipts not commonly found" as well as more familiar ones. The bread section includes a significant number of recipes prepared with graham and whole wheat flour and bran. Fruit and vegetable recipes make up a large part of the collection. Mixed with the many familiar recipes in the cookbook, Missouri cooks will find many new recipes, especially in the "Meat Substitute" section. Recipes rely on the Unity list of preferred protein foods: eggs, milk, cheese, nuts, gluten, dried ripe peas, lentils, and beans in such dishes as peanut meat, vegetarian roast, and vegetable tamale loaf to nutmeat hash, mock chicken croquettes, and butter bean cutlets. Cooks also find recipes for corn mock oysters, mock crab, mock chicken stew, and mock sausage. Chili lovers might be willing to try the nut chili, which includes all the familiar ingredients found in a pot of Missouri chili plus a half pound nut meats in place of ground beef.

Eleanor Richey Johnston, serving as editor of *How I Cook It,* by Virginia McDonald, owner of the Gallatin Tea Room, comments on McDonald's impact on her community by quoting a prominent Missouri businessman:

"Indians, early settlers, Mormons and the James boys came and went." He continues, "But it took Virginia McDonald's Tea Room to put Gallatin on the map permanently." By 1949, when the cookbook was published, citizens had been involved in conflicts associated with the settlement of Mormons in close proximity to the small town. Gallatin, located in northwest Missouri on the Grand River, weathered two encounters with the James gang. In 1869 Gallatin "was thrust into dubious fame by becoming the scene of a bank robbery staged by the notorious Jesse James, his brother Frank and their buddy Cole Younger." Johnston points out that the robbery took place not far from the McDonald home place and that "the mother of Charles McDonald, Virginia's husband . . . watched the escape of the James boys after the robbery." A second event involved the trial of Frank James after a train robbery close to Gallatin a few years later. Since Gallatin is the county seat, it became the location of the trial after Frank surrendered. He was, however, acquitted when during the trial Gen. Jo Shelby, Frank's commanding officer during the Civil War, spoke up for him.[7]

Johnston includes the story of the birth and growth of the nationally known Tea Room. After moving from Texas to Gallatin with her new husband from Missouri, Mrs. McDonald planned to help out with family bills by opening a food business on one side of her husband's small hardware store. Her project began as a lunch counter for area school children, but she was soon dreaming of a tearoom. She replaced the counter with several bright red tables, began drawing customers who were traveling through town, and satisfied travelers spread the word of the tasty dishes served at "Mrs. Mac's." The eating establishment went through several upgrades and expansions until, at the time of the publication of the cookbook, the restaurant included five rooms.[8]

Foods served in the tearoom and recorded in her cookbook brought accolades from newspapers around the country. The dust cover of the cookbook offers praise from writers associated with the *Saturday Evening Post,* the *Christian Science Monitor,* the *Chicago Tribune,* and the *Kansas City Star.* Besides her delicious dishes, the press praised her positive work ethic and her eye for detail in food preparation.

Duncan Hines, a noted food critic of the day, placed his stamp of approval on foods offered at the tearoom. He compliments McDonald and her cookbook in his glowing introduction, approving her "frank remarks about many of the recipes" which "give an additional spice of interest to the book," and concerning food presentation skills, "She has also included recipes for the artistic touches which, in combination with the delectable foods, make each meal a never-to-be-forgotten experience."[9] He seems to be referring to the opening section of the book on garnishes, where she details techniques ranging from how to frost mint leaves to be served with favorite beverages to how to construct sailboats out of halves of hard-cooked eggs with sails made of toothpicks and triangles of white tuna that sail out to customers on a crisp salad.

Hines discusses the style of cooking delivered in her restaurant and on the pages of the cookbook. "Now, like so many other Missourians whose ancestors came from the South, she has combined her knowledge of Southern cooking with the fresh, vigorous tastes of the Mid-West, and the result is a truly American culinary art."[10] Missouri's favorites show up in the main course sections—fried chicken, baked ham, Swiss steak, salmon croquettes, fried frog legs, and roast beef—along with more elegant dishes such as fresh lobster and crab meat au gratin, chicken chartreuse, and Creole shrimp.

A Celebration of Cooking 20 Years of Blessings, the most recent in a series of nine cookbooks available at the Blue Owl Restaurant and Bakery in Kimmswick, Missouri, currently one of Missouri's most popular "off the beaten path" eating establishments, briefly shares the story of the two founders, Mary Hostetter and Mrs. Lucianna Ross. Hostetter established From the Kitchen with Mary, a homemade bakery business in the St. Louis area in August of 1983. The holiday season of 1984 found her filling orders for thirty thousand Christmas cookies and pastries. A new location with a commercial kitchen and few hired employees proved to be the next step in Hostetter's business dream. In June 1985 she met with Ross, the "matriarch of Kimmswick," to discuss the possibility of joining Hostetter's baking business with a country tearoom. The site for the project became the Blue Owl Restaurant, a quaint old Kimmswick building owned by Ross.[11]

Kimmswick had been rescued by Ross, one of its community members. Writer Wade Rouse details how she saved her hometown. Although she lived in St. Louis, Ross had grown up in Kimmswick, and she maintained her connection with the town. In the late '60s, she realized that the town was falling into disrepair and took on what became a thirty-five-year project to save the small Missouri River community. Aware of the historic value of the town, which was chartered in 1868, she began buying old buildings, despite their being in bad shape, with a plan to restore them. Her original purchases included the old post office, a church, brick buildings, and log cabins. Rouse explains Ross's overall plan of action designed to bring her town back. "Ross not only infused the buildings she bought with new architectural life she also literally helped breath business life back into the town, launching a core of Kimmswick entrepreneurs who are still successful today." Rouse credits the success of her other local business development projects to Ross's "mix of personal nurturing and business savvy."[12]

The Blue Owl, at one time Ma Green's Tavern, had been purchased by Ross in the late '70s and was ready to operate as a restaurant by 1980. The Blue Owl Restaurant changed management five times before June 1985 when the two women met and decided to "give it a try." In her cookbook Hostetter explains that she optimistically predicted that one day "People will have to wait in line to get a table at the Blue Owl." She opened the doors of the Blue Owl Restaurant and Bakery in August of 1985 with five employees and the goal of serving thirty customers per day. By 2006, the restaurant was serving three hundred per day and many more on weekends and had a staff of seventy-five. The kitchen and dining spaces have been expanded to accommodate the establishment's popularity.[13]

The series of Blue Owl cookbooks shares recipes for items from the bakery and includes recipes for favorite soups, salads, sides, and entrees in addition to narratives of significant events relating to the restaurant in its twenty-year history. One story recounts the events of 1993, when Kimmswick and other river communities in Missouri were affected by the "Great Flood" along the Mississippi River. When floodwaters threatened the entire town, the Blue Owl had to be evacuated. Heroic sandbagging efforts by volunteers and members of the National Guard resulted in an earthen levee built to protect the restaurant and other structures in the community. *Let's Do Lunch*, one of the cookbooks in the series, is dedicated to the flood workers. That cookbook includes recipes for "sandbag" butter cookies and "Levee-High Apple Pie." Apple lovers may still experience a slice of "Levee-High Apple Pie"; Hostetter says that "the Pie" is made daily in the restaurant. Each pie uses eighteen apples, and the end product weighs seven and one half pounds.[14]

In recent months, the Blue Owl and Hostetter's "Levee-High Apple Pie" have been in a national TV spotlight. *Road Tasted*, a Food Network show hosted by Bobbie and Jamie Deen, visited the Blue Owl in May 2006 to learn how to make Hostetter's popular pie. Before the duo would visit, Hostetter had to agree to ship the food featured on the show to viewers who wished to order it. Many viewers did, and currently, instead of preparing four

Mary Hostetter, owner of the popular Blue Owl Restaurant and Bakery in
Kimmswick, displays one of the restaurant's signature desserts, a Levee-High
Apple Pie. (Photo by John Fisher)

to five apple pies daily, the restaurant uses extra staff to prepare for shipping up to seventy-five pies a day. The unbaked pies are shipped frozen and packed in dry ice.[15]

The national spotlight on the Blue Owl then shifted to Savannah, Georgia, to the set of popular food show host Paula Deen. Hostetter was once again invited to demonstrate her baking skills and, furthermore, challenged to create "an even bigger and better" version of the popular pie for food show host Paula Deen. Bigger was easy but better required a bit of culinary creativity. Hostetter's answer to the challenge resulted in a twelve-pound "Paula Deen's Savannah High Apple Pie" made of twenty-four apples with an added streusel topping placed between layers of apples and generous amounts of butter and pecans, two of the host's favorite recipe ingredients.[16]

Missouri, like states across the country, has experienced the growth of bed and breakfast accommodations. B and B enthusiast Elizabeth Arneson comments on the increasing popularity of these establishments. "Bed and breakfasts have grown from serving a small niche market to being a wildly popular lodging alternative."[17] Before the upsurge of bed and breakfasts, some of Missouri's earliest travelers, the pioneers, spent nights along the way during their westward trek in homes, inns, and taverns such as the Old Tavern in Arrow Rock. Older Missourians recall the Great Depression of the '30s when families shared homes to make ends meet.

Families traveling to the Missouri State Fair in the '50s often had trouble finding accommodations in Sedalia. The large influx of people during fair week quickly filled up the available lodging. Local residents stepped in and opened their homes to visitors. Traveling families took advantage of this type of lodging, sometimes staying at the same home year after year.

Innkeepers, scattered around the state, have placed cookbooks on the table for Missouri cooks to learn about their establishments and to sample recipes enjoyed at the inns. The association of Bed and Breakfast Inns of Missouri delivered two cookbooks featuring several of their member inns, *Be Our Guest* in 1991 and *Sunrise Inn Missouri* in 2002. Bed and Breakfast Inns of Missouri, a monitoring association, inspects properties' exteriors, common rooms, and guest baths and evaluates the innkeeper hospitality practices of member inn owners.

Both cookbooks tempt readers to take advantage of these popular accommodations through descriptions of the inns and through recipes for dishes served at their establishments. The books pinpoint participating inns on a Missouri map conveniently placed in the cookbook. For the traveler's convenience, *Be Our Guest* lists annual events in the area around each inn (i.e., in St. Genevieve, the Jour de Fete; in Hannibal, National Tom Sawyer Days; in Liberty, Horse, Buggy and Old Time Dance Days). Recipes featured in these cookbooks assure guests that they won't want to skip breakfast before moving on to experience another area of Missouri.

In addition to comfort and good food, at the time of the publication of *Sunrise Inn Missouri*, diversity and history seem to be a significant element of the Missouri bed and breakfast establishments featured in this publication. The cookbook indicates that at the Dauphine Hotel Bed and Breakfast in Bonnots Mill, guests enjoy beignets with a cup of café au lait for breakfast or for a snack. Innkeepers Sandra and Scott Holder explain the French connection. "Early settlers in Bonnots Mill would have eaten these, having first arrived in New Orleans before traveling up the Mississippi and Missouri Rivers to Bonnots Mill." B and B enthusiasts relax and enjoy "Mom's Blueberry Coffee Cake" at the Rivercene Bed and Breakfast in Boonville, built in 1899 and owned by riverboat captain Kinney. Nancy Marford, host at Recess Inn located in Ethel, offers sure-to-please apple dumplings on her menu. Cleverly named, her B and B gives "guests an opportunity to step back in time and experience the 3 r's: resting, relaxing, and reminiscing in an old time historic schoolhouse." The Red Oak Inn Bed and Breakfast in Fordland started as a dairy barn.[18]

Missouri Bootheel cookbook author Patricia Shell admits that once she was introduced to the Victorian era, she was "hooked." Since she was living in Dexter, this didn't happen until she was exposed to the *Victoria* magazine. Her country décor took a backseat to the decorating styles of the Victorian age as she continued her study of the era. "I loved the beautiful tea pots and teacups that were featured along with the many wonderful articles about the simple things of life that were so interesting." She began to see this period as a time that was "slow paced and stressed family values" but also a time when women had "a very active social life." Her dream of creating a tearoom grew out of a goal "to provide a sanctuary for women, a place that provides a soothing atmosphere that, when accompanied by a pot of tea, is especially welcome in this hectic world."[19]

In 1994 Shell selected a grocery and gas station property located on Cox's Corner in historic downtown Dexter as the site of a Victorian tearoom. The longtime Dexter business at that location was established in 1949 and was believed to have been the first convenience store in the area. After bringing the property up to environmental standards, Shell opened Lady Patricia's Tea Room in May 1995. With the tearoom came good food and a slate of Victorian activities designed for area women. In her cookbook, *Teatime Friendships at Patricia's,* the author shares information gleaned from research on the Victorian era and details related to activities hosted in the tearoom and in a Victorian garden developed at the site. Activities reminiscent of the Victorian era include afternoon teas, violin concerts, garden parties, themed parties, children's tea parties, games of croquet, and special tea gatherings with authentic dress for guests of all ages being an important aspect of certain events. A yearly Victorian Faire allows visitors to experience the era through exhibits set up under tents in the garden. According to the author, "Afternoon tea was a large part of Victorian lives. Tea parties were an opportunity to strengthen desirable acquaintanceships and to show excellent taste." Recipes in the cookbook reflect menu items—"delicate quiches, soups that delight, beautiful salads, and scrumptious casseroles . . . filling sandwiches, unnerving desserts and the pleasant flavor of the signature house tea." The cookbook shares information about tea, including a brief explanation of the origin of the afternoon tea. "Afternoon tea was invented by the Duchess of Bedford in the mid 1800s. To tide herself over for a very late dinner, she asked her maid to serve small sandwiches and cakes with her afternoon tea, and a new fashion was born."[20]

Since 1972, through their Food Service Hall of Fame, the Missouri Restaurant Association has recognized individuals "whose foresight was instrumental in shaping the future of the restaurant industry"[21] in the state. The number of yearly winners ranges from one to four with only one year not showing an inductee. Fortunately, cookbooks published by two past inductees preserve recipes once served in their now-closed restaurants.

Florence Hulling Apted earned the only Food Service Hall of Fame recognition delivered in 1974. Apted's business, Miss Hulling's Cafeteria, located at Eleventh and Locust, served good food, cafeteria style, to downtown department store shoppers and city workers for over sixty years. Longtime St. Louis residents John and Mary German fondly recall their lunch and dinner visits to Miss Hulling's. Both worked at the headquarters of the Missouri Pacific Railroad then located at Thirteenth and Olive. Miss Hulling's was just a few blocks away. The two generally ate lunch in the lower-level cafeteria. On leisurely occasions, they would go up to the restaurant on the ground floor. John recalls two of his favorite dishes at the cafeteria in his over twenty years of making selections along the cafeteria line: chicken pot pie and creamed spinach. Miss Hulling's split layer cake, Mary's dessert of choice, unless the glazed strawberry pie was available, came out of the kitchen in a variety of versions: chocolate, lemon, strawberry, caramel, and coconut.

Mary, herself an accomplished cook, still prepares dishes using her copy of *Miss Hulling's Own Cook Book,* a now-rare forty-page project apparently self-published by Apted in 1962. A second cookbook, *Miss Hulling's Favorite Recipes,* followed in 1969. In the first the author explains the reason for the cookbook and also delivers the key to Miss Hulling's popularity as an eating establishment. "Rarely a day passes which does not bring a request or two for one of our recipes." After commenting on their recipe searching, testing, and tasting procedures, she adds, "We at Miss Hulling's feel that no dish is better than the raw materials from which it is made. Choice meats and poultry, country fresh eggs and dairy products, fresh fruits and vegetables when available, pure spices and flavorings; all these are necessary to make a perfect product."[22]

The 1962 cookbook features recipes from simple to gourmet. It includes the St. Louis couple's favorite recipes for the glazed strawberry pie and the creamed spinach. Apted flags four recipes as Gourmet Award–winning recipes, awarded that honor by the Missouri Restaurant Association: champignons parisienne (mushrooms stuffed with crabmeat—on savory rice), cheese cake salad, orange ambrosia pie, and lemon ice box pudding with lemon sauce. Additional recipe titles reflect Apted's creativity in the kitchen: potato walnut loaf cake, fruit mayonnaise, and Spanish onions with almonds. Recipes for Missouri foods prepared across the state also indicate her insight into simple foods that Missourians love and appreciate: fried chicken and country gravy, old-fashioned sugar cookies, and Dutch apple pie. Even though Miss Hulling's Cafeteria is no longer in business, the word about her skill in the kitchen continues to grow thanks to Missouri Internet users who search for leads to locate Miss Hulling's recipes: German chocolate cake, banana-coconut cream pie, chicken pot pie, cottage cheese pie, and potato pancakes.

The Missouri Restaurant Association inducted Leslie and Loyd Stephenson, twin brothers and owners of Stephenson's Apple Farm Restaurant, into the Food Service Hall of Fame in 1985. In 1972, their restaurant also received the Ivy Award, a project organized by *Restaurants and Institu-*

tions magazine. This prestigious national award presented yearly acknowledges excellence in food service. Since the beginning of the award in 1971, over three hundred food establishments have been honored, seven of them from Missouri.[23]

Stephenson's Apple Farm Restaurant Receipts, first published in 1967 and in its fifth edition in 1973, offers a brief history supplied by the owners of the restaurant. "In 1870, when Highway 40 was a mud road, the Stephenson fruit and vegetable farm had its beginning. From a little, one-room stone building, our grandparents sold home-grown produce to folks traveling between Lee's Summit and Independence." They also discuss the development of the family orchards that supplied food items for the restaurant. "From these orchards come our fresh apples, peaches, berries and the sweet cider which we serve all year long."[24]

As they set up their restaurant, the Stephensons remembered the times when their grandparents smoked meats and preserved fruits and vegetables; they wanted to serve these same types of foods in their new restaurant. The history comments on the opening of the eating establishment. "And so, on April 16, 1946, when we opened our restaurant in the original stone building, it seemed natural to call it The Apple Farm. We had 10 booths then and served only 38 people the first day." Additional information in this section of the cookbook indicates that restaurant was remodeled seven times, although each time the original stone building remained a part of the updated facility.[25] The final design is reminiscent of the country barns that have long dotted Missouri's landscape.

After moving to Kansas City in 1960, Dean and Lois Preuett, at the recommendation of their new neighbors, celebrated their first wedding anniversary at Stephenson's Apple Farm Restaurant. Twenty-five years later, their three children joined them for a meal at the restaurant as they acknowledged this marriage milestone. In 2005 the couple received a gift certificate from friends for a dinner at Stephenson's in honor of their forty-fifth wedding anniversary. Before its closing in 2007, locals like the Preuetts and travelers to the area looked forward to visits to the restaurant, where they enjoyed hickory-smoked meats, brisket, steaks, and baked chicken and a variety of memorable sides, desserts, breads, and relishes, all in the restaurant's comfortable homey atmosphere. Complimentary servings of cold cider greeted guests in the waiting area as they contemplated whether to try a new dish or to stick with their favorites. Ask Missourians who have eaten at the popular restaurant to share their food thoughts on Stevenson's bill of fare and talk will turn to fritters, green rice, and apple butter.

In the preparation of their collection of recipes for their customers, own-ers Les and Loyd indicate in introductory comments that they selected "heirloom recipes" as well as newer ones "developed and altered as we have grown."[26] Regrettably, they were not able to include a recipe for the hickory-smoked meats because they require preparation in such large quantities. However, they do include instructions for their barbecue sauce, used in preparing the smoked meats. The cookbook includes recipes for peach, banana, and apple butter pumpkin fritters. An added comment by the "Baked Chicken'n'Butter and Cream" recipe indicates that this dish is always on the menu and information included with the green rice recipe promotes this dish as the specialty of the house. Les and Loyd generously share their recipes for homemade salad dressings, including the Apple Farm cheese dressing. A recipe for cinnamon apple salad instructs that it be garnished with watercress or a real apple leaf. Loyd's frozen blue cheese salad blends an interesting mix of ingredients. "Grandma Murphy's Apple Butter" keeps company with recipes for "End-O'-Summer Dill Tomatoes," spiced peach jam, and "Mom's Bread and Butter Pickles."

It might be difficult for Missouri cooks to decide which recipe in the dessert section of this small cookbook to try first. The section begins with a recipe for apple dumplings complete with instructions for modifying the recipe to make peach dumplings. Les includes his recipe for egg and vinegar pie crust to be used in making the pastry desserts, including his dutch apple or peach cobbler and his hickory nut pie and pumpkin pie. The Stephensons also include a recipe for warm cider sauce to top ice cream, pies, and fruit dumplings. For warmer seasons, dessert selections include chilled "Apri-cream Pie," pineapple cheese custard pie, and frozen lemon dessert.

Missourians have had their appetites stimulated and their hunger satis-fied by dishes prepared and served in their favorite eating establishments in their hometowns and as they travel the state's backroads and highways. Some of these restaurants have chosen to share their culinary secrets with their guests through cookbooks. These cookbooks allow both those who have experienced the menu in person and those who have only heard about it an opportunity to prepare and enjoy signature dishes in their own kitchens.

Chapter 10

World Events and Politics in Missouri Cookbooks

All the blood, all the heroism, all the money and munitions in the world
will not win this war unless our associates and the armies behind them
are fed.—*Patriotic Food Show Official Recipe Book,* Women's Central
Committee on Food Conservation, 1918

The St. Louis Convention and Visitors Commission proudly describes
the 1904 World's Fair, officially named the Louisiana Purchase Exposition,
as "the biggest party ever thrown by St. Louis, and it was the grandest world
exposition ever held—before or since." The city, by then well equipped to
host the event, had grown from a trading post established by the Lacledes
and Chouteaus into the fourth largest city in America. The "party" lasted 184
days from April 30 to December 1, 1904. Guests attending the "party" numbered about twenty million. The total cost of the fair rang in at fifty million
dollars. Notable guests who attended included President and Mrs. Theodore
Roosevelt, Secretary of War William Howard Taft, Prince Pu Lun from
China, Helen Keller, William Jennings Bryan, Guglielmo Marconi, Thomas
Edison, and sharpshooter Annie Oakley.[1]

The fair offered Missourians and their guests from around the world an
unbelievable assortment of entertainment from the new and amazing
twentieth-century technological wizardry to popular music. Likewise, the
event introduced its visitors to cultures from around the world. Attendees
experienced electricity for the first time and learned about X-rays, flying
machines, coin changers, electric clocks and automatic telephone answering

machines, and automobiles. The "palaces," or large exhibition halls, offered industrial exhibits as well as cultural and ethnic exhibitions presented by global participants. Entertainment featured the musical talents of ragtime performer Scott Joplin and John Philip Sousa and his band as well as the western humor of Will Rogers. The Festival Hall housed the largest pipe organ in existence at that time. Military and concert band performances were on the entertainment bill of fare.[2]

And what is a "party" without food? The St. Louis Convention and Visitors Commission's tally of food stops at the fair appears to be eighty snack concessions and thirty-five "fashionable" restaurants. They indicate on their site that the ice cream cone, referred to as "World's Fair Cornucopias," and iced tea were created at the event and that the hot dog and hamburger emerged as two popular American foods. "There were so many food options it was said some 36,000 people could be seated and dine at once at the Fair. Among the cuisines offered were Mexican, Philippine, Japanese, Egyptian and Indian. One restaurant, the American Inn, served 'real home cooking' in a family atmosphere."[3]

Several cookbooks originated at the fair or evolved from it. The Model Restaurant, under the charge of Mrs. Sarah Tyson Rorer, could seat twelve hundred customers. Rorer, a popular cooking-school teacher from Philadelphia and prolific cookbook author and popular magazine writer of the time, presented cooking demonstrations and sold autographed copies of her cookbook, *World's Fair Souvenir Cook Book*, at the fair. In *Beyond the Ice Cream Cone: The Whole Scoop on Food at the 1904 World's Fair*, Pamela J. Vaccaro supplies information about the cookbook and the author. She indicates that the committee formed to select the concessionaires at the fair immediately approved Rorer's application as well as her request to locate her restaurant at the East Pavilion on Art Hill.[4]

Rorer explains the goals of her project in her preface. "The object of this book is twofold: first, to present in a compact form a few of the choice recipes used at the Eastern Pavilion, at the Louisiana Purchase Exposition, St. Louis, 1904; and, secondly, to show how simply and easily all foods may be prepared."[5] Even though she hailed from the Northeast, Missouri cooks find familiar recipes that they would enjoy cooking in the *World's Fair Souvenir Cook Book:* cream of potato soup, beef stew, fried chicken with cream gravy, cheese straws, and baked macaroni. She offers simple recipes for stewed rhubarb, green gooseberry pie, soft gingerbread, and doughnuts. On a more elegant note, she includes a recipe for macédoine de fruits glacés and one for plumbiere.

Rorer delivers several recipes for ice cream, advising when making good Philadelphia ice cream to use the best materials and indicating that she prefers not to use gelatins and other thickening substances. "Good pure cream, ripe fruit, or the best canned in winter, and granulated sugar, make a perfect ice cream." For the inexperienced cook, she lines out exact instructions for managing the ice cream freezer and even details how to make an "impromptu ice cream freezer" if a store-bought one isn't available. "One may be made by using a tin pail for the can and a bucket or cask for the tub. In this case it will have to be stirred occasionally, while freezing, with a wooden spoon or flat stick, replacing the lid of the kettle after each stirring, and give the pail a rotary motion in the ice."[6]

In the final section of the cookbook, Rorer discusses how to develop menus. "An appropriate and healthful bill of fare implies both taste and discrimination."[7] She offers simple and elaborate menu plans, the first for everyday family meals and the second for company luncheons and dinners. Upon returning home from the fair, some Missouri cooks, depending upon their cooking and eating styles, and upon the seasonal availability of ingredients in their area of the state, be it rural or city, would have related more to Mrs. Rorer's techniques for putting a meal together more than would others. It would seem that Missouri cooks certainly would have enjoyed taking Mrs. Rorer's cookbook home with them as a souvenir, especially if they had sampled her cooking while visiting the event. To have experienced the cooking and teaching of the author of one of their cookbooks and the author of articles on food that they had read in their ladies magazines was certainly something to talk about when they returned to their homes and shared their "fair experience" with their neighbors. An autographed copy of Mrs. Rorer's cookbook was simply the icing on the cake.

Additional cookbooks came from the fair. In her work, Vaccaro mentions a thirty-two-page recipe booklet handed out by Pillsbury; visitors to the company's display could also sample freshly baked bread. Many companies provided fairgoers with something to enjoy there and something to take home as a reminder of the product. Vaccaro points out that in addition to getting samples of Jell-O when attending the event, "Fairgoers took home complimentary recipe booklets of the 'fast-food' product" and she also indicates that Towles Log Cabin Syrup Company provided recipe books as prizes in a contest that they held at the fair.[8] Following the fair, Pillsbury put out two cookbooks in 1905, *A Book for a Cook* and *A Little Book for a Little Cook,* both compiled by Mrs. Nellie Duling Gans. In the first, readers learn that Gans "demonstrated her superiority as a baker and a cook [at the World's Fair in St. Louis in 1904] by making the bread that took the Grand Prize, the highest award possible, using PILLSBURY'S BEST flour, and secured for her personally the Medal of Honor for 'perfect Bread'" and the cookbook represents "some of her well-tried and popular recipes" offered "as a help to the average housekeeper, in the hope that they will make easier her search after variety without calling too much upon her means."[9] The second, a small cookbook for young cooks, includes ten recipes. Additionally, little cooks may read the tale, written in poetic form, of a loaf of homemade bread from wheat grown in the field to kitchen table. The coordinated covers of the two cookbooks feature images from the same kitchen. The first shows a cook tending to her cooking, and the second depicts the same cook offering cooking instruction to two attentive young chefs.

Thirteen years after the St. Louis World's Fair, Missourians once again became involved in a world event, this time World War I. Women in Missouri became a part of a nationwide effort to assist with war efforts. In *American Women and the World War* Ida Clyde Clarke documents the "golden deeds by twenty million loyal-hearted women in every state of the American Union." She points out that "America was the first country in the world to give formal official recognition to women in the construction of its war machine, and to recognize immediately, upon a declaration of war, its woman power as one of its most valuable assets." Congress formally declared that a state of war existed between the United States and Germany on April 3, 1917. Clarke points out that fifteen days after this decision by Congress, the Council of National Defense appointed a "committee of women of national prominence to consider and advise how the assistance of the women of America may be made available in the prosecution of the war." Dr. Anna Howard Shaw, a respected physician, the first female Methodist minister, and a noted orator who supported causes in the areas of religion, women's rights, and medicine, spearheaded the entire women's effort. Mrs. Philip N. Moore of St. Louis, then president of the National Council of Women, was also appointed to the national committee officially named the Committee on Women's Defense Work. Other prominent women on the committee came from California, Rhode Island, New York, Atlanta, and Chicago.[10]

The primary purpose of the committee was "to coordinate the activities and the resources of the organized and unorganized women of the country . . . and to supply a new and direct channel of communication and cooperation between women and governmental departments."[11] State by state American women united, especially in the area of food conservation, developing their organizational structures and projects to help supply the necessary food for soldiers sent to the areas of conflict during the war. Clarke praises Missouri regarding organization of efforts to help with war concerns as being "worthy of especial study by those states who may still be in the process of organization." In addition to getting women across the state involved through excellent organization, Missouri is cited by Clarke as adopting a "unique and strikingly successful method of conducting its food conservation campaign." Clarke explains that in conjunction with Missouri Pacific Railway, the Women's Committee on Food Conservation, chaired by Mrs. Philip N. Moore with Mrs. B. F. Bush as vice chair, both of St. Louis, sent their message out via a "Woman's Patriotic Service Special" train. The railway car, staffed with experts on methods of cold pack canning and drying fruits and vegetables, traveled to cities and towns along the railway. Mr. Benjamin F. Bush, president of the Missouri-Pacific Railroad, provided the private car used. The car was sidetracked at twelve different locations while Missouri women held patriotic meetings and offered canning and drying demonstrations. Reports of the project showed that every time the train stopped it was enthusiastically received by patriotic citizens and by the mayors of the communities. During the stops women were encouraged to establish local organizations of the Red Cross and the Women's Council of National Defense as well as local Food Conservation Committees.[12]

From February 2 through 10, 1918, the Women's Central Committee of Food Conservation sponsored the Patriotic Food Show in St. Louis. Introductory information in the *Patriotic Food Show Official Recipe Book* explains that the publication is a compilation of recipes furnished by the University of Missouri, the Saint Louis Public Schools and the Community Cannery of the Women's Central Committee on Food Conservation of Saint Louis. Editors also include recipe suggestions from the *Official Recipe Book of the Chicago Food Show*. A line on the cover sets the tone: "Every Kitchen is a Fort of National Defense."

This Missouri World War I cookbook opens with a combination of patriotic fervor and food conservation talk.

Your Country Calls. Your Government does not ask you to give up three square meals a day—nor even one. All it asks is that you eat less of the foods needed to keep our armies going and eat all you want of the other things that we have in plenty. America and her associates in the war must not run out of meat, wheat, fats, sugar and milk. All the blood, all the heroism, all the money and munitions in the world will not win this war unless our associates and the armies behind them are fed. They will not be fed unless we take care; indeed, if we are not prudent, we, too, shall go hungry. So do you stand guard in you kitchen each day over the Nation's food supplies that the sacrifice of life and money be not in vain. . . . Let this book be your guide—in making yours a Patriot's Kitchen. Now's the time. Get in line.[13]

A sense of urgency flows through the text.

Let us remember that every flag that flies opposite the enemy's is by proxy the American flag, and that the armies fighting in our defense under these flags can not [sic] be maintained throughout this winter unless there is food enough for them and for their women and children at home. There can be food enough only if America provides it. And America can provide it only by the personal service and patriotic co-operation of all of us.[14]

Information focuses on the food needs of soldiers: wheat, butter/lard, sugar, beef, bacon, mutton and pork. Food indicated for use in Missouri kitchens includes corn, oats, barley, and rye; cottonseed, peanut, and corn oil; molasses, honey, and syrups; chicken, eggs, cottage cheese; and fish, nuts peas, and beans.[15]

In the protein section, readers are asked to reduce consumption of beef, pork, and mutton. "There are to be two meatless days, and on the other days we are asked to use mutton in preference to either beef or pork." The cookbook proposes serving smaller portions, using all parts of the animal, and using tougher parts of meat usually trimmed off. These, they instruct, can be made tender by pounding, grinding, and slow cooking.[16] The line up of recipes in this section includes those for liver, sweetbreads, kidneys, tongue, heart, pig's feet, headcheese, and scrapple as well as those for rabbit, fish, and fowl.

The section on how to save fats ties this food conservation effort to World War I weapon technology. The cookbook explains, "Authorities are warning

During World War I women across the state were involved in food conservation efforts. This cookbook was part of a 1918 food show organized by the Women's Central Committee on Food Conservation held in St. Louis.

us that fats, particularly animal fats, are very scarce. Americans have long been extravagant users and wasters of fats. Now, in this world shortage we must save, not only that our soldiers and our Allies may have a sufficient supply of this most necessary food, but that fats may be available to furnish the glycerine required in making ammunition."[17] Tips for the conservative use of fats in the kitchen include the following: one crust pies, no fried foods, use of drippings from meat as seasonings, and substitution of rendered poultry fat, suet, mutton fat, vegetable fat, or oil for butter in cooking and baking.

The conservation plan presented for breads calls for a reduction of the use of wheat by "one-fourth if we are to have enough to send the Allies" with the bread section detailing information concerning Liberty Breads. Missouri cooks are instructed to use three-fourths, two-thirds, or one-half of the amount of wheat flour and substitute the amount needed of some other kind of flour or meal. Possibilities listed include whole wheat flour, cornmeal, rice, potatoes, shorts, cotton-seed meal, buckwheat, bran, rye, peanut-meal, bean-meal, barley, and oats. A reminder before the bread recipes warns, "Share your WHEAT with the Allies. Better eat war bread now than eat the black bread of Germany later." The Liberty Bread introduction also indicates, ironically, that using this creative mix of flours and meals "will give you new kinds of breads which you will find to be appetizing, wholesome, and in many cases of even higher food value in certain respects than your customary white loaf."[18] Missouri cooks find creative new recipes for rolled oats bread, peanut and raisin bread, hominy bread, cottonseed meal bread, banana flour bread, and cornmeal wheat biscuit.

The cookbook then addresses the use of sugar and sugar substitutes. Missouri cooks find themselves trying out modified recipes for their typical desserts resulting in such creations as cottonseed devil's food cake, corn flour cookies, and bean molasses cookies as they utilized honey, corn syrup, sorghum, and maple syrup to get the desired flavor and taste. The cookbook offers an explanation as to why sugar was the preferred sweetener to be shipped during the war. "The concentrated energy and form makes it easy to ship. Soldiers often need quick sources of energy, and we have [at home] for flavor the syrups which cannot be so readily shipped."[19]

The final section provides the U.S. Department of Agriculture Time Table of Canning used in the Saint Louis Community Cannery during the summer of 1917. In addition to techniques for canning fruits and vegetables, cooks locate instructions for canning chicken, chicken gumbo, and chicken stock. Information encourages cooks to can mixed vegetables without chicken stock during the summer when vegetables are plentiful in their gardens. In the winter the canned vegetables can be added to soup stock for a quick pot of soup.

Approved Enduring Favorites, published in 1932 by the St. Louis Unit of the Women's Overseas Service League (WOSL), explains the purpose of the World War I–related cookbook. "First, to remind us of the days when we were part of the A.E.F. [Army Expeditionary Forces] Second, to construct a useful and enduring bond between the members of our organization, although we are scattered to the corners of the earth."[20] The general cookbook, compiled by Lorraine Livingstone, a member of the St. Louis WOSL Unit, also includes a collection of foreign recipes in the last section. Carol Habgood, current national spokesperson for WOSL, indicates that in the organization's history, only two units were established in Missouri, one in Kansas City from 1922 to 2003 and another in St. Louis from 1923 to 1969.[21]

Through their signed recipes, members of the St. Louis unit are well represented in the cookbook. Along with their names are service details, which show Missouri women representing the Army Nurse Corps, the American Red Cross, and the YMCA.

Information relating to WOSL, archived in the history section of their Web site, provides organizational and statistical information about American women who served overseas during World War I. The organization came into existence in 1921 after 90,000 American women had served with the U.S. Army Expeditionary Forces, 348 of whom gave their lives. "Over 11,000 Red Cross nurses served with the Army and Navy Nurse Corps. Others were assigned duties in the Ordnance, Quartermaster and Signal corps, and the Treasury Department."[22]

The WOSL history addresses the return of the women who had served in the war. "The women returned home and scattered across the country, most without the assistance and benefits afforded male soldiers." The organization developed as a "women's self-help group" with the group lobbying for members to be able to "gain admittance to veterans' hospitals . . . . for needed treatment and domiciliary care." With American women continuing their patriotic service during World War II, membership was extended to these 350,000 volunteers. "The majority of the membership is World War II era, although in recent years more women from the Vietnam and Gulf Wars have become members . . . with 31 units active in the continental United States."[23]

World War II kitchen guidelines reminiscent of those encouraged during World War I brought adjustments to meal preparation on the home front. Cooks nationwide were required to adjust their meal plans in accordance with a mandatory ration program put in place by the government. The Office of Price Administration (OPA) was established in 1941 with goal of controlling supply and demand as well as prices, thus assuring that all citizens whether poor or rich were able to purchase their share of foods and other products in demand. The government supplied instructional flyers and leaflets explaining the rationing system that controlled the purchase of such food items as coffee, meats, and processed foods. Charts printed in Missouri newspapers noted ration point values by can and weight with instructions to "clip and save" as a help when purchasing foods to be prepared in the kitchen. The St. Louis Independent Packing Company offered recipes from Dorothy Stuart's Mayrose Test Kitchen developed in cooperation with the information division of OPA. Their recipe flyer printed in 1943 details recipes for preparing old-fashioned beef stew, cabbage rolls, macaroni casserole, lamb burgers, baked stuffed spareribs, and breaded sweetbreads. The stew recipe utilized eleven ration points for meat and lard, the lamb burgers seven to eight points for the meat, and the breaded sweetbreads required three points for the meat.[24] Laclede Gas Light Company in St. Louis offered their customers a ration chart for meat cuts indicating points per pound and per cut including diagrams of veal, lamb, pork, and beef. Cooks purchasing meat found a hind pork foot tallied one point while a ham came to nine points, a round steak eight points, and a beef brisket four points.[25]

Although not printed in Missouri, several small war-related cookbooks certainly seem to have circulated in kitchens in the state during the war years since they can be found in numerous private collections. Among them General Foods Corporation delivered *How to Bake by the Ration Book,* assuring cooks that "You *can* have cakes as light, tender, and delicious as in the gold old unrationed days!"[26] That is if they follow modified recipes lined out in their cookbook. *Recipes for Today,* also by the General Foods Corporation, offers rule-friendly recipes in their sections on meat stretchers, meatless dishes, and baking. Kerr Glass Manufacturing Corporation delivered the National Nutrition Edition of their *Kerr Home Canning Book* in 1943 with an introductory message from Franklin D. Roosevelt. "FOOD is no less a weapon than tanks, guns, and planes." The cover and additional comments encourage patriotic support of the war through participation in the canning process. Kerr dedicates the cookbook "To the women who serve without banners . . . the Homemakers of America."[27]

Although the sense of urgency doesn't seem to be as prevalent compared to the St. Louis World War I *Patriot Food Show Cookbook* previously discussed, actions taken to deal with the war are evident in *The Victory Handbook for Health and Home Defense*, published by an unnamed Kirkwood organization during World War II. The cover sets a patriotic tone with a red, white, and blue victory theme complete with an American eagle. Comments in the cookbook emphasize the importance of home and personal health. The compilers include instructions for a nine-day reducing diet and a information regarding a program designed for gaining weight. The editors see those at home marching "shoulder to shoulder with the armed forces of our nation toward certain victory in the creation of a new world of democracy and freedom." Continuing a patriotic theme, the Kirkwood cookbook includes a quote by Calvin Coolidge explaining what the flag means to him, followed by instructions for properly displaying of the flag, noting that the rules "are based on the Flag Code adopted by the Flag Convention on June 14, 1923, and should be observed by all." The next section in the cookbook tells the reader "How to Add 5000 Miles to Your Tires" through a chemical plan "worked out by Dr. S. D. Lesesne, head of the Oklahoma City University," which involves a process of rubbing dirt-free tires twice each month with glycerine followed by powdered sulphur.[28] Suggestions for the use of leftover foods include saving cooked vegetables for use in salads, using leftover soups as a base for gravies and sauces, saving liquid from cooked vegetables to be used in soups, and using sour milk or sour cream in pancake batter for Sunday breakfasts.

Recipe names reflect the war effort. In the baking/dessert section, cooks find recipes for Sugarless Two-Egg Cake, Honey Pound Cake, World War Cake, Victory Lemon Cake, and Defense Apples, all of which include sugar alternatives in the ingredient list. Alluding to the use of sugar in making explosives, the cookbook offers a recipe for "Torpedo Frosting." This frosting combines heavy whipped cream, coconut, candied pineapple or cherries, vanilla, and grated orange rind. Compilers strongly recommend the use of sweetening alternatives.

At least two of Missouri's modern cookbooks have entered the political arena. In 1986 Carolyn Bond, wife of Missouri politician Kit Bond, introduced *A Taste of Missouri*, a collection of Bond family favorites featuring her husband and young son, Sam, in a family photo on the cover. Kit Bond, elected to the office of state auditor in 1970, became Missouri's governor in 1973 (at the time, he was the youngest the state had ever had). When the cookbook was published, Bond was running for the United States Senate, stressing his "common sense government" and his willingness to talk to and listen to the people of the state. The family theme and political message are also carried through a collection of Bond family photos depicting the candidate involved in backyard barbecuing, fishing, and garden planting sessions with son Sam. Photos show Bond and his family positively involved in activities around the state. The last recipe, "Peanut Butter in a Bowl" is contributed by young Sam. In the final section of the cookbook, Bond directly asks for support in his bid for the 1986 Senate election, lining out several of his political goals. Among them he proposes a strong voice for the people of Missouri, the family farmer, single mothers, retired people, young couples, and a strong voice for a defense budget that protects national security but cuts out fraud and waste.[29] Bond won his senate seat in 1986 and continues to represent Missourians in this position.

Sally Danforth's Cookbook also uses a family theme geared toward political success with a cover photo of the author and her husband sampling a favorite recipe in their kitchen followed by a recipe for "My Favorite Peanut Butter Sandwich" by the couple's young daughter, Eleanor. Mrs. Danforth delivers a message of Missouri foods and Missouri cooking by including recipes from friends and relatives around the state. She addresses the busy life of political husband Jack, then state attorney general, encouraging families to eat together whenever possible, making mealtime a special occasion. "We try to make our meals a family affair with some special dishes."[30] As in the Bond cookbook, photos of the family deliver an image of family involvement to the voters, not a bad image for a Missouri politician. Missouri cooks enjoyed reading the recipes and meeting the families indirectly through their cookbooks.

Chapter 11

Kitchen Medicine, Housekeeping Tips, and Cookbook Literature

For earache there is nothing more effective than a hot griddle cake baked in plenty of grease and applied as hot as can be endured.—*A Household Guide*, Cape Girardeau, Missouri, Presbyterian Church Ladies' Aid Society, 1904

Late-nineteenth- and early-twentieth-century cookbooks published in various sections of the United States typically include helpful information that is not necessarily directly related to cooking. Missouri cookbooks are no exception. In addition to new and favorite cooking instructions, doses of kitchen medicine and servings of housekeeping tips find their way into the state's cookbooks. Likewise, Missouri cookbook authors and compilers add literary tidbits in the form of quotes, creative recipes, poems, and narrative pieces designed to brighten the day and inspire the hardworking cook.

Compared to modern-day medicine with its miracle cures, wonder drugs, and medical advancements launched with the discovery of penicillin, simple home remedies recorded in early Missouri cookbook seem strange, odd, and sometimes questionable. What challenges the early Missouri cooks must have faced as they not only prepared three meals each day, managed a household, and helped with farm chores, but also cared for sick family members. Home remedies and medicinal recipes in the state's late-nineteenth- and early-twentieth-century cookbooks find cooks attempting to deal with a bevy of health problems. Some even offer preventive measures. Martha M. Williams in *The Capitol Cook Book*, writing from Monroe City in 1895, is concerned about preventing sunstrokes. "A wet handkerchief or brown paper—saturated with water and worn on top of the hat will prevent sun stroke, no matter how much one is exposed to the sun."[1]

The *Julia Clark Household Memoranda Book* and the *Harriet O'Fallon's Cook Book* include instructions for dealing with such common medical problems as bowel complaints in children, eruptions of the surface (of the skin), burns, bleeding piles, coughs, puking, and dysentery. "To Stop Pukeing Heat a Iron red hot and put it in cold water, and use the water." Instructions for preparing a salve for a burn direct the cook to "Scrap[e] the inside bark of elder slice in sheep suet and a little wax." For relief of croup, "Bind a large tobacco leaf to the breast, it cures the child instantly, before any medicine could have affect." For a sore head, "Tar and Butter Stewed together" or "The Yelk of an Egg & Sulphur made into a salve."[2] Harriet O'Fallon explains how to deal with dysentery. "Take common salts as much as will dissolve in a gill of shory [?] vinegar—after the vinegar is fully saturated with the salt, add three times the quantity of water—or strong mint tea—Dose—a small wine glass full every two hours."[3]

Addressing a wide range of health issues in *My Mother's Cook Book* (1880), the Ladies of St. Louis deliver a section titled "Remedies to Apply While Waiting for the doctor." Their suggestions begin with how to settle a stomach and follow with directions for dealing with convulsions, cholera, apoplexy, asthma, epileptic fits, poison vine eruption, and wounds, among other conditions. For rheumatism they say "Carry a potato on the person, the side diseased; also bathe the parts in hot potato water," and an earache "will be relieved by equal parts of chloroform and laudanum, a little being introduced on a piece of cotton."[4]

Spices and herbs as well as unusual and sometimes questionable ingredients become ingredients in remedies. Using spices from their kitchen, the Ladies of St. Louis suggest using salt and ground mustard for an emetic, a tea made of allspice for night sweats, and the essence of peppermint to cure weak eyes. The compilers recommend boiling mullen leaves to cure hip disease and suggest frying mullen leaves in hot lard and then applying them as a poultice for swollen limbs. Their cure for a cough includes the "Whites of two eggs, two tablespoonfuls of powdered sugar, two of honey, one wineglass of whisky, beaten well together" with the dose prescribed as "A dessertspoonful every time you cough."[5]

In Campbell, the Ladies of the Baptist Church introduce their medicinal section with this thought. "We all, when we are well, give advice to the sick."

The first item tells Missourians how to cure their corns. "Rub your corns with castor oil. It will take the soreness out, and beats all the 'corn cures' made." Mrs. Winnie Oxley from Malden shares her recipe for cough medicine: "One teacupful of good vinegar, one-half cupful honey, 1 teaspoonful cayenne pepper. Mix well and let simmer on the fire. When cold take 1 teaspoonful every hour until cough is cured." She also donates her remedy for heart trouble. "Take a pint bottle, put 1 tablespoonful of cream of tarter, 2 tablespoonfuls sulphur, a piece or assafoetida as large as a hickory nut and fill the bottle a little over half full of rain water warm; shake until all is nearly dissolves. Take one tablespoonful three times a day." For frostbitten feet, one contributor suggests using "One-half plug tobacco in a bowl of warm water."[6]

The senior citizens of Freistatt turned back the clock in their historic cookbook in 1981, sharing medicinal remedies from their community's kitchens of the past. For an abscess, the cook is instructed to "Mash a raw beet into a pulp, and apply it often, it will heal and take the soreness out." They suggest taking the soreness out of an ingrown nail by applying a poultice made of finely chopped onion, and they believe if pure apple cider vinegar is applied to a burn quickly enough, it will not blister. "A tablespoon of pineapple juice with a little salt is very good" for getting rid of hiccups. Crushed tomato leaves bound on a bee or wasp sting "draws it out at once." A tea prepared with black walnut leaves is a "wonderful blood builder." "The milk from the milkweed plant will kill the itching of ivy poisoning" and "Wild touch-me-not will do the same thing." An additional remedy from the field suggests that a syrup using the bark of wild plum can be made by boiling down "a handful of wild plum bark to a quart of water." For diarrhea, "Just chew a few leaves of ragweed," make a tea out of strawberry leaves, or "Take one teaspoon of ground nutmeg." A teaspoon of vanilla extract or a mixture of soda and water will work for toothache pain and a tea prepared with celery seed may be used for nervousness.[7]

In addition to providing recipes and suggestions for home remedies, Missouri cookbooks supply guidelines for "Invalid Cooking," "Cookery for the Sick," or "Receipts for the Sick-Room." Missouri cookbooks include recipes for simple, easy-to-digest foods in these sections. Mrs. Willis and Mrs. Bird in *Housekeeping and Dinner Giving in Kansas City* handle the "Cookery for the Sick" section of their work. Mrs. Willis offers recipes for beef tea and chicken broth, the first prepared by boiling a pound of lean round steak and the second by boiling a cut-up fowl in water and then seasoning lightly (the cook is to crack the bones before boiling). She also details how to prepare a beef sandwich for the sickly made with scraped uncooked steak and buttered bread, believing it to be "very nourishing, and quite palatable." Mrs. Bird, wrapping up the section, notes in her recipe for broiled tomatoes, "These are excellent for invalids suffering from constipation."[8] Overall, these recipes are similar to those found in other early Missouri cookbooks: recipes for panada, egg and milk Punch, herb teas, cornmeal gruel, wine whey, and cracker toast.

Missouri cooks also took advantage of recipes in medical cookbook almanacs and medically themed cookbooks distributed by patent medicine companies and drug companies. The Wolff-Wilson Drug Company in St. Louis offered its customers *How to Have Good Health and Make Good Candy* (nd). This small cookbook heavily promotes a line of drugs including Vinol Cod Liver and Iron Tonic, Vinlax Tablets, and Saxo Soap and Saxo Salve. A somewhat bittersweet project, the publication addresses a multitude of ailments and cures but sweetens the text with tasty candy recipes for such favorites as penuche, peanut fudge, creamed peppermints, seafoam candy, and coconut drops. The text proposes that Vinol is a remedy for stomach troubles, coughs, colds, bronchitis, and throat and lung troubles, as well as a body-builder for recovering patients male or female, young or old.

Moving on to the section promoting Vinlax Tablets, the project includes a detailed list of disorders attributed to constipation—among them, sick headache, facial humors, dizziness, depressed sprits, loss of appetite, impure blood, flushed face, rheumatism, disturbed sleep, hives, and typhoid and other fevers. The drug company believes its product to be a remedy for constipation problems and contends that skin problems such as pimples, boils, ring worms, and "The Itch" (scabies) will benefit from applications of two of their products, Saxo Salve and Saxo Soap.

Dr. W. H. Bull's Herbs and Iron 1904 almanac published in St. Louis includes monthly calendars, the moon's phases, monthly weather forecasts, and occasional jokes used as fillers. Like the Wolf-Wilson Drug Company publication, the almanac strongly promotes a line of patent medicines through descriptions of ailments and testimonials of successful cures attributed to the products being advertised. Dr. W. H. Bull's Herbs and Iron is recommended for liver, kidney, and heart problems and for promoting pure blood. Of interest is a discussion of the treatment the company suggests for the individual suffering from a condition called "Tobacco Heart."

Hoping to appeal to the Missouri cook, *Dr. W. H. Bull's Herbs and Iron 1904*, a company almanac, combined recipes, monthly calendars, weather forecasts, and the moon's phases blended with ads and testimonials for medicinal products.

Tobacco Heart so called because the nerves of the heart are weakened by the excessive use of tobacco by which the blood becomes saturated with nicotine poison. Persons addicted to the use of tobacco in any form, and finding heart action failing, should abstain from its use and take Dr. W. H. Bull's Herbs and Iron with occasional doses of Blood and Liver Pills to cleanse the blood of nicotine poison and stimulate the heart to its normal action.[9]

The following vivid ailment description titled "The Sign of Worms" must have caught the cook's attention as she perused recipes for custard, pumpkin and mince pies listed under "Granny's Good Receipts" on the opposite page. If worms are present in a child, they might demonstrate "hardness of the belly with colicky pains and diarrhoea [*sic*] at times, picking of the nose, restless broken sleep, low spirited and unusually fretful, feverish with frequent desire for water." The text continues, "Worms are restless creatures, continually groping about in the stomach and not unfrequently find their way into the throat, seeking passage through the mouth and nostrils."[10]

A satisfied Missouri customer supposedly sent this testimonial to the company.

Gentlemen:—For fifteen years I was troubled with granulated lids that nearly made me blind. The suffering from the awful scratching pains makes me shudder when I think about it, and it hardly seems possible that any one could have endured so much pain. The doctors here could not do anything for me, except to cause greater suffering in their effort to effect a cure. I was advised to try Dr. W. H. Bull's Golden Eye Salve, but must admit I had no faith in it, yet you know a 'drowning man will grasp at a straw' . . . I got two bottles of Dr. Bull's Golden Eye Salve and after using it my eyes were cured and I now see as well as ever; you will think so too when I tell you that I was at a "turkey shoot" a few days ago and won most of the turkeys. Simmons, Mo. Dec. 26, 1902[11]

Through their projects, Missouri cookbook authors and compilers have likewise been eager to share housekeeping tips concerned with cleaning, sewing, and gardening as well as pest control and laundry duties. Food preparation and preservation techniques often fall into housekeeping sections.

In 1951, the Rockview Methodist Church sponsored *Your Household Guide,* offering a collection of 1,001 helpful household hints gleaned from several hundred Walsworth Brothers *Home Recipe Books*. Honing in on the popularity of baking in Missouri kitchens, the project opens with pie- and cake-making tips. "Brush the bottom crust of meat pie, with the white of an egg to prevent the gravy soaking in." "For consistency, when making pie crust; Add water with clothes sprinkler." "Do not grease the sides of cake pans. How would you like to climb a greased pole?"[12]

Gardening suggestions in the same book are both creative and practical. "Plant sunflowers with your pole beans. Saves time spent in cutting poles and also protects beans from frost." "Tiny seeds are easier to plant in an even row if sprinkled from a salt shaker." "Before working in the garden, or doing other rough work, rub your finger nails over a piece of soap. This will prevent the earth from getting in under the nails, and when you wash your hands, the soap comes out easily."[13]

The Women's Progressive Farmers' Association members in the *Pure Food Cook Book* address herb preservation. "While the earth is filled with the warmth and glow of the midsummer sun, and vegetation is in its prime, the housekeeper should make provision against the time when frost shall have blighted all delicate green things." In the same section, they propose that herbs should be gathered on warm, sunny afternoons so that they are free from moisture and suggest that the herbs be tied in small bundles and placed in a bag to protect them from insects and dust. Bags are then tied and hung "in a current of air in the shade." They believe this method to be better than drying herbs in the open air because more flavor is retained. They go on to say that "Summer savory, sweet marjoram, thyme, parsley and sage are herbs that should be found in every kitchen pantry." After harvesting fresh herbs, Missouri cooks often made herb vinegars for use in their kitchens. The compilers conclude, "The garden and the country fields and roadsides supply nearly all the herbs that are required in the ordinary household."[14]

Besides keeping bugs out of drying herbs, Missouri cooks often had to deal with pests in their homes and gardens and were interested in reading about how other cooks in the state dealt with these problems. The Ladies of the Union Avenue Christian Church are convinced that gasoline is a "sovereign remedy for bugs." According to one church member, "It can be literally poured on the mattress, springs and bed without injuring the most delicate carpet, and every bug will disappear."[15] The Ladies of St. Louis in *My Mother's Cook Book* deliver advice for ridding a house of ants: "A strong solution of carbolic acid and water poured into holes kills all the ants it touches, and the survivors take themselves off."[16] A Missouri cook from Pilot Knob in the Iron County *Centennial Cookbook,* edited by Reese, includes a tip for dealing with ants. "Scatter cayenne pepper all over the pantry shelves, and not an ant will molest you."[17] Editors of the *Juanita Kitchen Guide* tell Sikeston cooks how to kill earthworms. "To exterminate earth worms from potted plants, thrust unburnt sulfur matchheads, heads down, into the earth around the plants."[18] Contributors to the Women's Progressive Farmers' Association cookbook recommend a mixture of lard or old butter and pine tar be added to a gallon of kerosene to be used as a fly spray. They also say that rats don't like sulphur and that mites among the chickens can be destroyed by painting roosts with house paint.[19]

Cooks turned the pages of their cookbooks to locate laundry tips, no doubt, to make this job easier and more efficient. The Rockview Methodist Church project supplies several pages of helpful bits on this topic. "An old pair of curling irons makes an excellent gripper to use in dyeing garments." "To keep the little tufts on a chenille bedspread fluffy, hang the wet spread on the line with the tufts inside." "Launder the laundry bag." "To keep handkerchiefs, socks or other small pieces from wrapping around washing machine wringers, fold them inside towel and run through." "Insert a teaspoon in the toe of your nylons when hanging them on the line to prevent blowing and snagging." "To remove a scorch from clothing, rub with a lemon and put in the sun."[20] The Women's Progressive Farmers' Association's *Pure Food Cook Book* compilers detail several helpful laundry tips. "Hang sheets and table linens by both hems. Hems will not fray out and articles will iron more easily." "Rub flat irons on cedar twigs and starch will not stick to them." "To remove trade marks from flour sacks: Soak sack in kerosene for about thirty minutes. Wash in hot suds, boil about fifteen minutes."[21]

The same cookbook extols the virtues of certain sewing techniques. "Darning is an important part of sewing." "Patching is another important art." Compilers remind readers, "Each week all clothing from the wash should be carefully examined and repaired; a rent should be mended at once, before the edges stretch or ravel." Likewise, worn-out items such as tablecloths "which have prolonged their existence by virtue of neat darns, can become napkins." Clever sewing tricks save time and frustration. "If your curtain rods are a little hard to get through the hem of your curtains try using a thimble over the end of the rod" and "A blunted sewing machine needle may be sharpened by sticking through a piece of sandpaper."[22]

Moving beyond sewing and pest and laundry management, information within household sections helps cooks in cleaning, polishing, and repairing items around the home. The contributors in the Women's Progressive Farmers' Association book use vinegar on their rusty stoves prior to polishing them. Kerosene added to the water helps get windows clean and keeps flies away. Clean window shades with a rough flannel cloth dipped in flour. "An old stocking is good" for cleaning oiled or varnished woodwork. To clean silver "Place silver in a pan, cover with buttermilk and let stand over night; wash and dry." To clean copper "Rub with salt and vinegar mixed together." "Orange juice," they say, "will be found a good polish for patent leather." One simple tip, "A little soap applied with the point of a lead pencil will remedy a squeaking hinge."[23]

Just as Missouri cooks enjoy sharing their kitchen tips today, Missouri cookbooks from the past have recorded lists of miscellaneous food preparation and preservation tips and techniques. The Ladies of St. Louis in *My Mother's Cook Book* note that rancid butter "May be remedied by putting in a saucepan and scalding, then put in a piece of toasted bread, which will absorb all of the bad part of the butter" and that summer eggs will "beat up much lighter" if placed in a pan of cold water for a while before beating.[24] Vinegar and salt were popular items in the kitchens of the ladies who compiled the *Union Avenue Cook Book*. Offering several suggestions, they explain, "In cooking a tough fowl or meat, one tablespoonful of vinegar in the water will save nearly two hours' boiling." Likewise, "If vinegar is added to prunes when stewing . . . it will improve their flavor." They believe that adding vinegar to the water when boiling ham "will improve it greatly, give the ham a bright red color and make it firm and compact" and suggest that the cook add a tablespoon of vinegar in lard when frying doughnuts "to prevent them from being greasy." They advocate using salt on hands when cleaning fowls, meat, or fish . . . "to prevent slipping," placing salt in the oven under baking tins to prevent "their scorching on the bottom," and finally throwing salt on a coal fire when broiling steak to "prevent blazing from the dripping fat."[25]

The cooking hints section in the *Pure Food Cook Book* shares numerous kitchen tips. Placing potatoes in hot water for about fifteen minutes before putting them in the oven "will hasten the baking." "When cooking *old potatoes*, add sweet milk to the water in which they are boiled." Dusting the frying pan with a small amount of white flour "will prevent the fat from popping out on your floor or stove." "A few turns of the egg beater will set it right" they say of a boiled salad dressing that has curdled. They also indicate, "Rose geranium leaves make nice *flavoring* for cakes and jellies." Finally, "To keep cake moist, put a good sound apple in the cake box."[26]

Missouri cookbook authors and compilers also seem to enjoy including a bit of literature in their cookbooks. These literary pieces generally are simple and folksy. Sometimes, however, compilers turn to the classics for their introductory quotes as in the case of a 1902 community cookbook in Caruthersville. The compilers introduce several sections with quotes from Shakespeare's plays. Missouri cookbook literature has sometimes taken the form of "recipe poems" where a recipe is actually written as a poem. Creative prose, novice entertaining, and sometimes inspirational pieces also enhance Missouri cookbooks.

Mrs. Dorritt Adams from Ironton contributes this poem for use in the *Centennial Cookbook* celebrating Iron County's one hundredth birthday.

How to Measure a Man

The man's no bigger than the way he treats his fellow man!
This standard has his measure been since time itself began!
He's measured not by tithes or creed big-sounding though they be;
Nor by the gold that's put aside, nor by his sanctity!
He's measured not be social Rank, when Character's the test;
Nor by his earthly pomp or show, displaying wealth possessed!
He's measured by his justice, right, his fairness at his play,
His squareness in all dealings made, his honest, upright way.
These are his measures, ever near to serve him when they can;
For man's no bigger than the way he treats his Fellow Man![27]

The "Scripture Cake" recipe has appeared in many Missouri cookbooks. In some versions the cook has to look up the verses to locate each ingredient. In other cases the compilers provide "verse answers" along with quantities and ingredients. Mrs. O. B. McCrea from Iantha contributes this version in the *Pure Food Cook Book*.

Scripture Cake

1 cup butter, Judges 5:25
3 cups flour, I Kings 4:22
2 cups sugar, Jeremiah 6:20
6 eggs, Isaiah 10:14

A little salt, Leviticus 2:13
Sweet spice to taste, I Kings 10:10
2 cups raisins, I Samuel 30:12
2 cups figs, I Samuel 30:12
1 cup water, Genesis 24:17
1 cup almonds, Genesis 43:11
1 tablespoon honey, Exodus 16:31
Follow Solomon's advice for making good boys and you will have a
good cake. Proverbs 23:14[28]

This motivational contribution by a member of the Helen Richardson
Mission Band examines the power of love. It appeared in their 1899 cookbook, *The Kitchen Oracle,* published in St. Louis.

A Cure for Love
Take two ounces of dislike, one ounce of resolution: one grin of common sense; two ounce of experience. Set them over a gentle fire of love;
sweeten with the sugar of forgetfulness; skim it with the spoon of
melancholy; put in it the bottom of your heart; cork it with the cork of
clear conscience; there let it remain, and you will immediately find ease
and be restored to your right senses. These things can be procured at
the apothecaries, of the house of understanding, next door to reason
street, in Village of Content.[29]

Cooks enjoyed this poetic recipe in *The Best in Cooking in Grandin* compiled by the members of the Order of Eastern Star.

Gingerbread
Pour a cupful of nice molasses
In a Bowl and mix it well
With a teaspoon of baking soda
Beat two eggs, all but the shell.
Now your butter slowly melted—
Just two tablespoons and then
Fill your cup with sifted flour
Once, and a half cupful again.
In the flour put some ginger
Half a teaspoon will do

Cinnamon I'd also put there—
Just a pinch if I were you,
Stir with a wooden spoon the mixture
Till you feel your shoulder ache,
Then in a butter pan I'd bake this
Simple, tempting ginger cake.[30]

Ova Johnson, the contributor, adds "I usually add 1/2 c nut meats."

And from the Ladies of the Union Avenue Christian Church—

Things to Remember
Sixteen tablespoons make one cup;
If milk or water, fill it up;
It takes but eight, heaped full and high,
If what you measure's fine an dry.[31]

A member of the Hebrew Ladies' Aid Society contributed a thoughtful recipe to *The Joplin Cook Book.*

And old fashioned recipe for home comfort
Take a thought of self one part, two parts of thoughts of others, equal parts of common sense and broad intelligence, a large sense of the fitness of things, a heaping measure of living above what your neighbors think of you, twice the quantity of keeping within your income, a sprinkling of what tends to refinement and beauty stirred thick with human principles and set to rise.[32]

The St. Louis Second Presbyterian Church Young Woman's Guild's *Cook Book* (1922) published a poem in the beverage section that seems to reflect their stand on Prohibition.

Beverages
Have a drink? "Yes, I will."
What ye got in the still?
What? No!Sho! Tee to?
Fill up that cup! Stop

Want to know my position?
Put it thar, pard: "Prohibition"[33]

A tasty recipe from *The Nettleton Cook Book,* compiled by Miss Grace L. Lawrence and the Geo. H. Nettleton Home Association in Kansas City offers a poem possibly inspired by a crisp fall Missouri morning.

Waffle iron hissing hot;
Coffee steaming in the pot;
Griddle cakes that spit and sputter;
Marmalade and apple butter
Country sausage, sage and spice;
Savory odors that entice;
Don't it seem that after all
The finest season is the fall.[34]

A brief prose piece in the Introduction of the St. Paul's Episcopal Church *Clinton Cook Book* (1898) tells the cook how to make her household run smoothly.

Let the mistress of the house take ten pounds of the very best self control, one and one half pounds of Justice, one pound of Consideration, five pounds of patience and one pound of Discipline. Let this be sweetened with Charity. Let it simmer well and let it be taken daily, (in extreme cases in hourly doses) and be kept always on hand. The domestic wheels will run smoothly.[35]

Mrs. Pierce introduces the bread section with a short poem in the *Columbia Cook Book* (1901) compiled by the ladies of the Methodist Episcopal Church, South.

If 'Bread is the staff of life,'
make sure that all the ingredients are pure.
And then, with a skillful hand combine
And watch the baking, or you will find
Your staff's to be but a broken reed
And a most untrusty prop indeed.[36]

Finally, one popular prose piece from a nineteenth-century cookbook reappeared in several twentieth-century Missouri cookbooks. Some organizers published sections of it, others included the longer version. Here Mrs. Thomas J. Mayes from Ironton delivers the longer piece for publication in the Iron County *Centennial Cook Book* in 1957. The same version appears in the *Pure Food Cook Book*.

How to Cook Husbands

A good many husbands are entirely spoiled by mismanagement in cooking and so are not tender and good. Some women go about it as if their husbands were bladders and blow them up. Others keep them constantly in hot water. Others let them freeze by their carelessness and indifference. Some keep them in a stew by irritating ways and words. Others roast them. Some keep them in pickles all their lives.

It cannot be supposed that any husband will be tender and good managed in this way, but they are really delicious when properly treated.

In selecting your husband, you should not be guided by the silvery appearance, as in buying mackerel, nor by the golden tint, as if you wanted salmon. Be sure and select him yourself, as tastes differ. Do not go to market for him, as the best is always brought to the door. It is far better to have none, unless you will patiently learn how to cook him. A preserving kettle of the finest Porcelain is the best, but if you have nothing but an earthenware pinkin it will do, with care. See that the linen in which you wrap him is nicely washed and mended, with the requisite number of buttons and strings nicely sewed on. Tie him in the kettle by a strong silken cord, called comfort; duty is apt to be weak. Husbands are apt to fly out of the kettle and be burned and crusty on the edge, since, like crabs and lobsters, you have to cook them while alive. Make a clear, steady fire out of love, neatness and cheerfulness. Set your husband as near this as seems to agree with him. If he sputters and fizzes, do not be ansious [anxious].Some husbands do this until they are quite done. Add a little sugar in the form of what confectioners call kisses, but no vinegar or pepper on any account. A little spice improves him, but it must be used with judgment. Do not stick any sharp instrument into him to see if he is becoming tender. Stir him gently; watch the while, lest he lie too flat and close to the kettle and so become useless. You cannot fail to know when he is done. If thus treated, you will find him very digestive, agreeing nicely with you and the children, and he will keep as long as you want, unless you become careless and set him in too cool a place.[37]

What better way to learn about the daily lives and cooking practices of the state's cooks and to experience their ever-changing daily lives than to peruse the pages of Missouri cookbooks? Authors and compilers not only delivered recipes, but also addressed daily home-management concerns. A close look at the nonculinary information shared and passed from cookbook to cookbook finds cooks eager to assist one another in their roles as doctors, nurses, exterminators, seamstresses, time-management specialists, and morale builders.

Chapter 12

A Final Perspective

Cookbooks have preserved for present-day Missourians a sense of times past in their kitchens and in their communities. Readers learn about food preparation on Missouri's early farms in one cookbook and in another they experience the culinary lifestyle of more urban settings such as St. Louis and Kansas City. In the state's cookbooks, time is marked in the kitchen through descriptions of cooking devices, kitchen equipment, and utensils. Cooking details chronicle the availability of food products used in dishes for family meals. Early cookbooks utilized basic staples from the store combined with homegrown fruits, meats, and vegetables in made-from-scratch meals. Modern life not only brought high-tech gadgets and appliances into the kitchen but also an increasing assortment of prepackaged and prepared food items, many of which have enticed Missouri cooks to trade homemade taste for convenience and efficiency.

An examination of the style in which a recipe is written provides information not only about the contributor of the recipe, but also about the intended reader. A pie or cake recipe in early Missouri cookbooks assumes a certain level of expertise and thus offers minimal mixing and measuring directions. On the other hand, recipes found in more recent cookbooks line out much more detailed directions, including exact measurements for the convenience of the not-so-savvy modern Missouri baker.

Even with fewer pots being stirred in modern kitchens, cookbooks continue to be popular with Missouri shoppers. It seems that many buyers simply read cookbooks much as they would novels or magazine articles. Today, armchair cooks, men and women, enjoy relaxing in the family room recliner while exploring, or reexploring, the pages of a cookbook. Likewise, they look forward to searching out vintage cookbooks at local flea markets and garage sales, for recipes like Grandma used to cook, all the while smiling over a recipe for pickled pigs' feet, scrambled eggs and brains, or fried poke stems. No doubt, readers also chuckle over the delightful prose and poetry pieces that explain "How to Cook a Husband" or "How to Make a Scripture Cake."

The state's cookbooks have an eclectic history. Individually authored cookbooks developed as a result of culinary interests and food experiences. Many of Missouri's cookbooks became available as civic-minded groups associated with churches, schools, historical societies, and various other charitable organizations throughout the state determined to raise funds for a wide range of worthwhile projects or businesses tried to raise awareness of, and profits on, their products. Cookbooks provide information about popular eateries from Missouri's past as well as those with their kitchens still open. Other works design recipes around Missouri-grown food products from pumpkins and walnuts to bison and honey. Likewise, Missouri-based companies have historically encouraged the use of their food products through promotional cookbooks and continue to do so using both traditional printing methods and high-tech digital delivery.

Missouri cookbooks continue to serve their intended purpose as cooking manuals. They are readily available, detailing styles of cooking from ethnic choices to health trends to the "short cut—fast and easy" style currently popular in today's kitchens. It seems likely that in the "Show Me" tradition, the state's "voices from the kitchen" will continue to guide Missourians while preserving their collective past. And future generations will puzzle over the social complexities of the twenty-first century, discovering and analyzing our present as their past—sometimes through the pages of one of their cherished old Missouri cookbooks.

Selected Recipes

Beaten Biscuits

Mrs. L. R. Moore, *Housekeeping and Dinner Giving in Kansas City,* 1887

Mrs. Moore, one of the contributors, takes a stand against the "old fashioned way" of preparing biscuits that called for beating the dough with a rolling pin for at least thirty minutes.

These biscuits to be well and easily made, should be kneaded with a machine made for that purpose. They cost from ten to fifteen dollars, according to finish. The labor of making the biscuit is trifling, compared with the old fashioned way of beating them. The receipt here given will make three dozen biscuits: Two quarts of flour, one pint of sweet milk and water, mixed in equal proportions; one-half a teacupful of fresh lard, two dessertspoonfuls of salt; mix the lard and flour thoroughly together, then add the salt and milk. Knead well with the hands for a few minutes, when it will be ready to be worked through the kneading machine. Roll the dough rather thin: prick on top with a fork; cut out and bake.

Plum-pudding, with Rum or Brandy

Mrs. Mary F. Henderson, *Practical Cooking and Dinner Giving,* St. Louis, 1877

Take three-quarters of a pound of chopped suet, three-quarters of a pound of stoned raisins, three-quarters of a pound of currants, quarter of a pound of citron, three-quarters of a pound of sugar, three-quarters of a pound of bread-crumbs, two apples cut into small dice, and the grated peel of a lemon; mix the whole in a basin, with three pounded cloves, a pinch of salt, six eggs and half a gill of rum or brandy. Butter a pudding-mold, fill it with the mixture and tie a cloth over the top. Place a plate at the bottom of a kettle which is three-parts full of boiling water. Put the pudding in, and boil for four hours, keeping the pot replenished with boiling water. Turn out the pudding on a hot dish; sprinkle over it sugar. Pour over half a pint of warm rum or brandy, and light it when putting the pudding on the table.

Black Cake

Mrs. R. W. Carr, *The Capitol Cook Book,* Calvary Episcopal Church Ladies, 1896, Sedalia

Twenty eggs, two pounds sugar, two pounds flour, one and one-half pounds butter, three pounds seeded raisins, three pounds currants, two pounds citron, one and one-half pounds blanched and chopped almonds, two nutmegs grated, two teaspoons of mace, two teaspoons cinnamon, one teaspoon cloves, two wine-glasses wine, two brandy, one teaspoon soda dissolved in a little water; cream butter and sugar together, beat egg separately, add first one then the other, put in spices, flour, liquor, and then the fruit, having floured well. Bake four or five hours.

Plain Beef Soup

Favorite Recipes, Ladies of the Baptist Church, Knob Noster, 1897

Place in kettle with plenty of cold water a 10 cent soup bone. When tender remove bone, strain soup, thicken with 10 cent cup flour mixed with water until smooth, season with salt and pepper. Boil up once and serve.

Corn Meal Mush

From "Granny's Good Receipts" in *Dr. W. H. Bull's Herbs and Iron 1904* almanac

Put two quarts of water in a pot with a cover, add a tablespoonful of salt and bring to a boil, have fresh yellow or white corn meal; take a handful of meal with the left hand and a flat stick or paddle to the right, then stir the water around and by degrees add the meal; continue stirring and adding meal until it is thick as you can stir easily, or until the paddle will stand upright without being held. Let it boil for two hours, then turn it into a deep pan. It is eaten cold or hot, with milk or with butter and syrup or sugar, or with meat and gravy, the same as potatoes or rice.

Fried Mush—Make it like the above recipe, turn into shallow pans, and when cold, slice it. Roll each piece in corn meal and fry brown in lard or butter. Most delicious when served hot.

Baked Pig

Mrs. S. S. Markey, *Twentieth Century Cook Book,* Caruthersville, 1902

Take a pig about six weeks or two months old, nicely prepared, score in squares, and rub lard all over it; make a dressing as you would for chicken or turkey. Fill the pig until plump, sew it up and place it on its knees in the pan, which fill with as much water as will cook it. Baste it very frequently with the gravy, also two red pepper pods. Turn while baking same as turkey, and continue to baste until done.

Bread and Potato Bread

Mrs. Nellie Duling Gans, *A Book for a Cook,* St. Louis, 1905

The loaf of bread which won the Grand Prize at the St. Louis World's Fair in 1904 was made from this recipe.

Materials:

    1 pint milk
    1 cup water
    9 cups Pillsbury's Best
    1 cake of yeast
    2 tablespoonfuls butter
    1 tablespoonful sugar
    1 teaspoonful salt
    ¼ cup lukewarm water

Way of Preparing:

Scald the milk and one cup of water, and while scalding hot pour the liquid over the butter, sugar and salt. Dissolve the yeast in ¼ cup of lukewarm water.

When the milk has cooled to lukewarm, beat into it four cups of flour and add the dissolved yeast. Mix thoroughly, cover and set to rise. When it is light and frothy add to it the other five cups of flour, until the dough ceases to stick to your hands and to the board. The quantity of flour to be added may be more or less than five cups; the moisture in the flour determines that: when the dough ceases to stick you have added enough.

Now knead the dough for about fifteen minutes and then set it to rise until it obtains twice its size, when you form it into loaves and place them into baking pans.

Let them rise again until they reach double their size, place them into an oven and bake forty-five minutes.

Quantity:

This will make three loaves in bread pans of ordinary size. To make the old-fashioned potato bread, add to the sponge of the above recipe two medium-sized white potatoes, boiled and mashed while warm.

Potted Ham

G. T. Hamel, *Modern Practice of Canning Meats*, 1911

Use ham trimmings which have been cured from 8 to 10 days and smoked on trays in the smoke-house. Cook these trimmings 15 minutes in boiling water, pass them through the 7/8 plate of the "Enterprise" chopper, then finish chopping it in the "Buffalo" cutter, adding to a 400 lbs. batch of meat the following spices:

Ground mustard 6 lbs.
White pepper 1 lb.
Red pepper 2 oz.
Mace, cloves and nutmeg to taste.
Water, up to the proportion of 4 lbs. per batch of 50 lbs., may be added during the chopping in the "Buffalo."

To Preserve Eggs

The Joplin Cook Book, Hebrew Ladies' Aid Society, 1912

To a pail of water add 2 pints of slacked lime and 1 pint common salt: mix well, fill your barrel ½ full of the fluid, put the eggs down in it any time after June, and they will keep 2 years if desired.

Liberty Bread

Patriotic Food Show Official Recipe Book, St. Louis, 1918

2 c. boiling water
⅓ c. molasses
1 c. rye flour
1 c. cornmeal
3 c. whole wheat flour
1½ t. salt
¼ c. lukewarm water
½ yeast cake

Mix, let rise, shape and bake as entire wheat bread.

Mock Sausage

Unity Inn Vegetarian Cook Book, Kansas City, 1923

½ c. dried lima beans
½ t. ground sage
¼ t. chili powder or few grains of cayenne
¼ c. corn meal
½ t. salt
2 T. butter

Soak beans for several hours; drain and cover with boiling water; cook until soft. Rub through a strainer. There should be 1¼ cups of pulp; add water if there is less. Return to saucepan and bring to boiling point. Stir in corn meal and boil 5 minutes, stirring constantly; then cook over water ½ hour, add seasonings and butter, and set aside to cool. When cold, form into flat cakes, roll in a mixture of corn meal and barley flour, and fry.

Cherry Rose Pie

Mrs. W. W. Reese, Ironton, Missouri, *Centennial Cook Book,* 1957

Line the pie plate with flakey pastry, sprinkle with flour and sugar, then fill with pitted and sugared pie cherries, dust with flour, sprinkle a handful of rose petals, the sweetest the garden affords, all over the fruit. Put on the upper crust and bake.

Calf Sale Chili

Neta Noel, *Favorite Recipes,* United Methodist Women, Unionville, 1976

    5 lbs. ground beef
    1 gal. can chili seasoned beans
    2 onions
    3 (46 oz.) cans tomato juice or 4 quarts
    1 T. chili powder

Brown meat and onions together (skim off excess fat, if desired), then add remaining ingredients. Simmer to improve flavor. Makes 3 gallons.

Margarine

Lucille Jones, *Missouri Ozarks Commodity Cookbook,* A Community Action Agency, no date

    1 lb. commodity butter
    1 can Pet milk

Combine one pound of commodity butter with one can Pet milk. Whip until smooth. This increases the volume of butter and cuts down on salt content.

Margee's Prize Zucchini Pancakes

This recipe, contributed by Margee Andrews from Kirkwood to *Missouri History on the Table* won first place in a statewide historic recipe contest celebrating Ste. Genevieve's Semiquincentennial Anniversary (1735–1985), 1985.

> 4½ c. grated zucchini
> 4 eggs, separated
> ¾ c crumbled blue cheese
> 1 t. minced garlic
> ¼ c. chopped green onion
> 3 T. sour cream
> ½ c. flour
> 1 T. chopped parsley

Squeeze out excess moisture in zucchini. Mix it, egg yolks, cheese, garlic, onion and sour cream. Mix well. Add flour. Beat egg whites in separate bowl till peaks form. Fold egg whites into the zucchini mixture. Using a nonstick skillet, fry 3-inch round cakes until nicely browned on one side. Turn. Sprinkle with parsley flakes. Serve with extra sour cream and/or blue cheese dressing.

Chitterlings

Josephine R. Lawrence, *Sharing Recipes,* Pennytown Freewill Baptist Church Cookbook, 1993

> About 20 lb. of fresh chitterlings
> 2 c. cold water
> 2 large onions
> salt, pepper, to taste

Clean chitterlings well, this means washing and removing excess fat. Rinse and rerinse several times. Place chitterlings in large pot (iron); add onion, water and seasoning. Cover kettle and cook over low heat for 6 to 7 hours or until chitterlings can be cut easily with a fork. Add a little more water if necessary to keep chitterlings from sticking. Stir often. Cook down low. Serve with coleslaw and hot water cornbread and chow-chow. May fry in batter.

Apple Dumplings

Mary Margaret Johnson, *The Fayette Apple Festival Cookbook,*
Sylvia Forbes, 1994

Sauce:

    1 c. sugar
    ½ T. butter
    1 heaping spoon flour
    1 c. water
    5–10 apples, peeled and halved
    Pie or biscuit dough, or canned uncooked biscuits

Add all sauce ingredients together in saucepan and cook till sauce thickens. Make pie or biscuit dough. Roll out and cut out in round 5" circles, or use premade uncooked canned biscuits from the store. Fill each circle with ½ apple, ½ t. sugar, and a dab of butter. Wrap apple in dough, seal edges, and place in cake pan. Pour sauce over dumplings. Bake at 350° until apples are tender. Serve hot or cold.

Irish Marmalade Bread Pudding

Angie Thompson Holtzhouser, *Drop Dumplin's and Pan-Fried Memories . . . along the Mississippi,* 1997. According to the author, Irish marmalade was a favorite Irish breakfast food. Her family recipe uses it to flavor a simple bread pudding.

    3½ c. sliced bread cubes
    2 T. melted butter
    3 eggs, lightly beaten
    ⅓ c. brown sugar, plus 1 T. for topping
    ½ c. Irish or other orange marmalade
    pinch of salt
    3 c. milk (skim or regular)

Preheat oven to 350 degrees.
1. Place the bread cubes in a mixing bowl.
2. Combine remaining ingredients (except 1 tablespoon of brown sugar for topping) and pour over the bread cubes. Stir to moisten. If bread is dry, let stand 15 minutes.

3. Pour pudding into a greased 2-quart soufflé dish. Sprinkle with remaining tablespoon of brown sugar. Bake 45–50 minutes, or until brown and knife inserted in center of pudding comes out clean. Yield: 4 servings

Kohleintopf (Cabbage Stew)

Augusta Historical Society, *German-Missouri Cookbook of "Duden Country,"* 1998. Missouri's German cooks, in order to save time and money, created "One Pot" (Eintopf) dishes.

> 4 lb. white cabbage
> 1 c. of tart apple cut up
> 4 onions
> 4 T. lard
> 1 T. vinegar
> A pinch each of sugar, pepper, paprika, caraway seeds, and salt
> 2 c. hot water
> 3 mealy potatoes

Remove outer leaves of cabbage and stem; divide into quarters and shred. Peel, core, and cut up apples. Sauté peeled and finely chopped onion in heated fat. Arrange alternating layers of cabbage and pieces of apple in a pot; pour over a mixture of vinegar, sugar, pepper, paprika, caraway, and salt; add water and steam covered for 20 min. Thicken the stew with the potatoes, peeled and grated, and simmer another 10 minutes.

Ozark Pudding

Bess Wallace Truman, *If You Can't Stand the Heat, Get out of the Kitchen,* vol. 2, Junior Service League, Independence, 1999. This is a popular recipe by Missouri's First Lady.

> 1 egg
> ¾ c. sugar
> 1 t. vanilla extract
> 2 T. flour
> ¼ t. baking powder
> 1/8 t. salt

½ c. chopped apples

½ c. chopped walnuts

Combine the egg and sugar in a mixer bowl. Beat until smooth. Add the vanilla and mix well. Sift the flour, baking powder and salt into a bowl. Add to the sugar mixture and mix well. Stir in the apples and walnuts. Spoon into a greased 8-inch-square baking pan. Bake at 350 degrees for 35 minutes. Yield: 9 servings

Mighty Mo Munchies Popeye Pesto

Missouri Soybean Merchandising Council, *The Best of Soy,* Jefferson City, 2001

3 c. spinach leaves, washed and stemmed

2 c. fresh basil leaves

1 c. soynuts, chopped

1 c. grated parmesan cheese

4 cloves garlic

¼ c. soy oil

Put spinach in container of food processor; briefly pulse. Add basil, soynuts, cheese, and garlic; pulse until ingredients are well mixed. Drizzle oil into the feeding tube with the processor running; process until ingredients are emulsified. Store in an airtight container in the refrigerator. Serve pesto on hot pasta or spread it on toasted French bread slices as an appetizer.

Almond Honey Dip

Rachel Nabors, 1994 MSBA Honey Queen, *Missouri Honey Recipes,* Missouri State Beekeepers Association, 2001

6 ounces cream cheese, softened

6 T. plain yogurt (or sour cream)

2 T. almond liqueur or ½ t. almond extract

3 to 5 T. honey

Cream the yogurt or sour cream with softened cream cheese. Add remaining ingredients, blending thoroughly. Serve with fresh fruit. Note: sour cream produces a thicker dip.

Pumpkin with Soup Inside

Pumpkin Festival Cookbook, Hartsburg

> 7–8 lb. pumpkin
> salt and pepper
> ½ c. minced carrots
> 4 c. beef broth
> ¼ c. rice
> bay leaf
> 3 T. chives
> 4 T. melted butter
> 1 c. minced leeks or onions
> ½ c. minced celery
> 1 c. chopped, peeled, seeded tomatoes
> 1 c. sour cream

Cut a lid from pumpkin, clean it out. Brush melted butter on pumpkin interior. Sprinkle pumpkin with salt and pepper. Replace lid and place pumpkin in a large pan. Bake for 20 minutes at 400 degrees. Meanwhile, sauté minced vegetables in 2 T. Butter 5–10 minutes. Add broth; heat to boiling point. Add tomatoes and season to taste. Place rice in pumpkin. Add boiling broth and vegetable mixture and float bay leaf on top. Cover and bake 45–60 minutes. Or until pumpkin is tender. Place on serving dish. To serve, ladle out the soup, scraping out a portion of pumpkin in each serving. Garnish with sour cream and chives.
[Yield 6–8 Servings].

Buffalo Chip Dip

Cooking with the American Buffalo, Missouri Bison Association, 2003

    2 lbs. ground buffalo meat
    1 onion, chopped
    1 (10.75-oz) can condensed cream of mushroom soup
    1 lb. processed cheese food, cubed
    1 (12-oz.) jar sliced jalapeño peppers, drained

Brown buffalo meat and onion until meat is no longer pink. Turn heat to medium-low. Pour in condensed cream of mushroom soup. Mix in processed cheese food and desired amount of jalapeño peppers. Cook and stir until all ingredients are well blended, about 10 minutes. Transfer the mixture to a medium bowl. Cover and chill in the refrigerator for 8 hours or overnight. Reheat the mixture in a slow cooker, mixing in about 1 tablespoon of water to thin, if necessary, before serving.

Blue Owl Stuffed Pepper Soup

Mary Hostetter, *A Celebration of Cooking 20 Years of Blessings,* The Blue Owl Restaurant and Bakery, Kimmswick, 2005

    1 lb. ground beef
    8 c. water
    4 c. tomato juice
    3 medium sweet red or green peppers, diced
    1½ c. chile sauce
    1 c. uncooked long grain rice
    2 celery ribs, diced
    1 large onion, diced
    2 T. Kitchen Bouquet browning sauce (optional)
    2 T. beef base
    2 garlic cloves, minced
    ½ t. salt

Cook ground beef until no longer pink. Drain. Add the remaining ingredients. Bring to a boil. Reduce heat. Simmer uncovered for one hour or until rice is tender. Yield: 12 servings.

Missouri Black Walnut and Bourbon Pie

Cooking with Black Walnuts, Hammons Pantry, Stockton, 2005

> 3 eggs
> 1¼ c. sugar, divided
> 4 T. cornstarch
> 5 T. bourbon
> 1 (9 in.) unbaked pie shell
> ½ c. butter, melted
> 1¼ c. Hammons Pantry black walnuts
> 1 (6 oz.) pkg. semi-sweet chocolate morsels

Beat eggs with ¾ cup sugar. Mix remaining ½ cup sugar with cornstarch and add to egg mixture. Fold in bourbon, butter, black walnuts and chocolate morsels. Pour filling into unbaked 9-inch pie shell. Bake in a preheated 375° oven for 15 minutes. Reduce oven temperature to 325° and bake 15 minutes or until filling is set and crust is golden.

Notes

Chapter 1 Cookbooks Come to Missouri

1. Robert G. Stone and David M. Hinkley, introduction to *Clark's Other Journal*.

2. Julia Clark, *Julia Clark Household Memoranda Book*.

3. Jerena East Giffen, "'Add a Pinch and a Lump': Missouri Women in the 1820s," 495, 497, 499.

4. Clark, *Household Memoranda Book;* Giffen, "Add a Pinch," 499; Clark, *Household Memoranda Book*.

5. City of St. Louis Community Information Network, "The History of O'Fallon," *http://stlouis.missouri.org/ofallon/history.htm*

6. Harriet O'Fallon, *Harriet O'Fallon's Cook Book*, 12, 14.

7. William E. Foley, *A History of Missouri*, vol. 1, *1673–1820*, 17, 23.

8. David D. March, *The History of Missouri*, 1:459.

9. Perry McCandless, *A History of Missouri*, vol. 2, *1820–1860*, 133.

10. G. K. Renner, "The Kansas City Meat Packing Industry before 1900," 19.

11. U.S. Bureau of Census, Population of the 100 Largest Urban Places 1870, Table 10 *http://www.census.gov/population/documentation/twps0027/tab10.txt*

12. Eleanor Lowenstein, *Bibliography of American Cookery Books 1742–1860*, 42, 114, 118.

13. Eleanor Brown and Bob Brown, *Culinary Americana*, 124.

Chapter 2 A Taste of Nineteenth-Century Publications

1. Ladies of St. Louis, *My Mother's Cook Book*, 17.

2. Ibid., 28.

3. Ibid., 184.

4. Ibid., preface, 184.

5. Ibid.

6. Mrs. Mary F. Henderson, preface to *Practical Cooking and Dinner Giving*.

7. Henderson, *Practical Cooking,* 14.

8. Ibid.

9. Ibid., 14, 15.

10. Ibid., 16.

11. "Why Mrs. John B. Henderson Offered Nation a Home for Vice-Presidents," *St. Louis Post-Dispatch,* Sunday section, 5.

12. Ibid., 5, 4.

13. Raymond P. Brandt, "Widow of Missouri Senator Rules Washington Diplomatic Society and Sells Her Houses," *St. Louis Post-Dispatch,* Sunday section.

14. "Why Mrs. John B. Henderson," 4.

15. Anne André Johnson, *Notable Women of St. Louis,* 58.

16. Ibid.

17. Ibid., 59.

18. Ibid.

19. Herbert M. Shelton, *Man's Pristine Way of Life,* chap. 52, *http://www.harvestfields.ca/HerbBooks/02/06/054.htm* (accessed Mar. 17, 2007).

20. Mrs. T. F. Willis and Mrs. W. S. Bird, eds., preface to *Housekeeping and Dinner Giving in Kansas City,* 7.

21. Ibid.

22. Ibid., 7–8.

23. Ibid., 8–9.

24. Ibid., 11–13.

25. Ibid., 13–14.

26. Ibid., 15–16.

27. Ibid., 16–17.

28. Ibid., 74.

29. Brown and Brown, *Culinary Americana,* 124.

30. *The Granite Iron Ware Cook Book,* 3.

31. Ibid., 5.

32. Ibid., 5–6.

33. Ibid., 45.

Chapter 3   Community Cookbooks

1. Ladies of the Union Avenue Christian Church, comp., preface to *Union Avenue Christian Church Cook Book.*

2. Ladies of the Fifth Presbyterian Church of Kansas City, comp., preface to *Choice and Tested Recipes.*

3. Woman's City Club, foreword to *Our Own Cook Book.*

4. *St. John's Evangelical Lutheran Church [Pocahontas, MO] Cook Book,* 2.

5. United Methodist Youth, comp., afterword to *Senath United Methodist Cookbook.*

6. Missouri Department of Natural Resources, "Elephant Rocks," *http:// www.dnr.mo.gov/pubs/pub683.pdf*

7. Russel L. Gerlach, *Settlement Patterns in Missouri: A Study of Population Origins,* 15–16.

8. William C. Hayes and Philip W. Guild, "Iron," in *Mineral and Water Resources of Missouri.*

9. David D. March, *The History of Missouri,* 1:611.

10. L. D. Fellows, "Granite and Felsite," in *Mineral and Water Resources of Missouri,* 157.

11. Ladies of the Baptist Church Campbell, *Campbell Cook Book,* 74.

12. Charter of Park College.

13. Ibid.

14. Carolyn McHenry Elwess, "George S. Park and Ella Park Lawrence," 5.

15. *Park College Record,* vol. 1, no. 3; vol. 8, no. 10; receipt, Park College Archives, Dec. 28, 1883.

16. Elwess, "George S. Park and Ella Park Lawrence," 11.

17. Principia Mothers' Club, comp., historical cover notes to *Kitchenology with Principia Friends,* collector's edition.

18. Principia, "100 Year Timeline," *http://www.prin.edu/about/history/ timeline.htm*

19. Bucklin R-II School Playground Committee, *Bucklin Alumni Cookbook,* preface, text (unpaginated).

20. MSTA Member Service Committee, introduction to *Schoolhouse Treats.*

21. Jewish Hospital Auxiliary, *Cooking in Clover,* introduction, foreword.

22. Albrecht-Kemper Museum of Art, *http://www.albrecht-kemper.org/ about.html*

23. Christopher Gordon, "Royal Booth and the Baby Chick Capital of the World," 192.

24. M. F. Miller, *A Century of Missouri Agriculture Bulletin,* 68.

25. Gordon, "Royal Booth," 192–203, 194.

26. Harter House Market Springfield, comp., introduction to *Harter House Cookbook.*

27. American Cancer Society Missouri Division, Inc., introduction to *The 1983 Show Me Missouri Four Seasons Cookbook.*

Chapter 4   A Serving of Ethnic Cookbooks

1. Augusta Historical Society, *German-Missouri Cookbook of "Duden Country,"* 1.

2. Ibid.

3. Ibid., 2, 3.

4. Ibid., 14, 32, 54, 72.

5. Senior Citizens of Freistatt, comp., *Authentic German Recipes, Old Time Remedies, and Historical Sketches of Freistatt,* 1.

6. Ibid., 2, 3.

7. Ibid., 10.

8. Ibid., 12–13.

9. Mary Harrison, ed., *The Art of Hermann-German Cooking,* introduction, 57.

10. Novinger Planned Progress, Inc., comp., *Ethnic Cookbook,* 7.

11. Ibid., 137.

12. Eleanore Berra Marfisi, *The Hill: Its History—Its Recipes,* 98.

13. Sue Hall, personal communication, Feb. 27, 2007.

14. Josephine Lawrence and Members of the Pennytown Freewill Baptist Church, comp., introduction to *Sharing Recipes: A Book of Favorite Recipes.*

15. Karen Grace, "Faith and Money: The Pennytown Project," *Preservation Issues, http://www.umsl.edu/~libweb/blackstudies/faith.htm*

16. Lawrence, introduction to *Sharing Recipes.*

17. Ibid., 45.

18. Shaare Zedek Sisterhood St. Louis, comp., introduction to *From Matzo Balls to Metrics: A Collection of Old and New Kosher Recipes.*

19. The Woman's Touch, B'nai Amoona Sisterhood, comp., introduction to *From Generation to Generation: B'nai Amoona Sisterhood Cookbook.*

20. Temple B'nai Jehudah, *Memories Good Enough to Eat,* 13.

21. Ibid., 14–15.

22. International Institute of St. Louis, "About Us—Introduction," *http://www.iistl.org*

23. International Institute of St. Louis, "Home—About Us—History," *http://www.iistl.org*

24. Harriette F. Ryan, foreword to *Foreign Cookery.*

Chapter 5 Missouri Cookbooks Record History

1. McDonald County Extension Council, comp., introduction to *McDonald County Native Foods Cookbook.*

2. Ibid., 1.

3. Ibid., 1–3.

4. Jean Mowrer, interview with the author, Apr. 19, 2006.

5. Ibid.

6. Ibid.

7. Duane Crawford, "Cooperation Made Calf Sales a Success," 11.

8. Missouri State University, "Hulston Mill History," *http://missouristate. edu/rls/hulston/hulhistory.htm*

9. Dade County Historical Society, comp., introduction to *Grandma's "Receets" from Missouri's Ozarks.*

10. Missouri State University, "Hulston Mill History."

11. Dade County Historical Society, *Grandma's "Receets,"* 10.

12. Ibid., 40, 46, 47.

13. *Albert E. Brumley's All-Day Singin' and Dinner on the Ground,* 2–3.

14. Ibid., 32, 34, 33.

15. Ibid.

16. Leon Howell, *Jesse James Cookbook,* 5.

17. Ibid., 7–8, 10, 9.

18. City of St. Joseph, "St. Joseph History—Jesse James," *http://www.ci. st-joseph.mo.us*

19. Ibid.

20. Junior Service League of Independence, front matter to *"If You Can't Stand the Heat, Get Out of the Kitchen!"*

21. Ibid., 24, 43, 44.

22. Ibid., 7, 23, 128.

23. Junior Service League of Independence, *The Bess Collection,* 5, 9.

24. Ibid., 9, 10.

25. Kurt W. Jefferson, "A Celebration of Churchill, the 'Iron Curtain' Speech, and Democracy," 6.

26. St. Louis Friends of the Winston Churchill Memorial and Library, *The Cookery Book,* 2nd division page, introduction.

27. Jefferson, "Celebration of Churchill," 3.

28. Don F. Pealer, comp., *The Old Tavern Book of Recipes,* 5.

29. Ibid., 9.

30. Ibid., 11.

31. Ibid.

32. Ibid., 12.

33. Jerena East Giffen, introduction to *Missouri Sesquicentennial Cook Book,* 6.

34. Ibid., 7.

35. Ibid., 342.

36. Ibid., 185.

37. Ibid.

38. Carolyn Reid Bond, ed., *Past and Repast,* 5.

39. Ibid., 11, 13, 21.

40. Ibid., 21, 22–23.

41. Ibid., 24–25, 28–29, 33–35.

42. Ibid., 41, 42–45.

43. Ibid., 47–48, and inside cover.

44. Introduction to *Odessa Centennial Edition Cookbook.*

45. Ibid.

46. Ibid.

47. William E. Foley, introduction to *Missouri History on the Table: 250 Years of Good Cooking and Good Eating,* edited by Jean Rissover.

48. Jean Rissover, ed., preface to *Missouri History on the Table.*

49. Ibid.

50. Rissover, *History on the Table,* 90.

51. Ibid., 98.

52. Ibid., 39.

53. Ibid., 15, 49, 22.

54. Rissover, preface to *History on the Table.*

Chapter 6   Individually Authored and Edited Cookbooks

1. George Herbert Walker, introduction to *The Ideal Bartender,* by Thomas Bullock.

2. Thomas Bullock, *The Ideal Bartender,* 3.

3. Ibid., 4.

4. Ibid., 15.

5. Irma S. Rombauer, *The Joy of Cooking,* 191.

6. St. Louis Walk of Fame, "Irma Rombauer," *http://www.stlouiswalkoffame. org/inductees/irma-rombauer.html*

7. Nils Larsen, introduction to *Rhythm in Foods: A Harmony between Fine Cooking and Scientific Food Values,* by Lamora Sauvinet Gary.

8. Max Lief, foreword to *The Missouri Traveler Cookbook* by Mary Hosford.

9. Mary Hosford, *The Missouri Traveler Cookbook,* 12.

10. Ibid., 63–64.

11. Ibid., 168–169.

12. Marian Maeve O'Brian, *The Bible Cookbook,* 11.

13. Werner O. Nagel, comp., *Cy Littlebee's Guide to Cooking Fish and Game,* 7, 13.

14. Ibid., 15, 31.

15. Ella Mae Tucker, *Dear Daughter Cookbook,* introduction, 25.

16. Beta Sigma Phi, "History of Beta Sigma Phi," *http://www.betasigmaphi. org/history.shtm*

17. Pauline Evans Pullen, introduction to *The Missouri Sampler: A Collection of Favorite Recipes from All Counties.*

18. Eula Mae Stratton, *Ozarks Cookery: A Collection of Pioneer Recipes,* introduction, afterword.

19. Ibid., 78.

20. Cherie Blanton, *A Little Fur in the Meringue Never Really Hurts the Filling,* 111.

21. Barbara Gibbs Ostmann, introduction to *The Best Recipes Cookbook.*

22. Charlie Knote and Ruthie Knote, *Barbecuing and Sausage-Making Secrets,* introduction, 91.

23. W. J. Walkley, introduction to *Grandma's Pie Pantry Cookbook.*

24. Angie Thompson Holtzhouser, *Drop Dumplin's and Pan-Fried Memories . . . along the Mississippi,* 35.

25. Laura Ingalls Wilder, introduction to *The Laura Ingalls Wilder Country Cookbook.*

26. Ibid.

27. Ibid.

28. Gwen McKee and Barbara Moseley, preface to *Best of the Best from Missouri: Selected Recipes from Missouri's Favorite Cookbooks.*

Chapter 7 Producer and Festival Cookbooks

1. Jay Gibb, "Public Markets in Old St. Louis," *http://stlouis.missouri.org/citygov/soulardmarket/oldmark.html*

2. Jay Gibb, "Welcome to Soulard: A Thumbnail Sketch," *http://stlouis.missouri.org/soulard/*

3. Suzanne Corbett, introduction to *Pushcarts and Stalls: The Soulard Market History Cookbook.*

4. City of Campbell, "Campbell the Peach Capitol of Missouri," *http://www.campbellmo.com/peach.html*

5. Ibid.

6. Jean Hamacher, introduction to *Mushroom Cookbook: Millennium Mushroom Festival—2000.*

7. *Pumpkin Festival Cookbook,* 1.

8. Ibid., 9.

9. University of Missouri, "Missouri Apple History," *http://horticulture.missouri.edu/apple/history.htm*

10. Sylvia Forbes, *The Fayette Apple Festival Cookbook,* 5.

11. Miller, *Century of Missouri Agriculture,* 54.

12. Missouri Corn Growers Association, "Missouri Corn Facts," *http://www.mocorn.org/facts.htm*

13. Miller, *Century of Missouri Agriculture,* 54.

14. Introduction to *The Best of Soy*.

15. Missouri State Beekeeper Association, *Missouri Honey Recipes*, 3, 4–5.

16. Missouri Beef Industry Council, "Producers," *http://www.mobeef.com*

17. Missouri Pork Association, "The Daily Pork," *http://www.otherwhite meat.com/aspx/recipes/*

18. Ibid.

19. Missouri Bison Association, *Cooking with American Buffalo*, 2.

20. Ibid.

21. Ibid., 3, 4, 5.

22. Ibid., 7.

Chapter 8   Company/Product Cookbooks

1. *Aristos Flour Cook Book*, 4.

2. Introduction to *Town Crier Ready Mixed Flour Recipes*, 2.

3. David A. Lossos, trans., "Statistical Facts about St. Louis in 1925," *http:// genealogyinstlouis.accessgenealogy.com/1925statistics.htm*

4. Culver-Stockton College, "Mary Culver and Robert Stockton," *http:// www.culver.edu/aboutcsc/history/*

5. *Majestic Range Cook Book*, 8–9.

6. Ibid., 10.

7. Ibid.

8. Culver-Stockton, "Mary Culver and Robert Stockton."

9. "Magic Chef," Wikipedia, 2007; *Answers.com*, Feb. 28, 2007, *http:// www.answers.com/topic/magic-chef*

10. Dorothy E. Shank, preface to *Magic Chef Cooking*.

11. *Home Comfort Cook Book*, 3.

12. Ibid., 4, 7, 8–9.

13. "The Rival Company," Encyclopedia of Company Histories, Answers Corporation, 2006, *http://www.answers.com/topic/the-rival-company*

14. *Crock-Pot Slow Electric Stoneware Cooker Cookbook*, cover, 46.

15. Theodore R. Gamble, *Seventy-Five Years of Pet Milk Company (1885–1960)*, 8, 9, 10.

16. Ibid., 10–11, 16–17.

17. *Pet Recipes*, 2–3; J. M. Smucker Company, "Pet Milk History," *http:// www.petmilk.com*

18. Built St. Louis, "The Beauty of Modernism," *http://www.builtstlouis. net/mod/mod18.html*

19. Urban St. Louis, "Pointe 400 Updates," *www.urbanstlouis.com/petbuilding. html*

20. Eagle Family Foods, Inc., "The Milnot Company History," personal communication, *www.milnotmilk.com*

21. Ibid.

22. Ibid.

23. *Tested and Tasted Recipes*, 3.

24. Hammons Products Company, *The Black Walnut People*, np.

25. Ibid.

26. Ott Food Products LLC, "Ott's History," *https://www.ottfoods.com/history.html*

27. G. T. Hamel, *Modern Practice of Canning Meats*, 100.

28. Ibid., introduction.

29. Ibid.

30. Ibid., 66.

31. Burgers' Smokehouse, "Burgers' Company and Family History," *www.smokehouse.com*

32. The California Chamber of Commerce, "Area Attractions: 'Burgers' Smokehouse' and 'Ozark Ham and Turkey Festival,'" *http://www.calmo.com/AreaAttractions.asp*

33. Wicker's Food Products, "Wicker's: The Great American Barbecue Sauce from the Little Missouri Town," *http://web.inetba.com/wickers/aboutus.ivnu*

34. Ibid.

35. Shifra Stein and Rich Davis, *All about Bar-B-Q Kansas City Style*, 11, 184.

36. Ibid.

37. Stone Hill Winery, "The History of Stone Hill Winery," *http://www.stonehillwinery.com/ourWinery/default.aspx*

38. Stone Hill Winery, "Wine 101—Recipes," *http://www.stonehillwinery.com/wine101/recipesintro.aspx*

39. St. James Winery, "Winery in the Ozark Highlands . . . ," *http://stjameswinery.com/winery.htm*

40. Ibid.

41. Missouri 4-H Foundation, *The Never Ending Season: The Cookbook of Missouri*, 19.

42. Ibid., 11, 13, 43, 40.

43. Ibid., 192.

Chapter 9 Cookbooks from Restaurants Past and Present

1. Dana Gatlin, *Unity's Fifty Golden Years*, 37.

2. Eric Page, Unity Library and Archives, personal communication, Mar. 27, 2006.

3. "From Our Archives: Unity and Vegeterianism," *Restoration News,* np.

4. Royal Fillmore, "The Unity Inn," *Weekly Unity* (Feb. 3, 1915): 1.

5. Ibid.

6. *Voice of Unity* (Oct 1, 1966): 5.

7. Virginia McDonald, *How I Cook It,* 17, 14, 15, 16.

8. Ibid., 10–11.

9. Duncan Hines, introduction to *How I Cook It* by Virginia McDonald.

10. Ibid.

11. Mary Hostetter, introduction to *A Celebration of Cooking.*

12. Wade Rouse, "The Matriarch of Kimmswick," 4.

13. Hostetter, personal communication; introduction to *A Celebration of Cooking.*

14. Hostetter, personal communication.

15. Ibid.

16. Ibid.

17. Elizabeth Arneson, "Bed and Breakfasts," *http://bandb.about.com/mbiopage.htm*

18. Bed and Breakfast Inns of Missouri, *Sunrise Inn Missouri,* 11, 34, 36.

19. Patricia Shell, introduction to *Teatime Friendships at Patricia's.*

20. Ibid.; Lady Patricia's Tea Room, "Gathering Places at Lady Patricia's," *http://www.morestaurants.org/hall_fame.php*

21. Missouri Restaurant Association, "Food Service Hall of Fame," *http://www.morestaurants.org/hall;fame.php*

22. Florence Hulling Apted, introduction to *Miss Hulling's Own Cook Book.*

23. "Ivy Awards," Restaurants and Institutions, *http://www.rimag.com/awards-events/ivy/winners-all.asp*

24. Les Stephenson and Loyd Stephenson, *Stephenson's Apple Farm Restaurant Receipts,* back cover.

25. Ibid.

26. Stephenson, introduction to *Restaurant Receipts.*

Chapter 10   World Events and Politics in Missouri Cookbooks

1. St. Louis Convention and Visitors Commission, "Louisiana Purchase Exposition," *http://www.explorestlouis.com/media/factsheets/fact_worldsFair.asp*

2. Ibid.

3. Ibid.

4. Pamela J. Vaccaro, *Beyond the Ice Cream Cone,* 31.

5. Mrs. S. T. Rorer, preface to *World's Fair Souvenir Cook Book.*

6. Ibid., 137, 138.

7. Ibid., 171.

8. Vaccaro, *Beyond the Ice Cream Cone,* 74, 76, 104.

9. Mrs. Nellie Duling Gans, introduction to *A Book for a Cook.*

10. Ida Clyde Clarke, *American Women and the World War,* http://www.lib.byu.edu/~rdh/wwi/comment/Clarke/Clarke00TC.htm (accessed Mar. 17, 2007) and *http://www.lib.byu.edu/~rdh/wwi/comment/Clarke/Clarke02.htm* (accessed Mar. 17, 2007).

11. Ibid.

12. Ibid., *http://www.lib.byu.edu/estu/wwi/comment/Clarke/Clarke22.htm* (accessed Feb. 27, 2007)

13. Introduction to *Patriotic Food Show Official Recipe Book.*

14. Ibid., 3.

15. Ibid.

16. Ibid., 6.

17. Ibid., 17.

18. Ibid., 20.

19. Ibid.

20. Lorraine Livingston, comp., foreword to *Approved Enduring Favorites.*

21. Carol Habgood, "Women's Overseas Service League," personal communication *http://www.wosl.org/contact.htm*

22. Women's Overseas Service League, "A Brief History: What Is WOSL?" *http://www.wosl.org/history.htm*

23. Ibid.

24. "Recipes from Dorothy Stuart's Mayrose Test Kitchen."

25. "Ration Chart for Meat Cuts," St. Louis: Laclede Gas Light Company.

26. *How to Bake by the Ration Book,* 2.

27. Introduction to *National Nutrition Edition Kerr Home Canning Book.*

28. *The Victory Handbook,* foreword, 33, 35.

29. Carolyn Bond, afterword to *A Taste of Missouri: Bond Family Favorites.*

30. Sally Danforth, *Sally Danforth's Cookbook*

Chapter 11   Kitchen Medicine, Housekeeping Tips, and Cookbook Literature

1. Martha M. Williams, *The Capitol Cook Book,* 274.

2. Clark, *Household Memoranda Book.*

3. O'Fallon, *Cook Book,* np.

4. Ladies of St. Louis, *Mother's Cook Book,* 217–19.

5. Ibid., 220.

6. Ladies of the Baptist Church, *Campbell Cook Book,* 70–71.

7. Senior Citizens, comp., *Authentic German Recipes Old Time Remedies Historical Sketches of Freistatt,* 63–67.

8. Mrs. T. F. Willis and Mrs. W. S. Bird, eds., *Housekeeping and Dinner Giving in Kansas City,* 220–224.

9. *Dr. W. H. Bull's Herbs and Iron 1904* [almanac], np.

10. Ibid.

11. Ibid.

12. Rockview Methodist Church, *Your Household Guide,* 3–6.

13. Ibid., 9–10.

14. Women's Progressive Farmers' Association, *Pure Food Cook Book,* 182–83.

15. Ladies of Union Avenue Christian Church, *Cook Book,* 103.

16. Ladies of St. Louis, *Mother's Cook Book,* 227.

17. Dorothy Reese, *Centennial Cookbook,* np.

18. *Jaunita Kitchen Guide,* 236.

19. Women's Progressive, *Pure Food,* 182.

20. Rockview Methodist Church, *Your Household Guide,* 21–25.

21. Women's Progressive, *Pure Food,* 179.

22. Ibid., 180–82.

23. Ibid., 180–81.

24. Ladies of St. Louis, *Mother's Cook Book,* 229–230, 233.

25. Ladies of Union Avenue Christian Church, *Cook Book,* 100, 101.

26. Ibid., 177–178.

27. Reese, *Centennial Cookbook,* 118.

28. Women's Progressive, *Pure Food,* 110.

29. Helen Richardson Mission Band of the Lafayette Park M.E. Church, South, comp., *The Kitchen Oracle,* 91–92.

30. Order of Eastern Star, *"The Best Cooking" in Grandin,* 24–25.

31. Ladies of Union Avenue Christian Church, *Cook Book,* 105.

32. Hebrew Ladies' Aid Society, introduction to *The Joplin Cook Book.*

33. St. Louis Second Presbyterian Church Young Woman's Guild, *Cook Book,* 9.

34. Miss Grace L. Lawrence and the Geo. H. Nettleton Home Association, *The Nettleton Cook Book,* 63.

35. St. Paul's Episcopal Church, introduction to *Clinton Cook Book.*

36. Ladies of the Methodist Episcopal Church, *The Columbia Cook Book.*

37. Reese, *Centennial Cookbook,* 120.

Bibliography

Albert E. Brumley's All-Day Singin' and Dinner on the Ground. Camdenton: Albert E. Brumley & Sons, 1972.

American Cancer Society Missouri Division, Inc. *The 1983 Show Me Missouri Four Seasons Cookbook.* Memphis: Wimmer Brothers Books, 1983.

Apted, Florence Hulling. *Miss Hulling's Own Cook Book.* St. Louis, 1962.

Aristos Flour Cook Book. Kansas City: The Southwestern Milling Company, 1911.

Augusta Historical Society. *German-Missouri Cookbook of "Duden Country."* Augusta: Friends of Historic Augusta, 2nd ed, 1998.

Beckner, Kathy, comp. *Home Cookin' Apple Recipes from Missouri Apple Growers.* Olathe, KS: Cookbook Publishers, Inc., 1990.

Bed and Breakfast Inns of Missouri. *Be Our Guest: Cooking with Missouri's Innkeepers.* St. Louis: Benita Crook, Creative Connections, 1991.

Bed and Breakfast Inns of Missouri. *Sunrise Inn Missouri.* Woodruff, WI: The Guest Cottage, Inc., 2002.

Beecher, Catharine E. *Miss Beecher's Domestic Receipt Book.* Mineola, N.Y.: Dover Publications, Inc., 2001. Reprint of 3rd edition originally printed in 1858 with introduction by Janice(Jan) Bluestein Longone.

Black Walnut People, The. Stockton: Hammons Products Company, nd.

Blanton, Cherie. *A Little Fur in the Meringue Never Really Hurts the Filling.* Memphis: Wimmer Brothers Books, 1979.

Bond, Carolyn. *A Taste of Missouri: Bond Family Favorites.* Jefferson City: Missourians for Kit Bond, 1986.

Bond, Carolyn Reid, ed. *Past and Repast.* Jefferson City: Missouri Mansion Preservation, Inc., 1984.

Bucklin R-II School Playground Committee, comp. *Bucklin Alumni Cookbook.* 1999.

Buege, Sandy. *Recipes from Missouri...with love.* Chanhassen, MN: New Boundary Designs, Inc., 1986.

Bullock, Tom. *The Ideal Bartender.* St. Louis: Buxton Printing and Stationery Co., 1917. *Feeding America. http://digital.lib.msu.edu/projects/cookbooks.* Also available in print.

Business and Professional Women's Club. *Peach Recipes from the Peach Capital of Missouri*. Campbell: Campbell Business and Professional Women's Club, 1975.

Calvary Episcopal Church Ladies. *The Capitol Cook Book*. Sedalia: Sedalia Printing, 1896.

Carter, Susannah. *The Frugal Housewife, or, Complete Woman Cook*. New York: G. and R. Waite, 1803. *Feeding America*. http://digital.lib.msu.edu/projects/cookbooks

Children's Hospital Auxiliary. *St. Louis Souvenirs*. Saint Louis: Adrian Typography, Inc., and Repco Printers and Lithographers, Inc., 1985.

Child, Lydia Maria. *The American Frugal Housewife*. Mineola, NJ: Dover Publications, Inc., 1999. with an introduction by Janice (Jan) Bluestein Longone. A reprint of the 29th edition originally printed in 1844 as *The Frugal Housewife* and changed to *The American Frugal Housewife* in the 8th edition.

Clark, Ida Clyde. *American Women and the World War*. New York: D. Appleton and Company, 1918. http://net.lib.byu.edu/~rdh7/wwi/comment/Clarke/Clarke00TC.htm Also available in print.

Clark, Julia. *Julia Clark Household Memoranda Book*. Clark Family Papers (Voorhis Collection), 1820, Missouri Historical Society Archives, St. Louis.

Community Action Agency. *Missouri Ozarks Commodity Cookbook*. np: nd.

Cooking with Black Walnuts. Stockton: Hammons Pantry, 2005. Jumbo Jack's Cookbooks, Audubon, IA

Corbett, Suzanne. *Pushcarts and Stalls The Soulard Market History Cookbook*. St. Louis: Palmerston & Reed Publishing Company, 1999.

Corson, Juliet. *The Cooking Manual*. New York: Dodd, Mead & Company, 1877.

Dade County Historical Society, comp. *Grandma's "Receets" from Missouri's Ozarks*. Greenfield: Vadette Printing Company, 1987.

Danforth, Sally. *Sally Danforth's Cookbook*. nd.

Dodds, Susanna W. *Health in the Household: Hygienic Cookery*. New York: Fowler & Wells Co., Publishers, 1886.

Dr. W. W. Bull's Herbs and Iron 1904. St. Louis: Stewart Scott Pressroom, 1904.

Eagle Family Foods Inc. "The Milnot Company History." *www.milnotmilk.com* personal communication.

Faithful Workers of the Presbyterian Church, comp. Caruthersville. *The Twentieth Century Cook Book*. Perryville: Cashion & Cashion, Printers, 1902.

Farmer, Fannie. *Fannie Merritt Farmer Original 1896 Boston Cooking—School Cook Book*. Mineola, NY: Dover Publication, Inc., 1997. A reprint of the 1896 edition.

Favorites from Farmland. np: nd.

Fellows, L. D. "Granite and Felsite," in *Mineral and Water Resources of Missouri*, Vol. XLIII, pp 157–164. Washington: USGPO, 1967.

Foley, William E. *A History of Missouri Vol. 1 1673–1820*. Columbia: University of Missouri Press, 1999.

Forbes, Sylvia. *The Fayette Apple Festival Cookbook*. Fayette: Sylvia Forbes, 1994.

Foreign Cookery. St. Louis: International Institute, 1932. 2nd revised.

Gamble, Theodore. *Seventy-five Years of Pet Milk Company (1885–1960)*. New York: The Newcomen Society in North America, 1960.

Gans, Mrs. Nellie Duling. *A Book for a Cook*. Minneapolis: Pillsbury, 1905.

Gans, Mrs. Nellie Duling. *A Little Book for a Little Cook*. Minneapolis: Pillsbury, 1905. Old Saybrook, CT: Applewood Books, The Globe Pequot Press, 1994. A facsimile reprint.

Gary, Lamora Sauvinet. *Rhythm in Foods: A Harmony between Fine Cooking and Scientific Food Values*. Kansas City, 1943. 2nd edition.

Gatlin, Dana. *Unity's Fifty Golden Years*. Kansas City: Unity School of Christianity, 1939. Material used by permission of Unity, *www.unityonline.org* and Unity Archives.

Gerlach, Russel L. *Settlement Patterns in Missouri: A Study of Population Origins*. Columbia: University of Missouri Press, 1986.

Glasse, Mrs. *The Art of Cookery Made Plain and Easy*. Bedford, MA: Applewood Books, 1997. Reprint of 1805 edition with introduction by Karen Hess.

The Granite Iron Ware Cook Book. St. Louis: St. Louis Stamping Co., 1896. Probable previous edition dating1878 i.e. testimonials in the 1896 (96th ed).

Hale, Sarah Josepha. *Early American Cookery: "The Good Housekeeper," 1841*. Mineola, N.Y.: Dover Publications, 1996. Reprint of 1841 edition with introduction by Janice Bluestein Longone.

Hamacher, Jean. *Mushroom Cookbook: Millennium Mushroom Festival—2000*. Richmond: Richmond Chamber of Commerce, 2000.

Hamel, G. T. *Modern Practice of Canning Meats*. St. Louis: The Brecht Company, 1911.

Hammons Pantry. *Cooking with Black Walnuts*. Stockton: Hammons Pantry, Printed by Jumbo Jack's Cookbooks, Audubon, LA, 2005 (1st printing 1993).

Hammons Products Company. *The Black Walnut People*. Stockton: Hammons Products Company.

Harland, Marion. *Common Sense in the Household: A Manual of Practical Housewifery*. Birmingham: Oxmoor House, Inc., 1985. Reprint of 1871 edition.

Harrison, Mary, ed. *The Art of Hermann-German Cooking*. Hermann: Historic Hermann, Inc. nd.

Harter House Market Springfield, comp. *Harter House Cookbook.* Kearney, NE: Morris Press Cookbooks, 2002.

Hayes, William C., and Philip W. Guild. "Iron," in *Mineral and Water Resources of Missouri,* Vol. XLIII, pp 74–88. Washington: USGPO, 1967.

Hebrew Ladies' Aid Society Joplin, comp. *The Joplin Cook Book.* Joplin: Joplin Printing Co., 1912.

Helen Richardson Mission Band of the Lafayette Park M.E. Church, South, comp. *The Kitchen Oracle.* St. Louis: F. H. Hesse Printing Co., 1899.

Henderson, Mrs. Mary F. *Practical Cooking and Dinner Giving.* New York: Harper & Brothers, Publishers, 1877.

Hillsboro P.T.A, comp. *Town and Country Cookie Book.* Hillsboro: Tri-State Printers, 1953.

Holtzhouser, Angie Thompson. *Drop Dumplin's and Pan-Fried Memories . . . along the Mississippi.* Memphis: Toof Cookbook Division, 1997.

Home Comfort Cook Book. St. Louis: Wrought Iron Range Co., 1952.

Hosford, Mary. *The Missouri Traveler Cookbook.* New York: Farrar, Straus and Cudahy, Inc., 1958. Foreword by Max Lief.

Hostetter, Mary. *A Celebration of Cooking 20 Years of Blessings.* Kimmswick: 2005. Illustrations by Cindy Aderman.

Howell, Leon. *Jesse James Cookbook.* Kansas City: Creative Cooking, 1975.

How to Bake by the Ration Book. General Foods Corporation, 1943.

How to Have Good Health and Make Good Candy. St. Louis: Wolff-Wilson Drug Co.:nd.

Hummel, Miss Elizabeth. *Menus from Abroad.* St. Louis: International Institute, 1927.

Jewish Hospital Auxiliary. *Cooking in Clover.* St. Louis: Universal Printing, 1977.

Johnson, Anne André (Mrs. Chas. P. Johnson). *Notable Women of St. Louis.* 1914.

Juanita Kitchen Guide. Sikeston: The Scott County Milling Company, 1934 The Bunting Publications, Inc. North Chicago.

Junior League of St. Joseph. *Palette to Palate.* St. Joseph: John W. Oxley & Sons, 1987.

Junior League of Kansas City. *Company's Coming Foods for Entertaining.* Kansas City: Junior League of Kansas City, 1975.

Junior League of Springfield. *Sassafras! The Ozarks Cookbook.* Springfield: S.C.Toof & Company, 1989.

Junior League of St. Joseph. *The Roux We Do.* Memphis: Wimmer Cookbooks, 2001.

Junior League of St Louis. *Meet Us in the Kitchen.* Memphis: Wimmer Cookbooks, 2000.

Junior League of St. Louis. *Saint Louis Days . . . Saint Louis Nights.* Memphis: Wimmer Cookbooks, 1994.

Junior League of Springfield. *Women Who Can Dish It Out: The Lighter Side of the Ozarks.* Memphis: Wimmer, 1998.

Junior Service League of Independence. *"If You Can't Stand the Heat, Get Out of the Kitchen!" Volume II.* Nashville: Favorite Recipes, 1999.

Junior Service League of Independence. *The Bess Collection.* Kansas City: Courtney Business Systems Kansas City, 1993.

The Kitchen Directory. St. Louis: Keith & Woods, 1858.

Knote, Charlie, and Ruthie Knote. *Barbecuing and Sausage-Making Secrets.* Cape Girardeau: The Culinary Institute of Smoke Cooking, 1992.

Knox Country Promotional Council Edina. *Knox County Corn Fest Second Annual Cookbook.* Leawood, Kansas: Circulation Service, 1988.

Ladies' Aid Society of the First Baptist Church, comp. Ironton. *Arcadia Valley Cook Book,* new and 3rd revised ed. Kansas City, The Western Bap. Pub. Co., 1920.

Ladies of the Circle of the Methodist Church Chaffee, comp. *Chaffee Cook Book.* 1926.

Ladies of the Baptist Church Campbell, comp. *Campbell Cook Book.* Campbell: Campbell Citizen Shop, [1910?].

Ladies of the Baptist Church Knob Noster. *Favorite Recipes.* Knob Noster: Gem Print, 1897.

Ladies of the Fifth Presbyterian Church of Kansas City, comp. *Choice and Tested Recipes.* Kansas City: Press of Standard Printing Company [1905/06?].

Ladies of the Methodist Episcopal Church, South, Columbia, comp. *The Columbia Cook Book.* Columbia: Press of E.W. Stephens, 1901.

Ladies of St. Louis, comp. *My Mother's Cookbook.* St. Louis: Hugh R. Hildreth Printing Company, 1880. 2nd edition/printing.

Ladies of the Union Avenue Christian Church, comp. *Union Avenue Christian Church Cook Book.* St. Louis: Christian Publishing Company, 1910.

Lawrence, Josephine, and Members of the Pennytown Freewill Baptist Church. *Sharing Recipes: A Book of Favorite Recipes.* Leawood, KS: Circulation Service, Inc., 1993.

Lawrence, Miss Grace L., and Geo. H. Nettleton Home Association Kansas City, comp. *The Nettleton Cook Book.* Kansas City: The Little Craft and Stationary Shop, Out West in Kansas City, 1909.

Leslie, Eliza. *Seventy-Five Receipts for Pastry, Cakes, and Sweetmeats.* Bedford, MA: Applewood Books, 1993. Reprint of the 1828 edition, Boston: Munroe & Francis.

Lessons in Cooking for the District Schools. St. Louis: St. Louis Public Schools, 1909

Lincoln, Mrs. D. A. *Boston Cooking School Cook Book.* Mineola, NY: Dover Publications Inc., 1996. A reprint of the 1884 edition.

Livingston, Lorraine, comp. *Approved Enduring Favorites*. St. Louis: St. Louis, MO. Unit, Women's Overseas Service League, 1932.

Majestic Range Cook Book. Majestic Manufacturing Company, St. Louis, nd.

March, David D. *The History of Missouri*. Vols. 1 and 2. New York: Lewis Historical Publishing Co., 1967.

Marfisi, Eleanore Berra. *The Hill: Its History—Its Recipes*. St. Louis: G. Bradley Publishing,Inc., 2003.

Martha Mary Circle of Belleview Methodist Church, comp. *Favorite Recipes*. Leawood, KS: Circulation Service, 1986.

Mayes, Dianne Stafford, and Dorothy Davenport Stafford. *It's Christmas*. Memphis: The Wimmer Companies, Inc., 1994.

McCandless, Perry. *A History of Missouri Vol 2 1820–1860*. Columbia: University of Missouri Press, 2000.

McDonald County Extension Council, comp. *McDonald County Native Foods Cookbook*. Pineville: The McDonald County Homemakers Council, 1969.

McDonald, Virginia. *How I Cook It,* Kansas City: Frank Glenn Publishing Co., Inc.,1949. Ed. by Eleanor Richey Johnston, printed by E.W.Stephens Co. Columbia. Introduction by Duncan Hines.

McKee, Gwen, and Barbara Moseley. *Best of the Best from Missouri: Selected Recipes from Missouri's Favorite Cookbooks*. Brandon, MS: Quail Ridge Press, 2001.

Menus and Recipes from Abroad. St. Louis: International Institute, 1927.

Miller, M. F. *A Century of Missouri Agriculture Bulletin* 701. Columbia: University of Missouri Agricultural Experiment Station, 1958.

Miriam Circle. *Favorite Recipes*. Kansas City: Ascension Lutheran Church, 1978.

McKee, Gwen, and Barbara Moseley, eds. *Best of the Best from Missouri: Selected Recipes from Missouri's Favorite Cookbooks*. Brandon, MS: Quail Ridge Press, 1992.

Missouri Bison Association, The. *Cooking with American Buffalo*. Kearney, NE: Morris Press Cookbooks, 2003.

Missouri 4-H Foundation. *The Never Ending Season: The Cookbook of Missouri*. Dallas: Missouri 4-H Foundation in association with Leisure Time Publishing, 1990.

Missouri Soybean Merchandising Council. *The Best of Soy*. Jefferson City: Missouri Soybean Merchandising Council, 2001.

Missouri State Beekeeper Association. *Missouri Honey Recipes*. Kearney, NE: Morris Press, 2001.

Missouri Sesquicentennial Cook Book. Jefferson City: The First State Capitol Restoration and Sesquicentennial Commission. Kansas City, MO: North American Press of Kansas City, Inc. 1971.

Moss, Maria. *A Poetical Cook-Book.* Philadelphia: Caxton Press of C. Sherman, Son & Co., 1864.

MSTA Member Service Committee. *Schoolhouse Treats.* MSTA, comp. Collierville, TN: Fundcraft, 2003.

Nagel, Werner O., comp. *Cy Littlebee's Guide to Cooking Fish and Game.* Missouri Conservation Commission, 1964.

National Nutrition Edition Kerr Home Canning Book. Sand Springs, OK: Kerr Glass Manufacturing Corp., 1943.

Novinger Planned Progress, Inc., comp. *Ethnic Cookbook.* Novinger: Novinger Planned Progress, Inc. Iowa Falls, IA: General Publishing and Binding, 1989.

O'Brien, Marian Maeve. *The Bible Cookbook.* St. Louis: The Bethany Press, 1958.

Odessa Area Centennial Inc. *Odessa Centennial Edition Cookbook.* Kansas City: North American Press of Kansas City Inc., 1978.

O'Fallon, Harriet. *Harriet O'Fallon's Cook Book.* John O'Fallon Collection, in Missouri Historical Society, St. Louis, 1821.

Order of Eastern Star. *"The Best Cooking" in Grandin.* Grandin: np, nd.

Ostmann, Barbara Gibbs, ed. *The Best Recipes Cookbook.* St. Louis: *St. Louis Post-Dispatch,* 1983.

Our Favorite Recipes. St. James: St. James Winery, nd.

Park, George S., and Ella Park. *Industrial Lessons* or *Park College Cook Book.* Parkville, MO: Park College, 1880 [published in 1883].

Parloa, Maria. *Miss Parloa's New Cook Book and Marketing Guide.* Boston: Estes and Lauriat, 1880.

Patriotic Food Show Official Recipe Book. St. Louis: Women's Central Committee on Food Conservation, 1918. Reprint edition, Louis Szathmary, ed. *Cookery Americana.* New York: Arno Press Inc., 1973.

Pealer, Don F., comp. *The Old Tavern Book of Recipes.* Arrow Rock: Arrow Rock Chapter of the Missouri Society Daughters of the American Revolution, 1927.

Pet Recipes. St. Louis: Pet Milk Company, 1930.

Presbyterian Church Ladies' Aid Society Cape Girardeau, comp. *A Household Guide.* Jefferson City: Tribune Ptg. Co., 1904.

Principia Mothers' Club, comp. *Kitchenology with Principia Friends.* St. Louis: Clark- Sprague, Inc., 1980. Collector's Edition. 1st printing 1933.

Principia Mothers' and Dads' Club St. Louis, comp. *Cooking with Principia.* Kearney, NE: Morris Press Cookbooks, 2003.

Pullen, Pauline Evans. *The Missouri Sampler: A Collection of Favorite Recipes from All Counties.* Springfield, Springfield: Mrs. Pauline E. Pullen, 1971.

Pumpkin Festival Cookbook. Hartsburg: nd. Introductory history written by Nancy Grant with Marjorie and Carl Thomas, and Henry Klemme.

Quick Meal Cook Book: A Collection of the Latest Tried Recipes. St. Louis: Ringen Stove Company, nd .

Raffald, Elizabeth. *The Experienced English Housekeeper.* East Sussex, England: Southover Press, 1997. Reprint of 1769 edition with introduction by Roy Shipperbottom.

Randolph, Mrs. Mary. *The Virginia Housewife or Methodical Cook.* New York: Dover Publications, Inc., 1993. Reprint of 1860 edition with introduction by Janice Bluestein Longone.

Recipes for Today. New York: General Foods Corporation, 1943.

Reese, Dorothy. *Centennial Cook Book: Tried and Tested Recipes of the Past Century.* Ironton, 1957.

Rissover, Jean, ed. *Missouri History on the Table: 250 Years of Good Cooking and Good Eating.* Ste. Genevieve: Ste. Genevieve 250th Celebration Commission,1985.

Rival Crock-Pot Cookbook. Kansas City: Rival Manufacturing Co., nd.

Rival Crock-Pot Cooking. Kansas City: Rival Manufacturing, 1975. Golden Press, New York.

Rival Crock-Pot Slow Electric Stoneware Cooker Cookbook. Kansas City: Rival Manufacturing, 1971.

Rockview Methodist Church, The. *Your Household Guide.* Marceline, MO: Walsworth Bros., 1951.

Rombauer, Irma S. *A Cookbook for Girls and Boys.* Indianapolis: The Bobbs-Merrill Company, 1946. 2nd ed. 1952.

Rombauer, Irma S. *The Joy of Cooking.* St. Louis: A. C. Clayton Printing Co., 1931.

_____ *The Joy of Cooking.* Indianapolis: The Bobbs-Merrill Company, 1936.

_____ *The Joy of Cooking.* Indianapolis: The Bobbs-Merrill Company, 1946.

Rorer, Sarah Tyson. *Mrs. Rorer's New Cook Book.* Philadelphia: Arnold and Company, 1902.

Rorer, Mrs. S. T. *World's Fair Souvenir Cook Book.* Philadelphia, PA: Arnold and Company, 1904. Reprint by Donald G. Uetrecht and Lin V. Uetrecht, Independence Publishing Corporation, St. Louis, 2003.

Ross, Dorothy. *Dorothy Ross' Cookbook.* Kansas City: Walter W. Ross and Co., Inc, 1969.

Ryan, Harriette F. *Foreign Cookery.* St. Louis: International Institute, 1932.

Sando, Shirleen. *Beyond Low-Fat Baking: Cancer Fighting Foods for the Millennium.* Dallas: Skyward Publishing, Inc., 2000.

Senior Citizens of Freistatt, comp. *Authentic German Recipes, Old Time Remedies, Historical Sketches of Freistatt.* Freistatt: Hal Schimke Litho, 1981.

Shaare Zedek Sisterhood St. Louis, comp. *From Matzo Balls to Metrics: A Collection of Old and New Kosher Recipes*. Lenexa, KS: Cookbook Publishers, 1976.

Shank, Dorothy E. *Lorain Cooking*. The American Stove Company, St. Louis. 1930. Printed Kingsport Press, Kingsport, Tennessee. 8th edition (1st edition 1924).

Shank, Dorothy. *Magic Chef Cooking*. St. Louis: American Stove Company, 1936. Printed by Kingsport Press, Inc. Kingsport, Tennessee, 16th edition (1st edition 1924).

Shell, Patricia. *Teatime Friendships at Patricia's*. Morris Press Cook Books, 2000.

Shelton, Herbert M. *Natural Hygeine: Man's Pristine Way of Life*. San Antonio, TX: Dr. Sheldon's Health School, 1968. "Women and Health," Chapter 52. Soil and Health.org *http://www.harvestfields.ca/HerbBooks/02/06/054.htm* Also available in print.

Silvernail, Lulu Thompson. *Nine Hundred Successful Recipes*. Kansas City: "S. & H. Cook Book," 1923.

Simmons, Amelia. *American Cookery*. Bedford, MA: Applewood Books, 1996. Reprint of 1796 second edition with introduction by Karen Hess.

Smith, Eliza. *The Compleat Housewife: or Accomplish'd Gentlewoman's Companion*. London: Literary Services and Production Ltd., 1973. Reprint of 1753 edition.

Stein, Shifra, and Rich Davis. *All About Bar-B-Q Kansas City Style*. Kansas City: Barbacoa Press, 1985.

Stephenson, Les and Loyd. *Stephenson's Apple Farm Restaurant Receipts*. Kansas City: Stephenson's Apple Farm Restaurant, 1973.

St. John's Evangelical Lutheran Church Cook Book [Pocahontas] Iowa Falls, IA: General Publishing and Binding, 1977.

St. Louis Friends of the Winston Churchill Memorial and Library. *The Cookery Book*. St. Louis: Wetterau Printing, 1977.

St. Louis Public Schools, *Outline of Lessons in Cooking for the District Schools*. 1909.

St. Louis Second Presbyterian Church Young Woman's Guild, comp. *Cook Book*. Saint Louis: Model Printing Company, [1922?].

Stone, Robert G. and David M. Hinkley. *Clark's Other Journal*. Lee's Summit, MO: The Fat Little Pudding Boys Press, 1995. Material printed as found in the 1820 *Julia Clark Household and Memoranda Book*. Foreword and introduction by the authors.

St. Paul's Episcopal Church. *Clinton Cook Book*. Clinton: Lingle & Lingle, 1898.

St. Paul's Lutheran Ladies Aid Society New Melle, comp. *St. Paul's Country Recipes*. Collierville, TN: Fundcraft Publishing, 1996.

Stratton, Eula Mae. *Ozarks Cookery: A Collection of Pioneer Recipes.* Forsythe, MO: The Ozarks Mountaineer, 1992 (1st printing 1976). 2nd printing

Temple B'nai Jehudah, comp. *Memories Good Enough to Eat.* Kansas City: nd

Tested and Tasted Recipes. np: Milnot, nd.

Tucker, Ella Mae. *Dear Daughter Cookbook.* Walnut Grove, MO: c 1965 (20th printing).

Town Crier Ready Mixed Flour Recipes. Kansas City: Town Crier Food Products Inc., nd.

United Methodist Youth, comp. *Senath United Methodist Cookbook.* Senath: Dunklin County Press, 1981.

United Methodist Church Women Unionville. *Favorite Recipes.* Iowa Falls, IA: General Publishing and Binding, 1975.

United Methodist Church Women Unionville. *Favorite Recipes II.* Collierville, TN: Fund Craft Publishing, 2000.

Unity School of Christianity. *Unity Inn Vegetarian Cook Book.* Kansas City: Unity School of Christianity, 1923.

Vaccaro, Pamela J. *Beyond the Ice Cream Cone.* St. Louis: Enid Press, 2004.

Victory Handbook, The. Kirkwood, MO: nd. Compiled by an unnamed Kirkwood organization.

Walkley, W. J. *Grandma's Pie Pantry Cookbook.* Olathe, KS: Cookbook Publishers, Inc., 1992.

Wilder, Laura Ingalls. *The Laura Ingalls Wilder Country Cookbook.* Mansfield: Laura Ingalls Wilder Home Association, 2003 (printed in Hong Kong by Terrell Creative) New Edition.

Williams, Martha M. *The Capitol Cook Book.* Monroe City: Frank L. Link, 1895.

Williams, Walter, and Floyd C. Shoemaker. *Missouri: Mother of the West.* Vol 2. Chicago: The American Historical Society, Inc. 1930.

Willis, Mrs. T. F., and Mrs. W. S. Bird, eds. *Housekeeping and Dinner Giving in Kansas City.* Kansas City: Press of Ramsey, Millett & Hudson, 1887.

Woman's City Club. *Our Own Cook Book.* Kansas City: Press of Spencer Printing Company, 1920.

Woman's Touch, The, B'nai Amoona Sisterhood, comp. *From Generation to Generation: B'nai Amoona Sisterhood Cookbook.* St. Louis: 1971.

Women of St. Paul's Episcopal Church, comp. *Clinton Cook Book.* Clinton: Lingle & Lingle, Printers, 1898.

Women's Club of Ste. Genevieve. *Recipes of Old Ste. Genevieve.* Ste. Genevieve: Ste. Genevieve Women's Club, 1997 (eighth printing). 1st printing 1959

Women's Progressive Farmers' Association, comp. *Pure Food Cook Book.* St. Joseph: Nelson-Hanne Printing Company, 1923.

Web Sites

Albrecht-Kemper Museum of Art. *http://www.albrecht-kemper.org/about.html* (accessed March 17, 2007).

Arneson, Elizabeth. "Bed and Breakfasts." *http://bandb.about.com/mbiopage.htm* (accessed March 17, 2007).

Beta Sigma Phi. "History of Beta Sigma Phi." *http://www.betasigmaphi.org/ history.shtm* (accessed March 17, 2007).

Bullock, Tom. Online Biography: *Feeding America The Historic American Cookbook Project.* http://digital.lib.msu.edu/projects/cookbooks/html/authors/ author_bullock.html (accessed March 17, 2007).

Built St. Louis. "The Beauty of Modernism." *http://www.builtstlouis.net/mod/ mod18.html* (accessed March 17, 2007).

Burgers' Smokehouse. "Burgers' Company and Family History." *www. smokehouse.com* (accessed March 17, 2007).

California Chamber of Commerce. "Area Attractions: 'Burgers' Smokehouse' and 'Missouri Ozark Ham & Turkey Festival.'" *http://www.calmo.com/ AreaAttractions.asp* (accessed March 17, 2007).

City of Campbell. "Campbell the Peach Capital of Missouri." *http://www.campbellmo.com/peach.html* (accessed March 17, 2007).

City of St. Joseph. "St. Joseph History—Jesse James." *http://www.stjoemo.info/ history/jessejames.cfm* (accessed March 17, 2007).

City of St. Louis Home Page. "Welcome to Soulard: A Thumbnail Sketch." *http://stlouis.missouri.org/soulard/* (accessed March 17, 2007).

City of St. Louis Community Information Network. "The History of O'Fallon." *http://stlouis.missouri.org/ofallon/history.htm* (accessed March 17, 2007).

Culver-Stockton College. "Mary Culver and Robert Stockton." *http://www. culver.edu/aboutcsc/history/* (accessed March 17, 2007).

Farmland Foods. "Recipe Box." *http://www.farmlandfoods.com/recipes/* (accessed March 17, 2007).

Gibb, Jay. "Public Markets in Old St. Louis." *http://stlouis.missouri.org/ citygov/soulardmarket/oldmark.html* (accessed March 17, 2007).

Gibb, Jay, "Welcome to Soulard: A Thumbnail Sketch." *http://stlouis.missouri. org/soulard/* (accessed March 17, 2007).

Grace, Karen. "Faith and Money: The Pennytown Project." *Preservation Issues,* Vol. 4 No 1 *http://www.umsl.edu/~libweb/blackstudies/faith.htm* (accessed March 17, 2007).

Habgood, Carol. "Women's Overseas Service League." *http://www.wosl.org/ contact.htm* personal contact. (accessed March 17, 2007)

International Institute St. Louis. "About Us—Introduction." *http://www. iistl.org/about* (accessed March 17, 2007).

International Institute of St. Louis, "Home—About Us—History." *http://www.iistl.org* (accessed March 17, 2007).

J.M. Smucker Company. "Pet Milk History." *http://www.petmilk.com* (accessed March 17, 2007).

Lossos, David A., trans. "Statistical Facts about St. Louis in 1925." *http://genealogyinstlouis.accessgenealogy.com/1925statistics.htm* (accessed March 17, 2007).

"Magic Chef." *Answers.com*, Feb. 28, 2007. *http://www.answers.com/topic/magic-chef* (accessed March 17, 2007).

Missouri Beef Industry Council. "Producers." *http://www.mobeef.org* (accessed March 17, 2007).

Missouri Corn Growers Association. "Missouri Corn Facts." *http://www.mocorn.org/facts.htm* (accessed March 17, 2007).

Missouri Department of Natural Resources. "Elephant Rocks." *http://www.dnr.mo.gov/pubs/pub683.pdf* (accessed March 17, 2007).

Missouri Pork Association. "The Daily Pork Recipe Finder." *http://www.otherwhitemeat.com/aspx/recipes/* (accessed March 17, 2007).

Missouri Restaurant Association. "Food Service Hall of Fame." *http://www.morestaurants.org/hall_fame.php* (accessed July16, 2007)

Missouri State University. "Hulston Mill History." *http://www.missouristate.edu/rls/hulston/hulhistory.htm* (accessed March 17, 2007).

Ott Food Products LLC. "Ott's History." *https://www.ottfoods.com/history.html* (accessed March 17, 2007).

Pet Milk Building *http://www.builtstlouis.net/mod/mod18.html* (accessed March 17, 2007).

Principia. "100-Year Timeline" *http://www.prin.edu/about/history/timeline.htm* (accessed March 17, 2007).

Restaurants and Institutions. "Ivy Awards." *http://www.rimag.com/awards-events/ivy/winners-all.asp* (accessed July 16, 2007)

The Rival Company. Answers.com.Encyclopedia of Company Histories, Answers Corporation,2006. *http://www.answers.com/topic/the-rival-company* (accessed March 17, 2007).

Soulard Market History *http://stlouis.missouri.org/citygov/soulardmarket/oldmark.html* (accessed March 17, 2007).

St. James Winery. "Winery in the Ozark Highlands . . ." *http://stjameswinery.com/winery.htm* (accessed March 17, 2007).

St. Louis Convention and Visitors Commission. "Louisiana Purchase Exposition (1904 World's Fair)." *http://www.explorestlouis.com/media/factsheets/fact_worldsfair.asp* (accessed March 17, 2007).

"St. Louis Walk of Fame Irma Rombauer." *http://www.stlouiswalkoffame.org/inductees/irma-rombauer.html* (accessed March 17, 2007).

Stone Hill Winery. "The History of Stone Hill Winery." *http://www.stonehill winery.com/ourWinery/default.aspx* (accessed March 17, 2007).

Stone Hill Winery. "Wine 101—Recipes." *http://www.stonehillwinery.com/ wine101/recipesintro.aspx* (accessed March 17, 2007).

University of Missouri. "Missouri Apple History." *http://horticulture.missouri. edu/apple/history.htm* (accessed March 17, 2007).

Urban St. Louis. "Pointe 400 Updates." *www.urbanstlouis.com/petbuilding.html* (accessed March 17, 2007).

U.S. Bureau of the Census. *Population of the 100 Largest Urban Places: 1870 Table 10 http://www.census.gov/population/documentation/twps0027/tab10.txt* (accessed March 17, 2007).

Wicker Food Products. "Wicker's: The Great American Barbecue Sauce from the Little Missouri Town." *http://web.inetba.com/wickers/aboutus.ivnu* (accessed March 17, 2007).

Women's Overseas Service League. "A Brief History: What Is WOSL?" *http://www.wosl.org/history.htm* (accessed March 17, 2007).

Newspapers, Articles, Journals, and Documents

Brandt, Raymond P. "Widow of Missouri Senator Rules Washington Diplomatic Society and Sells Her Houses." *St. Louis Post-Dispatch,* April 26, 1925. Sunday Section. 23–34

Charter of Park College. June 21, 1879. Historical materials courtesy of Fishburn Archives, Park University, Parkville, Missouri, Carolyn McHenry Elwess, '71, Archivist.

Crawford, Duane. "Cooperation Made Calf Sales a Success." *The Unionville Republican,* May 9, 2001, p 10–11.

Elwess, Carolyn McHenry. "George S. Park and Ella Park Lawrence." Unpublished biographical compilation dated February, 2006. Historical materials courtesy of Fishburn Archives, Park University, Parkville, Missouri, Carolyn McHenry Elwess, '71, Archivist.

Fillmore, Royal. "The Unity Inn." *Weekly Unity* vol. 6, no. 40 (Feb. 3, 1915): 1–2. Material used by permission of Unity, *www.unityonline.org* and Unity Archives.

"From Our Archives, Unity & Vegetarianism." *Restoration News,* vol 2 no 4, (Spring 1995). Material used by permission of Unity, *www.unityonline.org* and Unity Archives.

Giffen, Jerena East. "'Add a Pinch and a Lump': Missouri Women in the 1820s." *Missouri Historical Review* vol 65 no 4, July 1971, 478–504.

Gordon, Christopher. "Royal Booth and the Baby Chick Capital of the World." *Missouri Historical Review,* vol 97 no 32 (April 2003): 192–203.

Jefferson, Kurt W. "A Celebration of Churchill, the 'Iron Curtain' Speech, and Democracy." *Memo,* Summer 2006, Special Commemorative Edition, 6

Page, Eric. Letter, March 26, 2006 (archivist and reference librarian), Unity Library and Archives.

Park College Record. Vol 8 no10 (August 9, 1883). Historical materials courtesy of Fishburn Archives, Park University, Parkville, Missouri. Carolyn McHenry Elwess,'71, Archivist.

Park College Record. Vol 1 no 3 (1879). Historical materials courtesy of Fishburn Archives, Park University, Parkville, Missouri. Carolyn McHenry Elwess,'71, Archivist.

Renner, G. K. "The Kansas City Meat Packing Industry before 1900." *Missouri Historical Review,* Vol 55 no 1 (October 1960), 18–29.

"Receipt," Park College Archives, December 28, 1883. Historical materials courtesy of Fishburn Archives, Park University, Parkville, Missouri. Carolyn McHenry Elwess,'71, Archivist.

Rouse, Wade. "The Matriarch of Kimmswick." *Class Notes, The Alumnae and Alumni Newsletter of Mary Institute and Saint Louis County Day School,* Vol 13 no 1 (Winter/Spring 2005), 4–5.

"Voice of Unity," October 1, 1966. Materials used by permission of Unity, *www.unityonline.org* and Unity Archives.

"Why Mrs. John B. Henderson Offered Nation a Home for Vice-Presidents." *St. Louis Post-Dispatch.* February 14, 1923. Sunday Edition, 4–5.

Collections Consulted

Clark Collection: Missouri Historical Society

John O'Fallon Collection: Missouri Historical Society

Cookbook Bibliographies

Bitting, Katherine Golden. *Gastronomic Bibliography.* San Francisco: 1939. Reprint by Martino Fine Books, Mansfield Centre, CT.

Brown, Eleanor, and Bob Brown. *Culinary Americana.* New York: Roving Eye Press, 1961.

Cagle, William R., and Lisa Killion Stafford. *American Books on Food & Drink .* New Castle, DE: Oak Knoll Press, 1998.

Cook, Margaret. *America's Charitable Cooks: A Bibliography of Fund-Raising Cook Books Published in the United States (1861–1915).* Kent, OH: Margaret Cook, 1971.

Lowenstein, Eleanor. *Bibliography of American Cookery Books 1742–1860.* New York: American Antiquarian Society, 1972. 3rd edition.

How to Identify and Locate Missouri Cookbooks

The search for Missouri cookbooks involves not only identifying the collections in which they're held but also finding the collections. The Internet is an excellent place to start. Collections of cookbooks that include Missouri publications may be found at the state's historical societies and at Missouri's academic and public libraries. Cookbooks at historical societies, unlike most found at university and public libraries, are primarily viewed in-house, and rare cookbooks may be restricted to in-house reading no matter where they are housed.

Publications discussed in this project are in a variety of locations with a significant number included in the author's private collection and others borrowed from or viewed at the state's libraries and historical societies. Rare editions, such as Clark's and O'Fallon manuscript cookbooks, may be accessed at the Missouri Historical Society in St. Louis. A quick search for "Missouri cookery" in the society's online catalog nets numerous cookbooks.

The State Historical Society of Missouri in Columbia houses a collection of nineteenth- and twentieth-century community and individually authored Missouri cookbooks. Late-nineteenth- and early-twentieth-century publications are listed in their card catalog. Later publications may be located by using Merlin, the University of Missouri's online catalog. The society's Web site has county-by-county contact information of local historical societies and museums in the state, allowing researchers looking for books from a specific area to easily find and contact these organizations.

The Internet has become a valuable tool for exploring the pool of Missouri cookbooks. Not only can it be used to identify where Missouri cookbooks are available in academic and public repositories, it can also lead cookbook enthusiasts to dealers stateside or abroad as well as give them access to distant lending libraries. MOBIUS is a consortium of sixty academic libraries and two cooperating partners in Missouri. Through its Common Library Platform, more than eighteen million items are available. Material requested is delivered to local libraries for patron use through the MOBIUS delivery system. World Cat, a consortium with a much larger scope, allows an individual to search collections in thousands of libraries worldwide via a personal or public Internet connection. With both of these systems, local member libraries process patron requests, and items are both shipped to and returned to local libraries. Although these services are free, patrons are required to pay a nominal postage fee determined by each library.

Individuals desiring to purchase cookbooks over the Internet benefit from online book search engines such as AddAll, AbeBooks, Alibris, and Book-Finder.com, which search for new, used, out-of-print, and rare books through a network of booksellers.

Notable cookbook bibliographies listed previously provide assistance in identifying and in some cases locating cookbooks. For those interested in expanding their cookbook knowledge beyond Missouri, Lowenstein's work lists early American cookbooks starting with the first cookbook printed in America. Mid-nineteenth-century entries in this work document cookbook publishing in St. Louis. Bitting's extensive work lists approximately six thousand gastronomic works from various parts of the world from the fifteenth through the twentieth centuries (up to the book's publication in 1939). The introduction to the Cagle and Stafford project which catalogs the cookbook collection housed in the Lilly Library at Indiana University lists the rare, privately printed first edition of Irma Rombauer's *The Joy of Cooking* as one of the famous cookbooks in that collection.

Two additional easy-to-use bibliographies aid those interested in cookbooks. The Browns and Cook organize their lists chronologically by state. Both projects include specifically American cookbooks. While *Culinary Americana* by the Browns includes a variety of types of cookbooks, Cook concentrates on fundraising cookbooks published between 1861 and 1915. She lists cookbooks by state and then by city or town and also indicates the library or historical society where they can be viewed.

Index

1904 World's Fair, 153
1983 Show Me Missouri Four Seasons Cookbook, 50–51

A. and G. Dodds Granite and Stone Company, 19
A. J. Sheahan Granite Company, 32
Advertising, in cookbooks, 24–25, 27, 32, 34–38, 46–47
African American history, in Missouri, 80
Albert E. Brumley's All-Day Singin' and Dinner on the Ground, 72–73
Albrecht Gallery, 46
Albrecht-Kemper Museum of Art, 46
Allen, Dorothy Conquest, 86
America's Charitable Cooks, 28
American cookbook development, 3, 4
American Cookery, 3
American Frugal Housewife, The, 4
American Poultry Association, 48
American Royal Barbecue Contest, 135
American Stove Company, 122
American Women and the World War, 156–57
Anderson, William, 102–3
Andrews, Margee, 86
Appert, Nicholas, 126
Apple history, 110–11
Approved Enduring Favorites, 161
Apted, Florence Hulling, 149–50
Arcadia, 33
Arcadia Valley, 32
Arcadia Valley Cook Book, 32, 33
Aristos Flour Cook Book, 119–21
Arneson, Elizabeth, 147
Arrow Rock, 77–79

Arrow Rock Inn, 94
Art of Cookery Made Plain and Easy, The, 3
Art of Hermann German Cooking, The, 57
Asher, Arnold, 62
Atchison, David Rice, 80
Augusta, 53, 136
Augusta Historical Society, 53
Aunt Nan of the Ozarks, 98
Authentic German Recipes: Old Time Remedies and Historical Sketches of Freistatt, 55–57, 167
Autogastronomy, 94

Baby Chick Capital, 49
Barbecuing, 133–36
Barbecuing and Sausage-Making Secrets, 100
Bar-B-Q Kansas City Style, 135
Be Our Guest, 147–48
Becker, Edgar, 91
Becker, Ethan, 91
Becker, Marion Rombauer, 91
Beckner, Kathy, 111
Bed and breakfast, 147–48
Beecher, Catharine, 4
Beef production, 115
Belleview, 33
Belleview Valley, 32, 33
Berra, Lawrence "Yogi," 59
Bess Collection, The, 75
Best Cooking in Grandin, The, 46–47, 175
Best of Soy, The, 113–14
Best of the Best from Missouri: Selected Recipes from Missouri's Favorite Cookbooks, 103–4

Best Yet Cookbook, The (Fayette First Christian Church), 111
Beta Sigma Phi, 97
Bettlach, Jerry, 50
Beyond Low-Fat Baking, 101–2
Beyond the Ice Cream Cone: The Whole Scoop on Food at the 1904 World's Fair, 154
Bible Cookbook, The, 95
Biebel, Lorraine, 50
Biggs, J. Paul, 77–79
Bingham, George C., 79
Bird, Mrs. W. S., 20, 167
Bison (buffalo) production, 116
Blackstone, T. B., 84
Blanton, Cherie, 98–99
Blue Owl Restaurant and Bakery, 144–47
Bolduc House, 53
Bollinger Mill, 79
Bond, Carolyn, 81, 83, 163–64
Bond, Kit, 83, 163–64
Bonnots Mill, 148
Book for a Cook, A, 156
Book of Favorite Recipes, A, 32
Boone, "Blind," 80
Boone, Daniel, 100
Boone's Lick Country, 132
Boonville, 148
Booth Hatchery and Farms, 49
Booth, Royal, 49
Borden, Gail, 126
Braille cookbook, 125
Brainerd, Dorothy, 99
"Break-through" sculpture, 77
Brown, B. Gratz, 81–82
Brown, Bob, 25
Brown, Eleanor, 25
Brown, John S., 32
Brown, Mary, 81
Brown, Molly, 100
Bryan, William Jennings, 153
Buck, Jack, 59
Bucklin Alumni Cookbook, 43–44
Buege, Sandy, 99
Bullock, Thomas, 88–90
Bumbry, Grace, 80
Burfordsville Covered Bridge, 79
Burger, E. M., 132

Burgers' Smokehouse, 132
Burnham, B. P., 138
Bush, Benjamin F., 157
Bush, George Herbert Walker, 88
Bush, George Walker, 88
Bush, Mrs. Benjamin F., 157
Butchering, 55–56

California, 132
Campbell, 107–8
Campbell Cook Book, 34, 166–67
Canary, Martha, 99
Canning and preserving, 13, 68, 160–62
Capitol Cookbook, The, 165
Carter, Susannah, 3
Carthage, 129
Carver, George Washington, 113
Celebration of Cooking: Twenty Years of Blessings, A, 144
Centennial Cookbook, 33, 174, 178
Center for Advancement of the American Black Walnut, 129
Chaffee Cook Book, 31
Child, Lydia Maria, 4
Choice and Tested Recipes, 29–30
Chouteau, Auguste, 8
Christian, Spencer, 101
Christian Scientists, 43
Christian University, 122
Church and social life, 30–31
Church cookbook organization, 31–39
Church of St. Mary, Aldermanbury, 76
Church, Harry, 140–42
Churches and social life, 30
Churchill, Sir Winston, 75–77
Claiborne, Craig, 134
Clark, Ida Clyde, 156–57
Clark, Julia Hancock, 5, 6–7
Clark, William, 5–6
Clark's Other Journal, 5
Clay, William L., 80
Clinton, 49
Clinton Cook Book, 177
Clothing and fashion, 5
Columbia, 86, 177
Columbia Cook Book, 177
Committee on Women's Defense Work, 156

Common Sense in the Household, 4
Community cookbooks: first of, 4; characteristics and growth of, 29; and societal changes, 51
Company's Coming: Foods for Entertaining, 46
Complete Housewife, The, 3
Cook, Margaret, 28
Cookbook publishing companies, 39
Cookery Book, The, 76
Cooking in Clover, 45
Cooking school cookbooks, 4
Cooking with Black Walnuts, 128
Cooking with Principia, 42–43
Cooking with the American Buffalo, 116–18
Cooperative Extension Service, 138
Corbett, Suzanne, 107
Corn clubs, 138
Corn Fests, 113
Corn history, 111, 113
Corson, Juliet, 4
Council of National Defense, 156
Country Song Writers Association, 72
Cox's Corner, 148–49
Crock-Pot Cooking, 125
Culver, L. L., 120, 122
Culver, Mary, 122
Culver-Stockton College, 122
Cured hams, 132
Cy Littlebee's Guide to Cooking Fish and Game, 95–96

Dade County Historical Society, 71
Dade County Home Guard, 70
Dallas, George, 80
Dalton, John M., 83
Danforth, Jack, 164
Danforth, Sally, 164
Daniel, Walter C., 80
Dauphine Hotel Bed and Breakfast, 148
Davis, Rich, 135
Dear Daughter Cookbook, 96–97
Deen, Bobbie, 145–46
Deen, Jamie, 145–46
Deen, Paula, 147
Dexter, 148–49
Diamond Grove, 113

Dinner-on-the-ground, 72–73
Disney, Walt, 100
Dodds, Andrew, 19
Dodds, Mary, 19, 20
Dodds, Susanna W., 19–20
Dodds' Hygeian Home, 19
Domestic Receipt Book, The, 4
Domestic science classrooms, 65
Doniphan, Alexander, 99
Dorothy Ross Cookbook, 97
Dr. W. H. Bull's Golden Eye Salve, 170
Dr. W. H. Bull's Herbs and Iron 1904, 168–70
Drop Dumplin's and Pan-Fried Memories . . . along the Mississippi, 101
Duden, Gottfried, 53–54
Duden country, 54
Dunklin, Daniel, 79
Dunklin, Emily, 79
Dutchess of Bedford, 149
Dutzow, 53

Eads Bridge, 10, 33
Eagle Family Foods, 127
Early farming, 105
Eastern American black walnut, 128
Edison, Thomas, 153
Eisenhower, Mary, 77
Elephant Rocks, 32
Elwess, Carolyn, 42
Emberson, R. H., 138
Engelbreit, Mary, 125
Ethel, 148
Ethnic Cookbook (Novinger), 57–58
Experienced English Housekeeper, The, 3

Farmer, Fannie, 4
Farmers' markets, 105–7
Farmers and Merchants Watermelon Festival, 134
Farmland Foods, 132
Favorite Recipes (Ascension Lutheran Church, K.C.), 33
Favorite Recipes (Unionville), 39, 69
Favorite Recipes II (Unionville), 39
Favorites from Farmland, 132
Fayette Apple Festival Cookbook, 111, 112
Fayette Methodist Cook Book, 111

Felix and Odille Pratte Vallé House, 53
Femme Osage, 54
Ferdinand Rozier House, 53
Festival of Nations, 63
Fillmore, Charles, 140
Fillmore, Myrtle, 140
Fillmore, Royal, 140–41
First American cookbook, 3
First Ladies of Missouri, 79
First state capitol, 81
First State Capitol Restoration and
    Sesquicentennial Commission, 79
Foley, William E., 84
Food Service Hall of Fame, 149–51
Forbes, Sylvia, 111
Ford, Robert, 73
Fordland, 148
Foreign Cookery, 63–64
Forrest Keeling Nursery, 129
Fort Davidson, 33
Fredericktown, 33
Freel, Sam, 108
Freistatt, 55–57
*From Generation to Generation: B'nai
    Amoona Sisterhood Cookbook,* 62
*From Matzo Balls to Metrics: A Collection
    of Old and New Kosher Recipes,* 52, 62
Frona, 86
Frugal Housewife, The, 3
Fulton, 75
Fund-raising cookbook project
    organization, 31–39

Gaines, Lloyd, 80
Gallatin Tea Room, 142–43
Gamble, Theodore R., 126
Gans, Nellie Duling, 156
Garagiola, Joe, 59
Gardening tips, 171
Gardner, Jeanette Vosburgh, 82
Gary, Lamora Sauvinet, 93
Gatlin, Dana, 140
Gee, David A., 45
Geo. H. Nettleton Home Association,
    177
*German-Missouri Cookbook of "Duden
    Country,"* 53–55
Gibb, Jay, 106

Gideon, Gene, 72–73
Giffen, Jerena East, 6, 7, 79
Glasse, Hannah, 3, 8
Good Housekeeper, The, 4
Good Morning America, 101
Gospel Music Association, 72
Government food assistance programs,
    66
Grace, Karen, 60
Grand Duke Alexis of Russia, 82
*Grandma's "Receets" from Missouri's
    Ozarks,* 71–72
Grandma's Pie Pantry Cookbook, 100–101
Granite Iron Ware Cook Book, The, 10, 25,
    26
Graniteville, 33
Grant, Nancy, 109
Grape and Wine Advisory Board, 136
Grape and wine industry, 136–38
Great Flood, 145
Great Majestic Range Cook Book, The,
    120–22
Great Sanitary Fair (Philadelphia), 4, 28
Green hunting, 68
Green Tree Tavern, 53
Green Valley Methodist Church, 60
Gregory, Dick, 80
Grennan, Adelaide, 19
Gristmills, 70–71

Habgood, Carol, 161
Hale, Sara Josepha, 4
Hall, Sue, 60
Hamacher, Jean, 109
Hamel, G. T., 130–32
Hammons, Brian, 128
Hammons, Ralph, 128
Hammons Pantry, 128
Hammons Products Company, 128–29
Handy, W. C., 80
Hardin, Mary Barr, 82
Harland, Marion, 4
Harriet O'Fallon Cook Book, 8, 166
Harter House Cookbook, 50
Hartsburg, 109
Hatcheries, 48–49
Hauser, Charles, 127
Haynes, Eugene, 80

Health and nutrition, 19–20, 93, 94, 100–102, 110, 113–14, 128–29, 142

Health in the Household: or Hygienic Cookery, 19, 20

Hearnes, Warren, 83

Held, Betty, 136–37

Held, Jim, 136–37

Helvetia Milk Condensing Company, 126

Henderson, John B., 18

Henderson, Mary Foote, 14–19

Hermann, 54, 57, 136

Highland Brand Condensed Milk, 126

Hill: Its History, Its Recipes, The, 58–59

Hill, The, 58–59

Hillcrest Cooking School, 87

Hillsboro, 43

Himes, Chester, 80

Hines, Duncan, 143–44

Hinkley, David, 5

Historic cooking contest, 84–87

Hixenbaugh, Ardella, 66

Hofherr, Andrew, 137

Hofherr, Jim, 137

Hofherr, John, 137

Hofherr, Patricia, 137

Hog production, 114–15

Holder, Sandra, 148

Holder, Scott, 148

Holmes, R. C., 79

Holtzhouser, Angie Thompson, 101

Home Comfort Cook Book, 119, 124

Home Comfort Range, 124

Home Cookin' Apple Recipes from Missouri Apple Growers, 111

Honeybee history, 114

Hornersville, 134

Horsbrugh, Patrick, 76

Horse and Buggy and Old Time Dance Days, 148

Hosford, Mary Schroeder, 94–95

Hostetter, Mary, 144–47

Household Guide, A (Cape Girardeau), 165

Housekeeping and Dinner Giving in Kansas City, 20–25, 167

How I Cook It, 140, 142–44

How to Bake by the Ration Book, 162

How to Cook Husbands, 178

How to Have Good Health and Make Good Candy, 168

Howell, Leon, 73

Hughes, Langston, 80

Hummel, Elizabeth, 63

Hunter, Ida Elizabeth, 86

Hussman, George, 136

Huston, Joseph, 78

HV Food Products Company, 135

Hygeo-Therapeutic College of New York, 19

Hygienic cookery, 19

Ideal Bartender, The, 88–90

If You Can't Stand the Heat, Get out of the Kitchen, 74

Industrial Lessons (Park College Cook Book), 40, 41, 42

International Folkfest, 63

International Institute movement, 63

International Institute of Saint Louis, 63

Iron County Centennial Cookbook, 172

Iron County, 138

Iron Curtain speech, 75

Iron Mountain, 33

Iron Mountain Railroad, 37

Ironton, 33, 138

It's Christmas, 101

Ivy Award, 150–51

Jackson, Claiborne Fox, 78

James, Frank, 143, 73

James, Jesse, 143, 73–74

Jean Baptiste Vallé House, 53

Jefferson, Kurt, 75

Jesse James Cookbook, 73

Jewish Hospital Auxiliary, 45

Jewish kitchen, 61–63

Jim the Wonder Dog, 99

Johnston, Eleanor Richey, 142–43

Joplin Cook Book, The, 176

Joplin, Scott, 154

Jour de Fete, 148

Joy of Cooking, The, 88, 91–93

Juanita Kitchen Guide, 172

Julia Clark Household Memoranda Book, 3, 5, 6, 7, 166

Junior League cookbooks, 45–46

Junior Service League of Independence, 74–75

K. C. Masterpiece Barbecue Sauce, 135
Kansas City development: meat packing, 10; milling, 10, 119
Keller, Helen, 153
Kelley, Leslie, 103
Keyserling, Mrs. Robert, 83
Kimmswick, 144–46
Kitchen and household equipment and utensils, 22, 24–26
Kitchen design, 22
Kitchen Directory and American Housewife, 10
Kitchen medicine, 8, 166–70
Kitchen Oracle, The, 29, 34–37, 175
Kitchen organization, 22
Kitchen utensils, 16
Kitchen, Inc., The, 50
Kitchenology with Principia Friends, 42
Knolte, Ruthie, 100
Knote, Charlie, 100
Knox County Corn Fest Second Annual Cookbook, 113
Kosher, 62

Laclede, Pierre, 8
Lady Patricia's Tea Room, 149
Lake Venita, 84
Lamar, 74
Lane, Rose Wilder, 102–3
Larsen, Nils, 93
Laura Ingalls Wilder–Rose Wilder Lane Home and Museum, 102
Laura Ingalls Wilder Country Cookbook, The, 102–3
Lawrence, Ella Park, 40–42
Lawrence, Grace L., 177
Lawrence, Josephine R., 59
Lavelle, Nancy, 19
Leif, Max, 94
Leslie, Eliza, 4
Lessons in Cooking, 65–67
Let's Do Lunch, 145
Levee-High Apple Pie, 145–47
Lewis, Meriwether, 6
Lewis and Clark Expedition, 5, 77

Liberty, 148
Lincoln, Mary Johnson, 4
Lindbergh, Charles, 100
Litchfield Creamery Company, 127
Little Book for a Little Cook, A, 156
Little Fur in the Meringue Never Really Hurts the Filling, A, 98–99
Little Italy of the Ozarks, 137
Livingstone, Lorraine, 161
Loeffler, Gisella, 64
Log cabin cooking, 7
Lorain Cooking, 122
Lorain Oven Heat Regulator, 122
Louisiana, 18
Louisiana Purchase Exposition, 153
Lun, Pu, 153

Ma Green's Tavern, 145
Magic Chef, 122–23
Magic Chef Cooking, 122
Majestic Manufacturing Company, 120–22
Majestic Stove Lofts, 122
Mansfield, 102
Manuscript cookbooks, 5
Marconi, Guglielmo, 153
Marfisi, Eleanore Berra, 58–59
Marford, Nancy, 148
Marmaduke, John S., 78
Marmaduke, Meredith M., 78
Marthasville, 54
Mayes, Diane, 101
McAfee, John A., 41
McDonald, Virginia, 143
McDonald County Native Foods Cookbook, 66
McKee, Gwen, 103–4
McNair, Alexander, 79, 90, 81
McNair, Lilburn G., 90
Meet Us in the Kitchen, 46
Memories Good Enough to Eat, 62–63
Mennonites, 119
Menus and Recipes from Abroad, 63–64
Meyenberg, John, 126
Miller, John, 82
Milnot Company, 127–28
Mine La Motte, 33
Miss Hulling's Cafeteria, 149–50

Miss Hulling's Favorite Recipes, 150
Miss Hulling's Own Cook Book, 150
Missouri 4-H Foundation, 138
Missouri Apple Site, 110
Missouri Beef Industry Council, 115
Missouri Corn Growers Association, 111
Missouri Dandy, 128
Missouri Department of Agriculture, 81
Missouri History on the Table—250 Years of Good Cooking and Good Eating, 65, 84–87
Missouri Honey Recipes, 114
Missouri Mansion Preservation, Inc., 81
Missouri Nut Growers Association, 129
Missouri Ozarks Commodity Cookbook, 66
Missouri Pork Association, 115–16
Missouri Restaurant Association, 149–51
Missouri Sampler: A Collection of Favorite Recipes from All Counties, The, 97
Missouri Sesquicentennial Cook Book, 79–83
Missouri settlement, 5, 32–33, 52, 57–58, 136
Missouri Soy Bean Merchandising Council, 113
Missouri State Bee Keepers Auxiliary, 114
Missouri State Suffrage Association, 18
Missouri State Teachers Association, 44
Missouri Traveler, 95
Missouri Traveler Cookbook, 94–95
Modern Practice of Canning Meats, 130–32
Modified recipes, 160, 162–63
Monroe City, 165
Moore, Mrs. Philip N., 156–57
Moore, Walthal M., 80
Morehouse, Martha McFadden, 82
Morgan, Mary Kimball, 43
Moseley, Barbara, 103–4
Moss, Maria J., 4, 28
Mountain Grove research center, 136
Mt. Hope, 84
Mulvill Lake, 84
My Mother's Cookbook, 11–14, 166, 171, 173

Nagel, Werner, 95–96
National Council of Women, 156
National Nutritional Edition Kerr Home Canning Book, 162
Nettleton Cook Book, 177
Never Ending Season: The Cookbook of Missouri, 138
New Melle, 54
Nine Hundred Successful Recipes, 90–91
Norton/Cynthiana, 136
Notable Women of St. Louis, 19
Novinger Planned Progress, Inc., 57

O'Brian, Marian Maeve, 95
O'Fallon, Harriet Stokes, 5, 7–9
O'Fallon, John R., 5, 7, 8
Odessa, 83–84
Odessa Centennial Edition Cookbook, 83
Office of Price Administration, 162
Old Brick Tavern and Restaurant, 53, 147
Old Mines, 33
Old Tavern, 78
Old Tavern Book of Recipes, The, 77–79
O'Neill, Rose, 99
Ostmann, Barbara Gibbs, 99
Ott's Famous Salad Dressing, 129
Ott's Foods, 129–30
Our Favorite Recipes (St. James Winery), 137
Our Own Cookbook, 30
Ozark Ham and Turkey Festival, 132
Ozarks Arts and Crafts Fair Association, 98
Ozarks Cookery: A Collection of Pioneer Recipes, 98
Ozarks Mountaineer, 98

Page, Eric, 140
Palette to Palate, 45
Park College (Park University), 40–42
Park College Cook Book (*Industrial Lessons*), 28, 40–42
Park, George S., 40, 41
Parkville, 41
Parloa, Maria, 4
Past and Repast, 81–83
Patent medicine, 34
Patriotic Food Show, 153, 157
Patriotic Food Show Official Recipe Book, 153, 157–61

Patriot's Kitchen, 158
Peach capital, 107
Peach Recipes from the Peach Capital of Missouri, 108
Pealer, Don F., 77
Penny, James Cash, 100
Penny, Joe, 60
Pennytown, 59–61
Pennytown Freewill Baptist Church, 59–61
Pershing, John J., 100
Pest control, 21, 22, 171–72
Pet Milk Building, 127
Pet Milk Company, 126–27
Pet Recipes, 126
Philadelphia (New Philadelphia), 78
Phoenix Opera House, 84
Pilot Knob, 33
Poetical Cookbook, A, 4, 28
Pointe, 400, 127
Polk, James K., 80
Potosi, 33
Poultry production, 48–49
Poultry shows, 48
Powers, Estelle, 86
Practical Cooking and Dinner Giving, 14
Preservation Issues, 60
Price, Anna Love, 95
Principia College, 42, 43
Principia Mothers' Club, 42
Printing and publishing cookbooks, 33–34, 39
Proetz, Erma, 126
Prohibition, 19, 136, 137
Pulitzer, Joseph, 100
Pullen, Pauline E., 97
Pumpkin Festival, 109
Pumpkin Festival Cookbook, 109–10
Pure Food Cook Book, The, 47- 49, 171–74, 178
Pushcarts and Stalls: The Soulard Market History Cookbook, 107
Putnam County Feeder Calf Sale, 69–70

Quinine fever pills, 78

Raffald, Elizabeth, 3
Railroads, 36, 52–53, 55, 119, 83–84

Randolph, Mary, 4
Rations, 162
Ray County, 108–9
Recess Inn, 148
Recipes for Today (WWII), 162
Recipes from Missouri . . . with Love, 99
Recipes of Old Ste. Genevieve, 53
Recipe style, 27, 180
Red Oak Inn Bed and Breakfast, 148
Red Wheel, The, 122–22
Reese, Dorothy, 33
Renault, Philip, 80
Report on a Journey to the Western States of North America, 53
Rhineland, 54
Rhythm in Foods, 93–94
Richmond Chamber of Commerce Mushroom Cookbook, The, 108–9
Richmond Mushroom Festival, 108–9
Riddle, James R., 76
Riley, Franklin Studebaker, Jr, 94
Ringen, John, 122
Rival Company, 124–25
Rival Crock-Pot Slow Electric Stoneware Cooker Cookbook, 125
Rival Crock-Pot, 124–25
Rivercene Bed and Breakfast, 148
Road Tasted, 145, 147
Rockview, 170–71
Rogers, Will, 154
Rombauer, Irma, 88, 91–93
Roosevelt, Edith, 153
Roosevelt, Franklin, D., 162
Roosevelt, Theodore, 153
Rorer, Sarah Tyson, 4, 154–55
Ross, Dorothy, 97
Ross, Lucianna, 144–45
Rouse, Wade, 144
Roux We Do, The, 46
Rowe, Anne B., 98
Royer, Sarah Tyson, 154–55
Ryan, Harriette R. 63

Saint Louis Days . . . Saint Louis Nights, 46
Sally Danforth's Cookbook, 165
Sando, Shirleen, 101–2
Sandys, Edwina, 76

Sappington, John, 78
Sassafras! The Ozarks Cookbook, 46
Savage, Geraldine, 87
Sawyer, Tom, 99
Schoolhouse Treats, 44–45
Scott, Dred, 8
Scripture cake
Senath United Methodist Church Cookbook, 32
Seneca, 127
Servant training, 21, 23
Serving styles, 14, 15, 18
Seventy-Five Receipts for Pastry Cakes and Sweetmeats, 4
Shank, Dorothy, 122
Sharing Recipes (Pennytown), 60
Shaw, Anna Howard, 156
Shelby, Jo, 143
Shell, Patricia, 148–49
Shelton, Herbert M., 20
Shoemaker, Floyd C., 79
Sho-Neff Black Walnut Farm, 128
Sibley, George S., 78
Silvernail, Lulu Thompson, 90–91
Simmons, Amelia, 3–5
Sinews of Peace, 75
Single-concept cookbook, 43
Smith, Eliza 3
Smith-Lever Act, 138
Soames, Mary, 76
Social etiquette, 25, 27
Soulard, Antoine, 106
Soulard, Julia, 106
Soulard Market, 106–7
Sousa, John Philip, 154
Southwestern Milling Company, 119
Soybean history, 113
Spring cleaning, 23
St. Charles, 81
St. Francois Mountains, 32
St. James Winery, 138
St. John's Evangelical Lutheran church Cookbook, 30
St. Joseph Art League, 46
St. Joseph Lead Company, 32
St. Louis and Iron Mountain Railroad, 33
St. Louis Convention and Visitors Commission, 153

St. Louis development, 8, 9
St. Louis Friends of the Winston Churchill Memorial, 76
St. Louis Hygienic College of Physicians and Surgeons, 20
St. Louis Post-Dispatch the Best Recipes Cookbook, 99
St. Louis School of Design, 18
St. Louis Second Presbyterian Church Cook Book, 176
St. Louis Walk of Fame, 93
St. Mary Aldermanbury Church, 76
St. Paul's Country Recipes, 32
Stafford, Dorothy, 101
Starr, Belle, 99
State Agricultural Experiment Station, 107
State grape, 136
Ste. Genevieve, 84, 87
Ste. Genevieve 250th Celebration Commission, 84
Stein, Shifra, 135
Stephenson, Leslie, 150–52
Stephenson, Loyd, 150–52
Stephenson's Apple Farm and Restaurant, 150–52
Stephenson's Apple Farm Restaurant Receipts, 151–52
Stockstrom, Charles, 122
Stockstrom, Louis, 122
Stockton, 128
Stockton, Robert Henry, 120
Stone Hill Winery, 137
Stone, Robert, 5
Stone, Sara, 82
Stone, William Joel, 82
Stratton, Eula Mae, 98
Stumph, Mildred, 87
Sunrise Inn Missouri, 147–48

Taft, William Howard, 153
Tandler, Rudolph, 42
Taste of Missouri, A, 163
Taylor, Mary Lee, 126
Taylor, Zachary, 80
Teatime Friendships at Patricia's, 149
Tested and Tasted Economical Recipes, 128
Tinnin, Mrs. Nelson B, 79

Tom Sawyer, 99
Town and Country Cookie Book, 43
Town Crier Ready Mixed Flour Recipes,
    120–21
Trinity Church, 55
Truman, Harry S., 74–75, 79
Truman, John, 76
Truman, Virginia Wallace Bess, 74–75
Tucker, Ella Mae, 96–97
Turkey Red Wheat (Red Turkey Wheat),
    119–20
Twain, Mark, 100
Twentieth Century Cook Book, The, 33, 36

*Union Avenue Christian Church Cook
    Book,* 29, 123, 171, 173, 176
Unity Inn, 140–42
Unity Inn Vegetarian Cook Book, The,
    140–42
Unity School of Christianity, 140
University of Missouri, 129
USDA Forest Service, 129

Vaccaro, Pamela J., 154–55
Vaughn, Sarah, 80
Victorian Faire, 149
*Victory Handbook for Health and Home
    Defense,* 163
Virginia Housewife, The, 4

Walker, George Herbert, 88
Walkley, Ruth, 100–101
Walkley, W. J., 100
War garden, 82
Washington, 54
Weapon technology, 158, 160
Weather, 50–51
Western Bible and Literary College, 84
Westminster College, 75

Westward travel, 94
White man's flies, 114
Whitney, Cornelius Vanderbilt, 95
Wicker, Walter (Peck), 134
Wicker's Food Products, 133–35
Wilder, Almanzo, 102–3
Wilder, Laura Ingalls, 102–3
Wilder, Rose. *See* Lane, Rose Wilder
William Jewell College, 73
Williams, Martha M., 165–66
Willis, Mrs. T. F., 20, 167
Wilson's Creek, 70
Wine and Dine with Frau Held, 137
Wine industry, 136–38
Winston Churchill Memorial, 76
Wolf-Wilson Drug Company, 168
Woman's Exchange of St. Louis, 18
Woman's Patriotic Service Special train,
    157
Women in the 1820s, 6
*Women Who Can Dish It Out—The
    Lighter Side of the Ozarks,* 46
Women's Overseas Service League, 161
Women's Central Committee on Food
    Conservation, 157
Women's Defense Group, 63
Women's Progressive Farmers'
    Association, 47–48, 172–73
Woodson, Jennie, 82
World's Fair cornucopias, 154
World's Fair Souvenir Cook Book, 154–55
WOS (radio station), 77
Wright, Harold Bell, 100
Wrought Iron Range Company, 124
Wyman's Hall, 44

Younger, Cole, 143
Your Household Guide (Rockview), 170,
    172

About the Authors

Photo by Sharron Paris

Carol Fisher is author of *The American Cookbook: A History*, winner of the Missouri Writers' Guild Walter Williams Major Work Award. John Fisher is author of *Catfish, Fiddles, Mules, and More: Missouri's State Symbols* (University of Missouri Press). The authors live in Kennett, Missouri.